PRAISE FOR *STRETCH*

"In today's fast-moving, multigenerational workplace, we all want more from our professional experiences. *Stretch* provides solid advice on how you can feel valued and in control of your career success. This book is one that will bolster your spirits and might just change your life."

—Lindsey Pollak, *New York Times* Bestselling Author of *Becoming the Boss: New Rules for the Next Generation of Leaders*

"Our neuroscience research has shown that experiencing hope and dreaming of your desired future helps a person to create a path to that future and ameliorate the ravages of stress and uncertainty. Willyerd and Mistick have converted complicated research and emerging trends into a delightful journey through their stories and guidance. Reading will do more than help you prepare for the future: it will help you make your dreams your reality!"

—Richard Boyatzis, Distinguished University Professor, Case Western Reserve University and Co-Author with Dan Goleman and Annie McKee of the International Bestseller, *Primal Leadership*

"Willyerd and Mistick have the courage to expose a raw nerve that many of today's employees feel. They don't shy away from the reality of the vulnerability many feel about not only keeping up with today, but also preparing for an ever-changing tomorrow. *Stretch* brings hope and inspiration to both individuals and organizations with specific tools, examples, and practical ideas to move forward."

—Joe Campbell, Talent Management Director, Nike, Inc.

"The future of work promises to be dramatically different over the next decade. Disruptive technologies, big data, demographic shifts, and demand for new skills will require new ways of thinking about careers and preparing a workforce for tomorrow. *Stretch* tackles these issues head on with practical advice for those in the workplace and for organizations that want to prepare their workforces for the future. Those who prepare will seize huge opportunities and, with the workplace changes underway, everyone who wants to participate in tomorrow's economy should read *Stretch* today."

—Eva Sage-Gavin, Vice Chair of the Aspen Institute's Skills for America's Future Advisory Board

STRETCH

HOW TO FUTURE-PROOF YOURSELF FOR TOMORROW'S WORKPLACE

Karie Willyerd

Barbara Mistick

WILEY

Library of Congress Cataloging-in-Publication Data:

Names: Willyerd, Karie. | Mistick, Barbara
Title: Stretch : how to future-proof yourself for tomorrow's workplace /
  Karie Willyerd, Barbara Mistick.
Description: 1 | Hoboken : Wiley, 2015. | Includes index.
Identifiers: LCCN 2015027971 (print) | LCCN 2015039560 (ebook) |
  ISBN 9781119087250 (hardback) | ISBN 9781119087151 (epdf) |
  ISBN 9781119087113 (epub)
Subjects: LCSH: Career development. | Organizational change. | Vocational
  guidance. | BISAC: BUSINESS & ECONOMICS / Careers / General. | BUSINESS
  & ECONOMICS / Workplace Culture.
Classification: LCC HF5381 .W695 2015 (print) | LCC HF5381 (ebook) | DDC
  650.1—dc23
LC record available at http://lccn.loc.gov/2015027971

Printed in the United States of America

10 9 8 7 6 5 4 3 2 1

To the girls we love,

our daughters,

Charis and Rena

Sloane, Tori, and Adriana

CONTENTS

FOREWORD

My life's work has been about helping people use social science to solve the most important problems of their lives —like breaking stubborn habits or holding high-stakes conversations with stubborn colleagues. Over the years I've been blessed to work with not only some of the finest scholars in the world, but some of the finest human beings as well. Which brings me to the pages that follow.

Stretch is a story-filled delightful read. It is timely and important. It pulls together what we know about staying relevant today and appropriately anticipating tomorrow. It is no ordinary book. The well-informed practices presented in *Stretch* will help you take control of your future and get the career and life you want.

Stretch is everything I strive for in my own work. It is the expression of careful but seductive academic rigor. You'll get smarter and feel pleasure while doing it. I would have happily endorsed the book on its own merits, but that it was co-authored by a person I deeply admire made it not only proper but an honor to comply.

In taking on this topic, the authors argue that we've moved past 330 B.C., when Aristotle wrote, "All paid jobs absorb and degrade the mind." In a refreshing nod to self-empowerment, the authors counter that full engagement of the mind at work is not just possible but life altering. Work matters. The two choices you make in life that most shape who you become are whom to live with and whom to work with. *Stretch* will not only help you create a fulfilling career—it will guide you in creating a meaningful life.

I've marveled at times at my dumb luck. The skills I've developed through my work have opened doors for me to influence social and global problems I care deeply about. I wish I could take credit for having been more intentional in that happy accident. *Stretch* offers a pattern for creating just that kind of intentional life.

Those who believe they can at least change their corner of the world are those most likely to make a difference for us all. The last two decades have revolutionized the old models of work. Today's pace of change requires new voices and new strategies to guide us in how to stay prepared and engaged. In reading this book you can prepare for what the future will bring. Compelling and rigorous, yet fresh in approach, the book comes within reach of extraordinary, not only as a guide for a successful career but also for making the most out of life.

Too many business books are authored by consultants who have never personally had a career in large organizations, started companies, led public institutions, or worked in non-profits. Their guidance falls apart when it comes to the practical realities of everyday life. In contrast, the authors here are uncommonly positioned to bring a practical voice to help you achieve your career dreams.

No matter what line of work you are in, or whether you are five years or 25 years into your career, this book can change your life. I found myself engaged, challenged, and provoked in my thinking by the compelling premise of this book. You'll be reminded of those essential life lessons that we tend to forget in the midst of our busy lives. I think you'll agree and discover, as I have, that *Stretch: How to Future-Proof Yourself for Tomorrow's Workplace* is destined to become an essential read.

> Joseph Grenny
> *New York Times* bestselling author of
> *Influencer* and *Crucial Conversations*

Learn why the world wags and what wags it. That is the only thing which the mind can never exhaust, never alienate, never be tortured by, never fear or distrust, and never dream of regretting. Learning is the only thing for you. Look what a lot of things there are to learn.
Merlin, in The Once and Future King

—T.H. White

PREFACE

Stretch: How to Future-Proof Yourself for Tomorrow Workplace, tackles the question: How do we stay relevant in our work lives? Our answer: stretch. Stretch how we learn, stretch to stay open in our thinking, stretch to build diverse networks and experiences, and stretch our motivation.

It's a tall order. While we don't have a silver bullet solution, we do have lots of suggestions that we've learned through trial and error, research and experience. We wrote this book to address a less predictable future workplace, one in which you need to have options to realize your dreams. Barbara Mistick and Karie Willyerd met pursuing their own dreams of a doctorate in a program aimed at working executives and designed to bridge the worlds of scholarship and practice. It's funny to think of a doctorate degree as the last degree you'll earn because it made us realize no one is ever finished learning.

When we met fifteen years ago in Cleveland at Case Western Reserve University, we were surprised to discover that we both lived in the same Pittsburgh neighborhood. At the time, Karie was working for a large multi-national organization and Barbara was sorting out the transition from entrepreneur to academic. It wasn't long before we were sharing rides and ideas.

We discovered that we had a tremendous amount in common: we both had daughters, we both had dropped out of college on the first go-around but persisted, succeeding as the first generation in our families to graduate college. Our lives would eventually become even more similar, as we both traversed across entrepreneurship, corporate and institutional roles, and academia. We struggled with work lives that were dramatically different from those of our parents and were in search of preparation to succeed in new and shifting jobs.

Interestingly, our research interests converged around how to help people grow. Because we became good friends, we also confided that, as the doctoral program progressed, at times we felt in over our heads, and that we each were stretching to our limits. About a third of the people in our doctoral program dropped out, all successful, wonderful people. But together, we finished. Over the summers we continued our research together by learning how to fly fish in the morning at beautiful locations and collaborating on research in the afternoon. Thus came the birth of Karie's twitter handle—@Angler.

What surprised us most in our research was how little insight the people we studied had about what had made their careers successful. Somehow they just did it, connected the dots, asked for promotions, and succeeded in leadership positions. The data from our interviews with them told us that there wasn't just one way to succeed but many. We were able to see patterns—patterns that formed the basis of all our future work and of this book.

Then last year we had the opportunity to dig deeper on workplace trends in a massive global survey in collaboration with SAP and Oxford Economics. The hard data from our research uncovered a tremendous tension in the workplace. Respondents told us that their biggest concern about their jobs, by far, was that they would become obsolete at work. As scholar practitioners, we believed we could target this concern and bring meaningful insights and practical, evidence-based solutions.

The advance of technology, rapid pace of change, threat of off-shoring, and the memory of record unemployment rates have obviously left an impact. People told us they are worried their company or their industry is dying and they might be at risk of lay-offs, unemployment, or underemployment if they don't refresh their skills and their personal brand. The longer you are in the workplace, the more vulnerable you become to obsolescence in a constantly evolving job market.

Suddenly our years of research and experience in roles as entrepreneurs, academics, and business executives had us rethinking our ideas about how to help people grow. The result is this book, an essential guide to staying relevant and engaged in the workplace.

We began with webinars and presentations to test our practices and sought input on blogs and from colleagues. We talked to heads of learning around the world and to some of the best thinkers in academia. From reviews of thousands of write-in comments and interviews, we found three recurring themes describing the realities of career aspirations. We call these the Stretch Imperatives.

The fear of falling behind affects every age. Most of us feel our hands are tied when it comes to seeking alternatives to shape our future. We also know from Gallup that most of the global workforce reports being unengaged or actively disengaged. We believe it's in your power to become engaged—to stretch into your best self—whether you have a great boss or a bad boss, are in a job you love or are still searching for bliss in the workplace, and we trust you will believe the same by the end of the book.

The book is organized to be user-friendly, so we have not inserted footnote notations in text. Instead, find out more about our sources and citations in the Supplemental Materials at the end of the book. The practices we present are backed by solid research, which we outline. And our futurists' view of megatrends and the implications for where work is headed lets you know what to expect in the future. At the end of each of the chapters on the five practices, we have also included best practices and tips for organizations and managers.

Some of the most powerful learning can be gained from the experiences of others. We include many of the stories of professionals who have successfully stretched in their work, how they went about it, the motivational strategies they used and the new meaning they found.

Stretching is the future imperative for us all. Whenever people stretch, in any area of their lives, they can achieve unimagined success. Sometimes all we need is a little guidance. You have dreams. We hope our findings, presented here in *Stretch: How to Future-Proof Yourself for Tomorrow's Workplace* will encourage you to reach for those dreams. We know your potential is limitless and we can't wait to hear your story.

To share your story or to find more resources, contact or write us at www.StretchTheBook.com

Part 1: Introduction

Chapter 1: The Stretch Imperative

Tomorrow's workplace is being shaped by megatrends underway now. As people work longer, it has become necessary to reshape the identities we form in our careers. The reality of today's environment leads us to three key career imperatives.

Dreams

Hold fast to dreams
For if dreams die
Life is a broken-winged bird
That cannot fly.
Hold fast to dreams
For when dreams go
Life is a barren field
Frozen with snow.
　　　　　　　　—Langston Hughes

1

THE STRETCH IMPERATIVE

Jade stepped out on her apartment's patio to survey the city peeping through the river fog. For the next three weeks, her apartment would be taken over by a couple from Chicago, arranged through AirBnB. Her Uber was ten minutes away, according to the app, to take her on the first step to Cuba. Her editor at the city's major daily had assigned her to do a story on how the recent trade policy changes impacted medical care practices for both that country and the United States. U.S.-made prescription drugs, once under embargo, were now saving people's lives in Cuba. Cuban medical practitioners had some advice on public health policy to share in return: Cuba had the highest average life expectancy rates in the region—almost 79 years.

When she graduated ten years ago, Jade had dreamed of traveling to foreign countries and reporting on important stories, but her chosen field of journalism was in great upheaval. Although college prepared her with the fundamental skills she needed, the massive technological changes and industry-wide job hemorrhaging left behind an uncertain career path. In the last ten years, she had held jobs with nine different employers and had dozens of side contracts to gain experience and make ends meet.

Along the way, she realized that, in order to create the career she wanted, she needed to look at new media jobs. In truth, the jobs were both exciting and daunting because she would have to personally morph to learn new skills. Jobs like website designer, media app developer, growth hacker, emerging media editor, audience strategist, blogger, and podcaster seemed to be everywhere. While she experimented working at startups in some of those roles, she also started a blog called *JournEmerge*, about the experiences of journalists and their journeys as they adapted to the changing world. Ironically, her shift to new kinds of journalism landed her a traditional role at one of the world's largest dailies. A hiring manager followed her blog and Twitter feed and reached out to her when a spot opened up.

From her feedback on her blog, she knew life could have ended up very differently, as one person who left a post on her blog said. "Hi, I'm David, and thanks so much for your blog. My story is a lot like others on this site. I just didn't see it coming. I was so clueless. When I got my pink slip and went out to sit in my car, I noticed the new-car smell. Only that morning I'd loved the smell, but now it felt like a chain around my neck.

"I don't want to sound overly proud, but I thought I was immune. I had been nominated for three Pulitzer Prizes, won numerous investigative awards, and worked in Tokyo, Beijing, London, and São Paulo. None of the writers on staff had as much global experience, and only a few had won as much journalistic recognition. Well, clearly that didn't work out.

"The paper hired a young newsroom chief who kept asking me about my social presence and what I was doing to promote my stories. Honestly, at the time I thought that was ridiculous and completely ignored her. Not a good idea.

"Fortunately I got a job pretty quickly with an international consulting firm. They thought my global experience, especially living in Asia, and writing skills would make me a good analyst. Looking back, they should have, but I just wasn't ready to leave my old mindset behind. I still wanted to report independently and with ruthless truthfulness.

The clients didn't always appreciate those values. I bombed out after only 18 months.

"Finally I had that apocryphal 'aha' moment. Two pink slips inside of two years will do that for you. Either I had to change, or my kids would be on their own for college. I had promised them a college education, and I am not a person to renege on my promises. I contacted the boss who had laid me off, took her to lunch, and asked her to mentor me.

"She was incredibly gracious and spent a half-dozen sessions with me. Her mentoring helped me see the new world of media. Not long after, I got a job with a global research firm and I've been there almost seven years. My kids have both now graduated. I just wanted to let your readers know that it is possible to transition at any age. You just have to be open."

David and Jade's stories are like those of so many of us who prepared for careers that have ended up far away from our original vision. With an eye toward the future, still early in her career, it was easier for Jade to adapt as her industry shifted. David took longer to let go of a world that no longer existed. Your story may be different from theirs, but no matter what company, field, industry, or geography you are in, to be ready for tomorrow, you will need to stretch beyond your capabilities of today.

Who Do You Want to Be Tomorrow?

Gallup reports that the majority of us are disengaged at work. Pointing the finger at leadership for this state of affairs is easy to do. According to the Gallup Chairman and CEO, Jim Clifton, "Of the approximately 100 million people in America who hold full-time jobs, 30 million (30 percent) are engaged and inspired at work. So we can assume they have a great boss. At the other end of the spectrum are roughly 20 million (20 percent) employees who are actively disengaged. These employees, who have bosses from hell that make them miserable, roam the halls spreading discontent. The other 50 million (50 percent) American workers are not engaged. They're just kind of present, but not inspired by their work or their managers."

Engagement, then, is all about the bosses, if you believe Gallup. Logically then, the only options you have are to change bosses or stay in an unhappy situation.

We disagree.

Engagement is not a one-way street and not all on the shoulders of the boss. That's like saying a marriage is all up to just one partner. We believe you have the power to change from disengaged to engaged and to realize your career dreams, no matter what kind of boss you have. Why leave your development, your happiness, and your career in the hands of someone else? Engagement scores have not shifted dramatically in the fifteen years Gallup has been measuring them, in spite of millions of dollars of training for managers. Something needs to change.

Studs Terkel, author and Pulitzer Prize winner, said, "Work is about a search for daily meaning as well as daily bread, for recognition as well as cash, for astonishment rather than torpor; in short, for a sort of life rather than a Monday through Friday sort of dying." Work is integral to a fulfilling life. Your only job satisfaction should not be direct deposit. You can find meaning, be engaged, and build a stunning career. Boss optional.

Earlier in her career, Barbara worked closely with Fred Rogers, a children's advocate and television host. Fred was completely engaged in his work and personally responded to every letter from the children of the world who wrote to him. After nearly four decades of work, suffering from cancer, Fred started working from home. He asked the staff to continue to send him the letters, and he answered his last letter the day before he died. This is more than a strong work ethic; this is engagement at its most empowering and compassionate.

Imagine if everyone, yourself included, was as engaged in your work as Fred Rogers. And we can be, regardless of present or past work situations, education level, or even childhood expectations. Perhaps you are the first generation to complete college, just as Barbara and Karie are in our families. The future you could imagine for yourself might have been defined by the experiences of your parents. You wouldn't be the first to get advice from your parents that limited your future. Leonard Nimoy, the late acclaimed actor who played the character Spock in *Star Trek*, was told by his Ukrainian-born father, Max, that if he wanted to pursue acting, he needed to get a practical skill that would serve him well throughout his life. "Learn to play the accordion," Max Nimoy urged. "You can always make a living with an accordion." Fortunately for *Star Trek* fans, he didn't follow his father's advice.

Even if your launch into your career was enabled by a strong financial and family support system, you may have found that your equivalent to Nimoy's accordion advice was pressure to get a practical degree, for which you hold no passion. Or perhaps you took that well-paying "tangent" job in order to pay down your college loans. Or maybe the job you held for years was sufficient, served its purpose, and you've only recently discovered your true passion.

As people live and therefore work longer lives, it becomes necessary to reshape the identities we formed in our careers. We absolutely can prepare for a new future, fulfill a reinvented set of dreams, and surpass any goals we set out at the beginning of our career journeys.

Our undertaking as authors is to share our extensive research and personal experiences in order to give you the capacity to be fully engaged, prepared for the future, and to stretch to the next level, no matter where you are in your career. We also want you to avoid career heartbreak, obsolescence, and loss of purpose.

We will help you:

1. Learn career management tools that you can implement on your own, without the need for big financial or company resources;

2. Choose from a broad set of options and strategies on how to approach work and develop your career, so that you have the flexibility to pick what works within your own situation; and

3. Assess your current reality and plot a path to achieve your dreams so you can be prepared for tomorrow's workplace.

The future beckons. Will you remain one of the 70 percent of the disengaged zombies at work? Or are you facing obsolescence, like

David, the Pulitzer Prize nominee? Instead, what if the life you are living is your bucket list, and all you want is to ensure that you get to live more of the life you have, work and all? It's time to stretch, to prepare for tomorrow's workplace, and put yourself in control of the career of your dreams.

The Workforce 2020 Research

Our research mission was to discover how changes in the global economy and shifting demographics will impact the employment and talent marketplace. We collaborated with SuccessFactors—an SAP company—and Oxford Economics to conduct twin studies of executives and employees across 27 countries to find out what the future workforce is thinking, wanting, and worrying over.

In addition to the global surveys, we interviewed and talked to over 300 people, and consulted with dozens of academic or corporate learning experts to refine and validate our practices. We reviewed over 1,000 academic papers, kept booksellers in business with book deliveries, and clicked through countless of the web's estimated trillion pages.

Survey respondents were clear that they need development in order to be prepared for tomorrow's workplace. Around the world, the number one concern people expressed was that their ability and skills to perform rapidly changing jobs would render them obsolete. Additionally, only 50 percent of the employees from our survey believe the skills they have today will be the skills they need just three years from now.

See more details about our research and findings in Appendix A.

Megatrends That Will Affect Your Future

In order to point ourselves in the right direction, first we need an idea of where we are going. When we plan for tomorrow, we have to assume the work environment will be different than it is today. That is truer now than ever. Before we get started in practical career tools to future-proof yourself, we'll give you an overview of the factors that are sure to change the world of work tomorrow.

We have identified seven megatrends that will certainly have an impact on the types of jobs, entrepreneurial opportunities, and skills needed for workers in the future. Entire books are written about these trends. This big picture review is meant to help you see how they might affect you and what you will need to do to prepare for the workplace of tomorrow.

Globalization

A major shift in where business is conducted is occurring now. McKinsey estimates that half of the world's largest companies will be headquartered in what are now emerging markets, such as Brazil, India, and eastern European countries. By 2030, nearly two-thirds of the global population could be middle class. As the world develops, the economic picture shifts radically. Pressure from global competition and other factors resulted in over 40 percent of the companies that were in the Fortune 500 in 2000 falling off the list by 2010. These were replaced largely by new global entrants and technology companies. Still, the Fortune 500 had revenues in 2014 equivalent to almost 72 percent of US GDP, double what it was in 1955.

In just the last decade, Brazilian company 3G has purchased established brands such as Kraft, Heinz, Anheuser-Busch InBev, Tim Hortons, and Burger King. Then, following an established 3G management pattern, they aggressively managed out costs and consolidated departments, resulting in the loss of thousands of jobs, while expanding to international markets and delivering increased profits.

Even high-achieving companies in growing industries face the pressure of globalization. For example, at the same time the visual effects company Rhythm and Hues was winning their third Academy Award, this time for *Life of Pi*, their bankruptcy proceedings were going through the court. *The Wall Street Journal* reported that "like most large U.S. visual effects firms, Rhythm & Hues already was under pressure because of generous tax subsidies in foreign countries including Canada, competition from lower-cost developing markets, and boutique shops that use off-the-shelf technology."

The types of jobs most affected by globalization will be ones that can be done anywhere in the world and shipped over the Internet, like the computer and digital graphics industry already has demonstrated. Paraphrasing John Donne, no person, company, industry, or country is an island in today's world, standing of themselves. We are all interconnected.

Demographics Shifts

In many economies around the world, advances in healthcare and declining birth rates have resulted in a population that is graying and a workforce that is shrinking. In the United States, 11,000 people a day turn 65 and this trend will continue until 2030. People are living and working longer, with the average retirement age for most people working now expected to be 66, up from 57 two decades ago. Among those people over 55 in the U.S., an astonishing 43 percent have less than $25,000 saved for retirement, and many see no end to working in the foreseeable future.

Japan's population continues to decrease and Europe experienced a 1 percent decline in the overall population in the last decade. According to the United Nations Population Division, Germany, Italy, and Spain are all expected to experience population declines ranging from 14 to 25 percent. By 2030, China will have nearly as many senior citizens aged 65 or older as children aged 15 and younger, resulting in a workforce deficit.

On the other end of the spectrum, Millennials are now the largest generation in the workplace in most countries, and their voices, connected through social media, will increasingly alter the workplace culture. The Millennials replacing the exiting older workers are generally more tech-savvy, with eight in ten believing that the Internet has changed life for the better, while less than half of the oldest generation of workers believe the same. Gen Xer's, born between 1964 and 1979, have also embraced technology, beginning in the 1990s with their BlackBerry devices. We expect that Millennials will increasingly assert their values and experiences on everything from an expectation of simplicity in work processes and technology to benefits, pay, and development requirements.

Diversity is also on an uptick. Women comprise about 47 percent of the U.S. workforce, up from 38 percent in 1970, and are outnumbering men in college attendance. Millennials are increasingly diverse, and U.S. demographers estimate that non-whites will be the majority by 2040. In many countries, immigration is also changing the face of the workforce. Shrinking workforces leave too few jobholders, especially in entry-level positions, requiring immigrants to sustain the economy. This increasingly diverse workforce will demand more representation in leadership positions and in pay equity.

Explosion of Data

When they call it "big data," they mean really big. Experts estimate that from 2009 to 2020, data will grow 4300 percent. That data will be in the form of content from the past that can be readily structured into a database, and will also increasingly include unstructured data such as that found in social media sites like Twitter, Instagram, Facebook, Vine, and so on.

Increasingly, the data will be generated by machines that are connected to one another via the Internet, also called the "Internet of Things." In 2011, 20 typical households generated more Internet traffic than the entire Internet in 2008. Organizations that can mine this data to reveal customer trends will lead the markets of the future.

Already, the demand for people who can make sense of all the data is soaring. In 2015, IBM estimated that the global need for data scientists is 4.4 million jobs, but only one-third will be filled. Cyber security and privacy are concerns as well, as more information becomes automatically connected without human intervention.

No matter what field you are in, the interface with data and machines will increasingly become a factor. Sensors, location-enabled applications, and machines from your car to your refrigeration will all be feeding you with personalized data to improve the productivity and quality of your life. Imagine having your hotel room set to your preferred temperature when your phone approaches within an hour of your arrival, or your fitness application sending a stream of data to your healthcare provider to create a personalized health plan.

The United Nations has declared access to the Internet to be a basic human right. So the Internet is here to stay. People of all generations worry that being constantly connected and monitored is a potential threat. It is, however, where we are headed.

Emerging Technologies

Already there are indicators of jobs that are going away based on new and emerging technologies. In April of 2015, the first driverless car to cross the United States arrived at its destination in Manhattan after nine days. Whether drivers or pilots are completely eliminated in the near future remains to be seen, but as one pilot sitting in coach next to Barbara said, "I'm only up front to make you feel comfortable that someone is there. I'm not really needed."

Another technology that is being used in unique ways is 3D printing. Manufacturing will move from being a subtractive process to an additive one, where objects are built in layers by printing rather than by machining away from a block of material. People have created an amazing array of objects on 3D printers, including shoes, acoustic guitars, drones, bionic ears, guns, and cars—the list goes on. Thus, imagine the role of designers in the future who can sell their printing instructions for anything to anywhere in the world.

One of the many emerging technologies worthy of mention is robotics. Japan is expecting one in three of its population to be over the age of 65 by 2030, and one in five to be over 75, creating a major requirement for the care of the elderly. Not surprisingly then, Japan is on the leading edge of using robots in service roles. A hotel opened in Japan in 2015 with lifelike robots, called actroids, serving as the check-in staff. Robots can also provide room-to-room delivery of food, newspapers, toiletries, and such items. Aid assistance in nursing facilities is on the horizon, meaning many of the entry-level jobs in those areas will become obsolete. How soon will you interact with a robot providing customer service? The answer may be sooner than you think.

Climate Change

Climate change will have a strong economic impact in the future. The OECD anticipates that by 2050, more than 40 percent of the world's population will live under severe water stress, resulting in floods or drought that, combined, can put the economic value of assets at risk at record highs. The 2015 mandated water controls in California are just an example of what we can expect in the future. The cost of water and the need to cut back on development could easily have, for example, California-based organizations eyeballing expansion locations near the rainforests of Oregon, or see the popping up of new businesses along the South-to-North Water Diversion Project in China. People follow economic development shifts, so expect people to migrate in search of jobs.

Consolidating and reducing facilities in favor of environmentally friendly buildings is a top priority at many organizations. Economically, it can only make sense to position corporate assets in locations at low risk of climate destruction.

Finally, becoming efficient with resources is socially responsible and cost beneficial. Organizations need to adapt to increasing regulations controlling energy efficiency, waste, water leakage, urban congestion, transportation efficiency, land degradation, freight impact, and other factors. Allowing employees to work virtually also reduces the need for facilities and helps organizations minimize their carbon footprints.

Redefined Jobs

What is a job? Look over a few definitions on the web and it's easy to see that few of us are still limited to Google's first meaning: "a paid position of regular employment." Sure, we have paid work, but from only one source and in a regular fashion? That is less likely due to the increase in part-time and contract work. The percentage of part-time workers to full-time workers remains high, possibly as employers resist hiring people for more than 30 hours a week to avoid paying benefits. The reality of the 40-hour workweek, single-employer job is elusive to many, and now experts estimate that one-third of all U.S. workers are freelancers or contractors.

Instead, the definition of a job looks more like the second meaning from Google: "a task or piece of work, especially one that is paid." Piecing together multiple gigs at the same time or freelancing in a series of work-for-hire roles is a new normal. According to Freelancer. com, some of the fastest growing opportunities are PowerPoint creation, accounting, report writing, designing Facebook landing pages, and community management.

Rarely are jobs assigned or taken on as a result of a strategic plan to build your skills and capability, thus preparing you for the future of work. Instead, the nature of fluctuating workloads requires moving to meet those needs, whether your skills and motivation match or not. Over 83 percent of executives told us they plan on increasing their use of contingent, part-time, or flexible workers in the next few years. The nature of work is going to be increasingly a trans-actional task exchange, which is to say, those with in-demand skills will be hired to accomplish one specific project, rather than given a full-time position.

Even if you have a full-time job or have started an entrepreneurial venture, you can build new skills by taking gigs on the side. Some of the many sites available that match people with project requests are Crowdspring, Upwork, or Freelancer. Technology advances and shift-ing market demands also create new categories of jobs. Just a few of the jobs that didn't exist ten years ago include app developer, market research data miner, admissions consultant, social media or commu-nity manager, cloud computing services—and the list is growing.

The nature of how work gets done is rapidly shifting. Co-location workspaces are popping up all over the place to allow people who don't work for the same organizations or in the same field to work in the same place and perhaps find ways to unexpectedly collaborate. Work is happening everywhere, all the time. Even the lines between workday and personal time are blurring, since work and personal time blend and overlap. Work is no longer a place, but a thing.

Complexity

Complexity is increasing for both organizations and individuals. At the organizational level, complexity multiplies with layers upon layers of government regulations, in multiple countries, combined with requirements from customers with their own unique specifications. In our survey of executives, increasing regulations was one of the top concerns for being able to compete in the future. Complicated regulations can create complex processes and policies.

The massive amounts of available data, although holding great promise for market insights or productivity gains, are only useful when paired with the capability to meaningfully understand and apply insights to decisions and processes. Organizations that can streamline and simplify structures, processes, systems, and cultures will have the competitive advantage in the future.

At the individual level, the need to master this complexity and balance competing demands is also on the increase. Stanford researchers identified a number of stressors that affect overall health and wellness for employees, including long hours, job insecurity, extraordinary job demands, work family conflict, unfair work situations, and others. Whether you are in a large or a small organization, the constant volatility, uncertainty, change, and ambiguity result in job complexity that make decisions more difficult and increase the demand for simplified processes.

Studies agree resoundingly that these megatrends are forging the working landscape of the future. Some trends may seem far removed from your everyday world; others you may already be experiencing. All of them have the potential to change the way we work in substantial ways, threatening to make many people and even experts in their fields obsolete. Do you know how soon you will be one of the affected, whether your skills are about to become irrelevant?

Do You Have a Sell-By Date?

Although incredibly accomplished and skilled in his field, our award-winning journalist David missed the signs pointing to his inability to maintain a job in the field he loved. When we originally talked to him and asked why he left journalism, he said, "I didn't leave journalism. Journalism left me." David had a sell-by date that he didn't realize existed until it had expired.

There were many indicators he should have picked up on, but his focus area was too narrow at the time. As Marshall Goldsmith, author and executive coach, says, "What got you here won't get you there." The skills and experience that made David successful early in his career didn't prepare him for a day when social marketing of his content was a necessary job requirement. Fortunately, he was able to reboot, fail at a major consulting firm in his next role, but then bounce forward into a successful career in a research firm, where his global experience and interviewing skills have served him well.

Today is not your grandfather's work world or even your mother's work world. Dynamic forces are at play, shifting even the world's largest corporations with a trickledown effect that hits you. Fifty years ago companies stayed on the Fortune 500 list an average of 75 years. Now it's 15 years. Only 67 companies stayed on the Fortune 500 list in the period from 1955 to 2011, as new companies with new market approaches displaced the old ways of doing business. And the rate of churn is increasing. The iconic gold watch presented as a retirement gift after 50 years of loyal service in your grandfather's work world is as antiquated as the white leisure suits of the 1970s or the boy bands of the 1990s.

David is only an example of one of many journalists who found they faced a completely evolving industry with no sure steps toward an employment future. Print media was one of the hardest hit industries during the financial crisis of 2008, but it wasn't the only one. According to Scott Timberg, music and culture writer, severe cuts across whole job categories included:

- 19.8 percent decrease in graphic design over four years

- 25.6 percent decrease in photography over seven years

- 29.8 percent decrease in architecture over three years

Although the total number of jobs lost was regained by 2014, the types of jobs regained were not of the same quality as those that had been

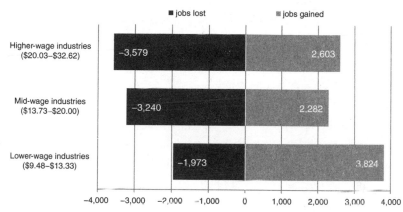

FIG 1.1 Net Change in Private-Sector Employment (in Thousands)

■ jobs lost   ■ jobs gained

Industry	jobs lost	jobs gained
Higher-wage industries ($20.03–$32.62)	−3,579	2,603
Mid-wage industries ($13.73–$20.00)	−3,240	2,282
Lower-wage industries ($9.48–$13.33)	−1,973	3,824

−4,000 −3,000 −2,000 −1,000 0 1,000 2,000 3,000 4,000

Jobs lost: January 2008 to February 2010
Jobs gained: February 2010 to February 2014

Source: National Employment Law Project

lost. Middle- and higher-income jobs were replaced by low-income jobs, as shown in Figure 1.1. As a result, from 2003 to 2013, the typical U.S. household experienced a 36 percent decline in inflation-adjusted net worth.

But as Jade's and David's stories showed, there is hope for those who reinvent themselves to stretch to the future. The effort is worth the payback.

The worry of becoming obsolete is not new. Change is just happening at a faster rate, making us worry about it far sooner in our careers. The concept of sell-by dates started in the most unlikely of places and was originated by a less-than-reputable character. During the 1920s, Chicago earned a reputation as a city where mobsters enjoyed free-range operations. The most notorious of these was Al Capone, also known as Scarface. He was believed to have ordered dozens, if not hundreds, of murders, including the St. Valentine's Day massacre. Bootlegging during Prohibition was an important part of his criminal empire.

But even gangsters face the threat of changing business models. Before his crimes caught up with him, Capone had made a few attempts to polish up his public reputation and go straight. None of them lasted long. As the repeal of Prohibition seemed inevitable, Capone sought to establish business alternatives to bootlegging. Given that he already owned a distribution system to get his illegal alcohol around the city, he considered how to use the equipment, skills, and contacts he already had for the inevitable day when alcohol was once again mainstream. "Do you know," he would say, "they got a bigger mark-up in legit fresh milk than we could ever get away with in booze? Honest to God, boys, we been in the wrong racket all along."

Realizing his impending obsolescence, Capone and his protégés first cornered the market on stamping equipment. They then lobbied the Chicago City Council to regulate milk cartons by stamping them with expiration dates. That innovation was the first time sell-by-dates were used on milk to indicate freshness. It is a practice that remains to this day. By no means is Capone a model of citizenship we would advocate to emulate, but his story does demonstrate that a scrappy approach to thinking about the future can be wildly effective.

Capone was interested in keeping his product visibly fresh in order to effectively market and sell it. An expired product is not sellable. Pass the sell-by date significantly, and the product heads for the waste fields. The same applies to workers. The importance of keeping our skills and abilities fresh in order to be competitive in the job marketplace is mandatory. To keep nudging our own sell-by date out further, we must be in constant refresh mode. We must constantly stretch.

stretch

streCH/verb

1. To reach beyond your capabilities of today to be ready for tomorrow
2. To expand your viewpoints and skills beyond your current state
3. To be relentlessly resourceful in pursuing your career dreams

The question is not whether you have a sell-by date. You do. The real question is what you are doing to extend that date. Depending on what field you are in and how up-to-date your experiences and education are, that sell-by date might be soon, or it might be a few years away. Even though your skills might have an expiration date, your dreams don't, which is why the practices offered in this book become critical.

The Stretch Imperatives

There is no future in any job. The future lies in the person who holds the job.

—George W. Crane

From write-in comments on our survey and interviews, we repeatedly heard three themes that represent the realities of today's workplace. These themes represent the climate that we address in this book. We call these the Stretch Imperatives. To provide you with the best set of practices to build a successful career, we must address the realities of today's environment.

 ## Stretch Imperative 1: It's All on You

Not only is your engagement all on you, but your development is too. In our research, the number one attribute executives valued in employees was a high degree of education and qualification. Yet fewer than one-third reported that their companies offered incentives or benefits related to obtaining more education, whether it was degree-oriented or job-specific. Only 34 percent of employees said their company was able to give them the training they need.

At a 2013 convention of Chicago's top chief human resources officers, one of the keynote speakers, an HR leader from a Fortune 500 company, proclaimed, "I am not responsible for anyone's development but my own." There was a moment of silence. Had he actually just said that out loud? Then the audience began cheering him. Resoundingly. Indeed, it's all on you.

If you want to become a leader, it's even more on you. We asked executives in our survey to rank their top employee attributes. They told us they value the willingness to follow more than leadership ability. As a result, you have to build leadership skills on your own if you want to be prepared for the demands of management roles. In a review of the

17,000 leaders who went through one firm's training programs, they reported that the average age managers received their first leadership training program was 42, even though the average age most became leaders for the first time was 30. For those first twelve years, leaders were on their own to manage with inherent skills or those they acquired independent of their organization's support.

Even though organizations may offer information on careers at their firms, few offer guidance or development at the personal level. The pressure of simply keeping up with the work in your queue today makes it difficult to proactively stretch in preparation for tomorrow. It's easy to fall behind.

Elaine typifies what can happen while being focused on delivering results day-to-day without an eye on the future. After college, she worked at a local manufacturing company in human resources. With two years of experience and her college loans paid off, she went back to earn an MBA. Networking through friends and family, she landed a job in a large aerospace company in the southwest. With regular promotions, a marriage, and two children, the years slipped away.

At the fifteen-year mark, the company decided to do a major reorganization and the department head announced that everyone in her department would have to reapply for his or her job. Elaine decided to test the market while the reorganization was underway. Feedback from the few recruiters she talked to seemed frightening. Being in the same industry and company for so long, they said, could limit her options and might even put off some potential employers.

Although she was able to hold onto her job, the experience helped her realize she could no longer be a passive sojourner in her career. She began to seek new opportunities at work, achieved a new certification in her field, and began to focus more on an external network. Never again, she vowed, would she feel so at the mercy of her employer for her livelihood.

To help you take on the responsibility for your own development we explore how to learn on the fly and be open in your thinking to new or different opportunities.

Stretch Imperative 2: You Need Options

One size definitely doesn't fit all when it comes to preparing for tomorrow. Even if you have a defined career path at your company, you may not be willing to follow that prescribed plan. For example, the first five years at a top-tier consulting firm can involve 100-hour weeks and constant traveling, only to have that exhausting schedule continue once the initial dues are paid. Or at some companies, there are strong rules about how long you have to be at a certain grade level before promotion, regardless of your capabilities or merit. You need options in order to maximize your personal development.

As one of our survey respondents said, "[I want] to move more towards working independently, taking project-based work that grows my skill set while giving me the opportunity to network further. I do not see myself continuing to work in an office 9 to 5 setting, and flexibility is my goal." Others thrive in the corporate world, or perhaps enjoy an entrepreneurial small business environment. Some naturally take to the 24/7 work life of the modern workplace, while others want the freedom to go home to their families after 6 p.m. without work following them.

To increase your options, we cover some key practices on building a network and in gaining experiences. We also include five to seven strategies in every practice, letting you custom-fit your stretch solution based on your situation. Pick the strategies that work best for you.

Stretch Imperative 3: You Have Dreams

Our survey respondents and interview subjects shared hopes and aspirations for building their careers now to achieve loftier goals in the future. That might be bigger and more significant roles at your company or another one, or it might mean starting your own business. What we heard loud and clear is that you want more for yourself and your family, and you are willing to take the steps to be career-ready.

Whether it is more money, development such as mentoring, or an opportunity for challenging work, you are clearly thinking about the future. As one respondent said, "I've been a marketing professional for some time and have a lot of contacts. I have a goal in mind, but I am not seeing light at the end of the tunnel in this company. I plan to switch jobs and get a good one in a bigger organization soon."

Performing today is important, but you care about the bigger picture. When we asked what is the most important factor influencing employees' job satisfaction, the number one response was "meeting overall career goals." As this respondent affirms, "I want to focus on developing as a person, not just improving job performance." You don't only want to be ready for a job tomorrow—you also want to grow as a person to have even more career options for the future. You want to stretch.

To help you realize your dreams, we look at how you can leverage your career experience to not just bounce back but also bounce forward to embrace your dreams for the future.

An Overview of the Five Practices

Our goal as authors is to help you stretch, avoid becoming obsolete, and be engaged at work. We have combined the lifetime of our experiences developing people, conducted original research, interpreted the extensive research of others, and now aim to deliver a practical set of solutions. From our research, we found five practices that people who stretch to their potential employ. The five practices connect to the Stretch Imperatives, as shown in the chart below.

STRETCH IMPERATIVE	STRETCH PRACTICE
It's all on you	Learn on the Fly Be Open
You need options	Build a Diverse Network Be Greedy About Experiences
You have dreams	Bounce Forward

Since the first Stretch Imperative confirms that it's all on you, you must be able to:

- Learn on the fly in any situation

- Open your thinking to a world beyond where you are now

Because you need options, these practices included in the second imperative will help you:

- Connect to the people who can help you make your future happen

- Seek experiences that will prepare you for tomorrow

Finally, to ensure you are able to fulfill your dreams, as cited in the third imperative, we offer some motivational strategies to:

- Bounce forward and stay motivated through the ups and downs of a career

These five practices form the foundation for supporting your ability to reach your career goals and to be resilient and prepared for a future you have yet to envision. We believe these are the five practices that will help you stay on the path to a flexible and sustainable future.

Stretch Imperative 1: It's All on You

Practice One: Learn on the Fly

How much time did you spend in training classes last year? Or in time with your manager or mentor? In the learning industry, there is a common maxim introduced by the Center for Creative Leadership called the 70-20-10 model, as shown in Figure 1.2. The model suggests that 70 percent of learning happens informally while on the job; 20 percent through relationship with others like coaches, managers, or mentors; and 10 percent from formal coursework or training.

Informal learning happens in many ways. These can include casual conversation with co-workers, experiences such as expanded roles and responsibilities, using new tools and technologies, working on teams or programs outside of your normal responsibilities, or taking on a completely new role in a volunteer position outside of work. Since

FIG 1.2 70-20-10 Model

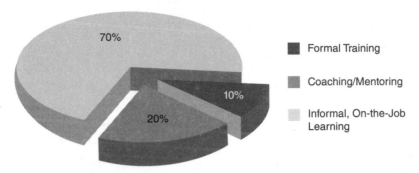

- 70%
- 20%
- 10%

Legend:
- Formal Training
- Coaching/Mentoring
- Informal, On-the-Job Learning

most of how you learn is unstructured, having strategies and tools to learn on the fly is one of the most important ways you can stretch to your potential.

Kurt is an example of someone unprepared to learn on the fly. Frustrated with feeling he was stagnating in his role as a project manager and knowing from feedback that people wanted him to be more "take charge," he knew he needed help. He went to the local bookstore and scanned the self-help and career titles to learn about being more decisive. Overwhelmed with the choices, ironically he walked out with nothing because the decision was too difficult.

Unlike Kurt, we have found that expert learners have a specific set of techniques they use to develop themselves. We will provide you with tools the experts use and also help you avoid the most significant learning traps people fall into when learning in the context of their work.

Practice Two: Be Open

Even though you may have the ability to learn, there is a mindset about approaching work and your environment that is either open or closed. Are you willing to be vulnerable about not knowing everything, or do you position yourself as already knowing everything there is to know about a topic? As Liz Wiseman, author of *Rookie Smarts*, says, "Rookies are unencumbered, with no baggage to weigh them down, no resources to burden them, and no track record to limit their thinking or aspirations. For today's knowledge workers, constant learning is more valuable than mastery." To be open, we must recognize that the world is shifting faster than we can possibly change ourselves.

In Chapter 3, "Be Open," we will give you techniques for soliciting feedback in safe and unconventional ways and help you assess how open you truly are. We provide key strategies for developing your skills to be open to seeing opportunities in new ways and to identify small decisions you can make along with big ones to move your career forward.

⊘ Stretch Imperative 2: You Need Options

Practice Three: Build a Diverse Network

Many of the people we interviewed told us that the strategy they used to stay current and stretch their own horizons was to hang around the right people. Those might be smart people, connected people, younger people, older people, or powerful people. But which of the following two networks would serve you best in getting a job?

The first option is a network of people who are close to you, friend ship, community, or family who are always there to see you through thick and thin. You know you can count on them to help make introductions and provide small favors in your job quest. You are strongly tied to these people.

The second option is a network of acquaintances with whom you are likely to have less frequent contact. We are not talking about your Facebook friend George Takei, but the people with whom you might have had lunch once or twice, or whom you met at a professional confer ence and kept up an occasional email exchange with or see at an annual holiday party. This network might be a little more geographically diverse and not as concentrated as the first network. Chapter 4, "Build a Diverse Network," explores the function and application of both your networks and the surprising answer to what networks you need when.

Depending on the type of job you have and your personal style, the strategies for building a network may differ. We will provide you a range of approaches and when to use each one, depending on your type of job and your personal style.

Practice Four: Be Greedy About Gaining Experiences

Given the same experiences, two different people might not each gain the same growth of knowledge and capability. As Douglas Adams wrote in *The Hitchhikers Guide to the Galaxy*, "Human beings, who are almost unique in having the ability to learn from the experience of others, are also remarkable for their apparent disinclination to do so."

The collection of meaningful experiences, with a deliberate approach can be the most powerful way to stay up-to-date and current in your role. Michael Webb, senior vice president at HSBC in Canada, passes on advice from his father: "Be absolutely greedy about experiences."

In Chapter 5, "Be Greedy About Experiences," we will provide you with ideas to consider to develop more capabilities both inside and outside the confines of your current job. We also help you contemplate what to do if your current experience is with a bad boss, or whether your good boss may be keeping you from stretching to your potential.

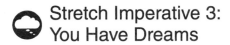 Stretch Imperative 3: You Have Dreams

Practice Five: Bounce Forward

One of the biggest factors determining how well you navigate your success in the future is how much grit you have. Grit is a combination of perseverance with a passion for long-term goals, needed to sustain you through setbacks. But we not only have to bounce back from setbacks, we must also bounce forward toward a goal that keeps us learning and growing. Being absolutely determined is a strong predictor of success, which is why perseverance through setbacks so often leads to success.

If you've ever said, "I'll never do that again," it is likely because the impact of the failure or bad event is bigger than any number of good events strung together. Negative events are powerful learning tools. Bad is stronger than good, at least when it comes to learning and locking in long-term memories.

The solution, if we are to move forward and avoid stagnation, is to recover from a downfall with a drive to achieve a goal in the future. Although failure is one of the worst setbacks, there are other types of setbacks that can be just as debilitating. False starts, such as declaring one academic major in college only to realize in your senior year that you have no passion for it, can be just as hard because of the sunk costs and the feeling that you are abandoning a set path.

Another type of setback is disruption, usually from events out of your control. The company you work for could be acquired, or regulatory environments could change, like the repeal of Prohibition affecting Al Capone's livelihood. And then there are the missed opportunities we each have in our past. These can cause us to look backward and dwell on what could have been instead of what can be. Determination and grit can see you through any of these setbacks, and Chapter 6 will provide some motivational strategies to help you persevere toward a long-term goal.

The Story of Brandon

Brandon, a director of training, is an example of someone who had to discover what goals he felt passionate about and then stretch to achieve them. Diagnosed with ADD and dyslexia, a psychologist told his mother that a high-school degree would be aiming high and college was out of the question. With strong support from his parents, he obtained a BS degree in psychology, but was unsure what he wanted to do. He first worked in construction, then as a camp counselor. As he worked various jobs, he realized he liked working with people more than working with his hands.

Upon returning from a year of traveling the world, he decided to go into sales. Quickly realizing he hated sales, that experience was chalked off to learning what he didn't want to do. Still unsure, he decided to earn an MBA, and then focused on finding a job in adult education.

His first boss in a corporate training position was, as he put it, "absolutely horrible," but when that boss moved on, he got the opportunity to move up. "Something clicked in," he said. "I struggled for six months, but then I realized that learning on the fly was okay."

Brandon has finally landed in a field that he can pursue in almost any industry, as all but the smallest companies have training departments. Looking back, he now sees how every one of his working experiences combined to make it possible for him to find the job that ultimately clicked.

Brandon learned how to bounce forward through a number of obstacles, false starts, and the disruption of a bad boss. He tried a variety of experiences to see what fit, all the while defining the working environment he liked best. He learned to use his network for both support and to find positions. Brandon is engaged. Are you ready to thrive as well?

Stretch Summary

- You are in charge of your engagement with your work.
- The number one concern of employees around the world is their position changing or their skills becoming obsolete.
- The stretch imperatives are the three resounding themes from employee and executive interviews and write-in comments. They are:

  It's all on you. You are the only one who can drive your career development. Don't rely on your boss or your organization to engage you.

  You need options. Not everyone is able or willing to relocate or make a major career shift if the company demands it. You need options from which to choose in considering how to prepare for tomorrow.

  You have dreams. Whether those dreams are in the organization you are in now, somewhere else, or as your own boss, you dream about doing more.

- The five practices to future proof yourself for tomorrow's workplace map to the Imperatives:

  It's all on you: Learn on the fly
                            Be open

  You need options: Build diverse networks
                            Be greedy about experiences

  You have dreams: Bounce forward

Part 2: It's All on You

Chapter 2: Learn on the Fly

Chapter 3: Be Open

The fundamental building blocks to stretch when development is all on you io to learn no matter where you are and to recognize the opportunities around you.

The illiterate of the 21st century will not be those who cannot read and write, but those who cannot learn, unlearn, and relearn.

—Alvin Toffler

2 LEARN ON THE FLY

If you've attended any of your high school reunions, you've no doubt realized that the same observations have been made by alumni across the country: Who looks good? Who's aged poorly? Who's transformed so much that we hardly recognize them?

Conversation regarding who's transformed extends to the professional realm as well. Most everyone in the class has reached the same milestones in their careers, but some have done really well. Some everyone expected, but there are always surprises—the people never predicted to do well but have somehow transformed into successes. How did they do it?

New studies show that what separates those who went beyond what everyone else achieved is something very simple: they maintained the ability to keep on learning. Those who stay on a quest to learn beyond school have an immeasurable potential. And they'll attend each subsequent reunion more successful, every time.

Jonah was voted the class slacker when he was in high school, so there were probably more than a few lifted eyebrows at his reunions. Getting his history degree was easy enough, he said, but it wasn't until he volunteered at a local school that he found his passion for education. Like a good portion of his generation, he decided to go into teaching.

He felt the ideal situation would be to develop young people in a high-integrity environment, so he took a position at a charter school. The first year was not what he expected. "It was so hard. I was miserable and thought I would quit, and I couldn't make it. I was working fourteen hours a day. People told me I was walking around looking miserable, and that's not good for school culture. I wanted to be really amazingly great. I had faith that I had enough potential to succeed."

The only recourse was to get better, and to do that, he needed to learn new skills for success. "I talked too much. And kids got sick of listening to me. So then they'd do other things, and I would get frustrated and it showed." He knew he had to make his second year better than his first. Not only did he read some books that shaped his thinking, but when the school year started, he also helped organize some professional development with the other teachers. "Even little tips, like how to handle the five minutes between classes, helped me improve. Learning is about practicing, I realized, and I looked for ways to practice so that I could get better."

By year three, he began to coach new teachers, and soon he realized that he got as much satisfaction coaching teachers as he did in teaching itself. Jonah is now in a principal development program. No one would call him the class slacker now.

Good Enough Isn't Good Enough for Long

Almost anyone can identify with Jonah's first year on the job and the effort it takes to get to a feeling of competency. But not everyone continues to push beyond the required job competencies in order to fulfill her potential. For some, stopping at "good enough" is enough. But "good enough" employees are the ones in peril of never advancing, of losing job satisfaction, becoming disengaged and of becoming obsolete over time.

According to our research, less than 40 percent of employees report being satisfied with their jobs. Interestingly, more than half of all employees say they are at least somewhat likely to leave their jobs in the next six months. Stuck in that mindset, it is easy to see why people might stop pressing forward and learning new capabilities. "What do you do," a manager asked recently, "when people will only give the minimum they need to get by on the job?"

Some, like Jonah, are eager to become competent early in their career tenure. But for many others, work is more of a habit than an opportunity. If you never acquire new capabilities or feel inspired to take on new challenges, you will simply level off in your field. Worse, new technologies, processes, and knowledge naturally erode the overall competency of any individual, no matter where he begins. The decay slope is stronger in some fields such as medicine, but over time, it is possible for someone with years of experience in almost any field to become less expert than a newcomer. Tenure doesn't guarantee expertise or high performance—in fact, quite the opposite.

Imagine two people who start their careers, both excited to learn their new jobs and both advancing early on at the same pace as shown in Figure 2.1. The first person continues learning on the job,

FIG **2.1** Learning a Living

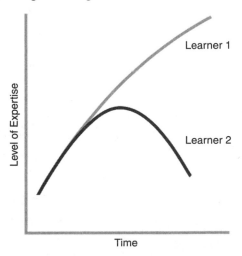

incrementally acquiring new knowledge, skills, and expertise. The second person becomes complacent, perhaps frustrated with the job, thus only putting in the minimal effort to stay employed. However, that minimal effort accumulates over time. New job content grows and old content continues to decay. Eventually, while likely earning more than a newcomer, their expertise is lower. The second person has become obsolete and a prime target for an employment crisis.

Learning a Living

To avoid becoming obsolete, you must continue to learn and not just in a classroom or in other formal learning settings. In a sense, we must all learn a living because, as people said repeatedly in our interviews, "It's on me to develop myself." The same refrain comes from human resource leaders and others. Gianpiero Petriglieri, INSEAD professor, confirms, "Everyone says that learning is essential for companies' success—and for your own. And yet, on a daily basis, who cares for your learning? No one. People care about what you have learned. They care about your results. Learning is great as long as you do it quietly, in your own time."

Companies that provide learning opportunities increase their employees' knowledge base and skill set, plus boost employee satisfaction. This benefits both the organization and the individual. However, the unfortunate reality is that companies are not providing enough training to keep employees up-to-date, much less prepared for tomorrow's workplace.

According to an Accenture 2011 study, nearly 80 percent of employees in today's workplace received no company-sponsored skills training in the past five years. None. This leaves many workers to fend for themselves. Today the average spent per employee is still just over $1,200 per year in the United States, primarily on compliance and leadership training. Fortunately there's a promising trend for organizations indicating they will spend more on formal training.

Certainly there are companies that are renowned and award-winning for providing extraordinary employee development opportunities, such as GE, TELUS, Cigna, Unilever, USAA, Hilton, Marriott,

Corning, and others. But as many have noted, including Professor Petriglieri at the beginning of this section, they are the exception and not the norm. You must assume it's on you to find your own way to get the development you need, especially while on the job. Most of the real learning you receive in your professional life will be on the job, and not in a classroom. You must learn on the job, often "on the fly" if you are to have any hope of keeping up.

What Does Excellence Look Like?

Being effective at what we value resonates with something beyond feeling competent. At some level, competence connects with our dreams, with that part of us that yearns for unity with something greater than ourselves. We want to matter.

—Raymond J. Wlodkowski

As far back as Greek civilization, the right to express an opinion in a public forum demanded a level of expertise. Socrates reported that when decisions were to be made at the assembly, the experts in respective domains were called forth. Builders were called for building discussions, shipwrights when the dialogue was about shipbuilding, and so on. "But if anyone else tried to give advice, no matter how handsome or well-born he is, they still will have none of him, but jeer at him and create an uproar, until either the would-be speaker is shouted down and gives up of his own accord, or else the guards drag him away or put him out on the order of the presidents." Being excellent in your chosen field matters if your voice is to be heard.

The Levels of Expertise

"Do you know wines?" Karie asked her friend Rick Harwell as they prepared for a business trip to northern California. In an era when Saturday night stays made airfare far less expensive, they had decided to extend the trip by one night and visit Napa Valley. "I know something about wine. One of my favorites is Pouilly-Fuissé," he said. Karie had never heard of Pouilly-Fuissé, and was glad to have a seeming expert along for the trip.

To start their Saturday off, they attended a two-hour class on wine tasting at a wine discovery center. The sommelier introduced the customs and practices for tasting wine and made the somewhat intimidating subject more accessible. At the end of the two hours, Rick turned to Karie and said, "Forget everything I said about knowing wine. I know nothing!"

When you approach a new subject area, you know nothing. Like Rick, you may think you know more than you do until you are in the company of an expert—in this case the sommelier.

Think of achieving excellence in your field as having five levels. When you first graduate from college, you might be at the novice level, well on your way to being competent in your field, as shown in Table 2.1. Unless you keep on learning, you are unlikely to progress much beyond that. Excellence requires deliberate and intentional effort.

Table 2.1 The Levels of Expertise

LEVEL	DEFINITION
Initiate	Minimal or no exposure
Novice	Some introductory instruction; may have taken formal courses, but little applied experience
Competent	Actively learning and working in the field; usually has five or fewer years' experience; in complex fields may take up to 12 years; relies on others for complex problem solving advice
Professional	Able to work with little to no direction at a high level; recognized with awards and recognition for outstanding contribution in the field; often has assumed substantial responsibility for decision making
Expert	Highly regarded by others; can handle difficult, rare situations; skilled across subdomains; offers groundbreaking solutions; rarely has less than a decade working in the field

How Many Areas Can You Be Great At?

You likely have multiple domains in which you operate. For example, if you are in a marketing role, you might specialize in marketing communications but also need a healthy dose of expertise in social media marketing. Out of the levels defined in Table 2.1, to work in a field, you will need to be at least at the Competent level, but to stand out you will need at least a Professional level for knowledge-based jobs. Most people can spend an entire career never going beyond the Professional level, since keeping up with changes in their field is challenging enough.

With that in mind, people early in their careers can usually only achieve a professional level of expertise in one functional area. You might start with just marketing communications, but you can move to deeper expertise while acquiring competence in another domain. Eventually, depending on your commitment to learning and the experiences you gain, you can decide to specialize and become a marketing expert, or begin cutting across functions to build your capacity toward being a general manager.

How long will it take? Some people get lucky with the right experiences and challenges and can achieve high levels in just a few years. For most, it will take longer, especially if you are in a complex field or organization. Chess masters, surgeons, and pilots take on average 10,000 hours of practice to become Experts, but not all fields require this level of dedication. The more complex your field, the more likely it will take you longer to become extraordinary.

Strategies for Learning on the Fly

I don't divide the world into the weak and the strong, or the successes and the failures, those who make it or those who don't. I divide the world into learners and non-learners.

—Benjamin Barber

Learn on the Fly Stretch Strategies

1. Adopt a growth mindset
2. Mindfully observe
3. Cultivate curiosity
4. Set aside time to reflect
5. Know when to unlearn

In job interviews, nearly all candidates are apt to declare that they are "quick learners." But how do they know they are good at learning on the fly? And aren't all humans built to be learners? Everyone breathes; is everyone a good breather? They might think so until they take their first yoga class and realize they know almost nothing about the different ways to approach inhaling and exhaling.

Researchers estimate that most of what adults learn is unconsciously absorbed through highly automated mental operations. Even teachers or masters, when asked to convey what they know, will believe they have given 100 percent of their knowledge, but have actually withheld 70 percent of their non-conscious expertise. Surely you've experienced this when you have asked someone to give you instructions for a task, only to find that important steps were left out. Years ago, Karie bought her first rowboat and asked a neighbor how to best launch from the dock. "Just step into it from your dock," he said. "It's very easy. You'll do fine."

The neighbor failed to mention the importance of keeping the boat tied to the dock, so with one foot in the boat and one on the dock, the growing split led to an inevitable spill in the water and a sunken boat. Twenty minutes later, after restoring the boat to floating capacity, Karie successfully sat in the boat and launched off, only to notice the oars remained on the dock. With yet another dunk in the lagoon water, she made the third try work.

If our advisors are withholding critical knowledge, whether intentional or not, we can't rely entirely on them to guide us in our learning; we must develop techniques and strategies of our own. We tend to remember what we practice. As skills become routine, it's easy to forget all of the inherent steps. That's why your potential to learn isn't always apparent on your first try.

Fortunately, there are strategies for improving your ability to learn and acquire new levels of expertise without having to take a dunk doing it. Here we offer some strategies to help you become more adept at learning on the fly.

Adopt a Growth Mindset

Among a host of possible reasons, the most important one that keeps people from achieving their dreams may be their innate beliefs about their potential. The first strategy to learn on the fly is to commit to a mindset that you have the capacity to learn and grow. Carol Dweck writes about this in *Mindset*. Those who believe that their potential is fixed, based on their genes or heritage, background, or the opportunities available to them, for good or for bad, will focus on proving their perceived capabilities. "I'm not a math person, so I should stay away from analyst jobs" or "I didn't go to the right school, so I don't fit in this culture" or "I'm a natural athlete so I don't need to practice as much." They have what Dweck calls a fixed mindset.

When observing first-year college students, Barbara often sees that they must shift their mindsets. High school might have been an easy path for them, one that required little effort, and suddenly they realize what is required of them in college is considerably more advanced. There is so much to learn and so much more competition. And plenty of other students are willing to work hard to achieve higher goals. If the fixed mindset of "I'm smart and do not have to study hard" is relied upon, they will likely flounder. They must reset their thinking to be more active learners.

A person with a growth mindset, in contrast, believes that true potential is "unknown and unknowable because it is impossible to foresee what can be accomplished with years of passion, toil, and training." People with a growth mindset, Dweck asserts, "don't just *seek* challenge, they thrive on it. The bigger the challenge, the more they stretch."

One of Barbara's colleagues introduced the concept of a growth mindset to her students through a TED talk by Dweck. Later, that student told her that she had been very close to dropping out because she could not see a quick fix or an immediate solution to passing her semester. The student had a fixed mindset that if the answer wasn't readily available, then she should drop out. Once she understood the concept of a growth mindset, she found some peace in knowing that she might not have the solution yet, but she would. "I will, but not yet," became her mantra.

The same thing applies to the workplace, whether you are in your first years with the company or are an established employee. With a growth mindset, opportunities to learn will abound and you will find yourself more open to new experiences, and you will be more likely to achieve the skill improvement and professional development goals you set out for yourself.

How do you change from a fixed mindset to a growth mindset? First recognize that you are never completely one or the other, because your thinking about a situation can change. When you feel helpless in a situation, is it possible you are in a fixed mindset? For example, have you ever said, "It won't do any good to try and get my boss to see my point of view because he doesn't like me." Once you have identified that you are in a fixed mindset, then ask yourself how you could approach the

STRETCH BREAK

Do you have an orientation to learn and to grow? Here are some questions to assess your learning orientation. Try to think about the last few job assignments as you consider the answers to these questions. Rate each item, with 1 being strongly disagree and 7 being strongly agree. Add your scores together, then divide by 5 to find your average.

Learning Goal Orientation	Strongly Disagree					Strongly Agree	
	1	2	3	4	5	6	7
I am willing to select a challenging work assignment that I can learn a lot from	1	2	3	4	5	6	7
I often look for opportunities to develop new skills and knowledge	1	2	3	4	5	6	7
I enjoy challenging and difficult tasks at work where I'll learn new skills	1	2	3	4	5	6	7
For me, development of my work ability is important enough to take risks	1	2	3	4	5	6	7
I prefer to work in situations that require a high level of ability and talent	1	2	3	4	5	6	7

Table excerpted from: Don VandeWalle, "Development and Validation of a Work Domain Goal Orientation Instrument", *Educational and Psychological Measurement*, December 1, 1997. This is one of three components from the instrument.

An average over 6 indicates a strong learning orientation. When you tally your numbers, are you satisfied? Can you readily see where you excel or where you might improve? If your boss or a close peer were to score you, what would he or she say?

situation from a growth mindset. "My boss and I don't see eye-to-eye on most things, but what would it take to persuade him to my point of view? Who can I enlist to help me?"

Mindfully Observe

You have probably had the experience of going to a meeting with a colleague and walking out with very different perspectives on what happened. Perhaps your colleague was checking his phone constantly and doodling, head down, while listening only partially, in a state of continuous partial attention. On the other hand, you watched the reactions of the people in the room, asked questions, and tried to synthesize the varying viewpoints. Your colleague might view the meeting as both routine and unnecessary, whereas you might have gained some new insights. The difference was mindfulness.

Mindfulness applied to learning involves focusing on the present experience, being intentionally aware and attentive, and recognizing that life is constantly changing.

One way to apply mindfulness to learning on the fly is to come to a situation open to viewing it from several perspectives. In school or in formal classrooms, we are often taught which perspective to adopt or use. On the job, it helps to have the ability to observe without immediate judgment.

By observing in the moment, without a need to immediately respond or jump to conclusions, we create an opportunity to see new or novel thoughts and ideas, reflect on their impact, and create new approaches to understanding the information. Clearly, it helps to have very good listening skills to be able to observe in the moment. Dave Ulrich, a professor and coach, talks about someone he once coached who had a tendency to interject a response before the person was through talking. When Dave asked the executive what he thought good listening was, the executive responded, "When I understand what they are trying to tell me." Dave said, "Wrong. It's not when you understand them. It's when they feel heard." Hearing others gives you the opportunity to adopt new perspectives. As Henry James said, "Try to be one of the people upon whom nothing is lost." Mindful observation enabled by careful listening will help you become someone upon whom nothing is lost.

Cultivate Curiosity

Committing to a learning mindset and observing in the moment are important, but they are stronger when followed up with curiosity about why. Curiosity helps us avoid complacency and disengagement. The more successful you become, whether as organizations or as individuals, the easier it is to become complacent about learning and lack curiosity about your work world.

Since we all work from a set of unconscious rules we have acquired from our experiences, asking "Why?" with a sense of curiosity can help you bring the unconscious rules to the conscious level. If Karie had asked more questions of her neighbor about how to climb in the boat, she might have avoided a couple of dunks in the lagoon. Being eternally curious leads to never completely being satisfied, but "not being satisfied is what makes curiosity so satisfying."

Curiosity makes us happy, too. "There's this paradoxical route to well-being," Todd Kashdan of George Mason University says. "Maybe the real way to make yourself happy is by doing something that challenges you, makes you stretch." In a sense, once we allow ourselves to be curious, life becomes astonishing.

One of the downsides of the incredible search engine capabilities available to us on the web is that we can be deluded into thinking we do not need to develop an array of knowledge and information for ourselves. But it is exactly that deep background knowledge that helps us ask good questions. The irony of the increased efficiency of search engines is that the precision in our questions has weakened. Amit Singhal, head of Google Search, says, "The more accurate the machine gets, the lazier the questions become. So actually our lives get harder." Our inability to ask precise questions yields such a broad and lengthy set of search results that we do not find the answers we are seeking.

STRETCH BREAK

In the checklist below, we have put together some questions you can ask yourself in almost any business situation to help stimulate your curiosity. Use them to help you understand more about the world around you and what piques your interest to help you set learning goals.

A Curiosity Stimulator Checklist

☐ *For someone who does work that is very different from your own:* What is one thing you think people don't know about what you do?

☐ *Ask of subject matter experts:* What is the most interesting project or idea you are working on now, or wish you were working on?

☐ *During meetings:* What is valid about the dissenting viewpoint in this discussion?

☐ *When listening to a proposal for something new:* How is this idea similar to other ideas that have worked? How is it different? (Tip: try to focus on similarities before differences or why something won't work.)

☐ *When you find yourself disagreeing with someone:* What assumptions or models am I using that causes me to agree or disagree in this situation?

Set Aside Time to Reflect

Do you remember that insight you had last month when you were at that conference and your colleague made an informative presentation on the marketplace? No? Neither do we. But Bob Cancalosi of GE Crotonville does. For over eleven years, Bob has kept work journals that he uses for reflecting and learning about his path as a leader. See Figure 2.2 for a picture of the level of detail that he puts into his journals.

When Bob is presented with an informative or inspirational piece of information, he may reduce the slide and insert it in his journal,

FIG 2.2 Journals Picture

or he may just copy the key points, adding actions and his own insights. Some topics are of special interest to Bob, so he codes entries across 30 unique categories, allowing him to go back and synthesize across time and subject matter. "I am up to journal 35 now, and for a while I thought I would make the transition to doing it all online. I learned from Scott G. Halford's book called *Activate the Brain* that it's been shown that we create better memory trails in our brain when we physically write the words versus type them. His research indicates that handwriting is like strength training for the brain."

Periodically, Bob looks back over his notes to think about what he has learned over the year, creating a triple loop of learning. The first insight is in the handwritten recording. Then, every 50 pages in his journal, he inserts a "stop and reflect" page to summarize the biggest insights, creating a second learning loop. The third loop is as the end of each book, where he synthesizes the best of the learnings in the "stop and reflects" into a single page per journal. So far Bob has 696 recorded learning events, and he uses his top 80 to help him prepare for speeches and in his coaching of other executives. He has turned his curiosity and note-taking into a wellspring for his frequent role as a mentor and coach. Bob's sharing of knowledge, insights, and connection of the dots from his plethora of journals to others could be considered a fourth or quadruple loop of learning.

Many people keep personal journals, but the practice of what Bob calls "leadership reflections" is almost entirely work-focused and creates a habit of reflection. At the start of every journal, Bob picks a few random pages to write in personal questions such as, "Am I happy?" "Am I achieving my health goals?" or "Am I following my ambition?" He likes the surprise factor of turning the page to remind himself of his personal goals.

If you are not the journaling type, at least consider setting some time aside to think about the past week and anticipate the next week while running on the treadmill or taking a lunchtime walk. Even better, find a learning partner to meet with every two to four weeks to share your learning goals and discuss what you have learned. Reflection leads to learning.

Know When to Unlearn

Does it feel like you are falling further and further behind in your reading and in keeping up with your field? That is not an illusion. When Buckminster Fuller named the "knowledge-doubling curve," it was based on his observation that for all of human history until 1900, knowledge doubled every century. Now it is estimated that knowledge is doubling every 13 months, but will soon lead to doubling every 12 hours.

EMC, the IT storage company, reports that by 2020, there will be more data bits available now than there are stars in the universe. If you considered just the knowledge you need to absorb in your field, the amount of content is beyond what any one individual can absorb in a lifetime. At the moment we do not have adequate tools to help sort new information and deliver it in a customized fashion, although a number of companies are making progress in designing ways to help us stay up-to-date.

Even if we could keep up, facts change. As Samuel Arbeson, a complex systems scientist reminds us, if you are a Baby Boomer who graduated from high school before 1970, over 10 percent of chemical elements are new, Pluto is no longer a planet, and the debate rages whether dinosaurs had feathers or scales. The half-life of facts is changing constantly and differs between fields, but what you learned in school or on the job might actually now be wrong or outdated. We have to be able to rapidly unlearn as well as learn new things.

New learning can replace old learning, but triggers are necessary to jar us into awareness of the need to learn or unlearn. As just a small example, Karie read a blog that said double spaces at the end of a sentence were a dead giveaway the writer was over 40. For this book we each had to unlearn putting in those two spaces, something anyone who learned to type before 1990 carries as an ingrained habit. Although unlearning slowed us down at first, eventually we broke through and formed the new one-space habit. By having an open mind, you will more readily see the triggers that alert you to unlearn.

How do you identify when you need to unlearn? We carry with us explicit and tacit knowledge that we've gained over the years, as well as frames of reference—mindsets—that form how we think about the world. Our deeply ingrained habits and the systems in which we work also can discourage us from changing.

Expect to be frustrated when you are unlearning, as that is a natural part of the process. Feeling like you are back to ground zero is the uncomfortable phase you have to go through when unlearning. Over the course of a career and of continuously updating yourself, you should feel those moments of frustration. Having your career goals in mind makes it worth the effort to push through. In the next chapter we will explore how to be open and aware of your frames of reference and how they affect what you choose to learn or to block.

STRETCH 2.4

There are times when you are in a situation where you have a strong reaction to something new, unusual, or discomforting at work. That strong reaction may be a sign that you are hanging on to an outdated way of thinking. Here are some questions to determine if it's time to unlearn something old.

The Unlearning Checklist

☐ Are people bringing up terms or concepts that are unfamiliar to me, and I counter with examples that are more than a few years old?

☐ Are the people I rely on the most at work up-to-date in their field? Do my closest associates challenge me to think in new ways and abandon old practices or tools?

☐ Do new people who come to work here seem to have ideas that are far different from my own? Could that be a sign I need to re-fresh my thinking?

☐ Do I tend to use the same arguments or stories year after year without retesting whether they are still valid?

☐ How am I working in different ways than I see people younger than me working? Is that difference because they are still new, or is it because I am not adopting new practices that might be more efficient?

☐ Is there a possibility that the way I am thinking about this is out-dated or wrong, and that I need to change my frame of thinking?

Learning Traps to Avoid

When you look at people who have successfully stretched and grown throughout their careers, take note that there were also traps they managed to avoid. Now that you have a few strategies to use to help you learn on the job, here are also some cautionary tales about what not to do.

Confusing Confidence with Competence

"I'm not sure how to handle this situation I have right now," the head of human resources of a large consumer goods company confided to Karie at a conference. He had just listened to a talk about Millennials in the workplace, and it had struck a chord with him. "There is a talented young man, two years out of college, who absolutely insists that he is ready to be a general manager. He thinks we are being bureaucratic because we want him to get more management depth, but he is absolutely confident he's ready. How do I tell him he's not, because I think his whole life, like many in his generation, has been about reinforcement and confidence building? But there is no way he is ready."

Paradoxically, less capable people tend to confidently overestimate their abilities, while more capable people tend to underestimate the difficulty of what they do. This phenomenon is called the Dunning-Kruger Effect, and you may have been at the brunt end of it at work when a manager pushes you to promise way more than you can deliver based on his or her own overconfidence.

Unless we are careful, we can live in the ignorant bliss of our relative inability. One of the biggest steps you can take to avoid this trap is to adopt a growth mindset, the first strategy in this section, because people with a growth mindset are more likely to be accurate about their capabilities and to understand what they need to do to improve their capabilities. Another way to avoid this trap is to assess yourself by seeking feedback from others, a topic we'll discuss in detail in the next chapter.

Unintentionally De-Skilling

Automation and technology can not only threaten to replace your job, but can also make you stupider in the job you are in. Many studies have shown that the more we rely on technology to do our jobs for us, the rustier we can become at manually handling work and at working at the edges of what automation can do. If you have a smart phone, how many numbers do you have memorized? In a sense, we have outsourced many cognitive skills to our devices, so that our ability to memorize, for example, becomes weaker over time for any type of memorization, not just phone numbers.

In jobs, consider airline pilots who rely on autopilot to do most of the flying for them. When an emergency strikes, unless they have been practicing on manual controls, they are not as prepared as you would hope. The same is true for many professions. For example, the act of sketching out designs seems to activate parts of our brain that inspires creative thinking and learning, as compared to relying solely on design software.

One solution is to periodically train manually. Captain Sullenberger, the pilot who miraculously landed a plane on the Hudson River, kept up his manual skills. His extensive experience and practice, including glider training, is partially credited for the survival of all 155 passengers and crew.

Another solution is to seek out challenges that are outside technology's capability. If you need to conduct some analysis and currently rely on reports that are generated from a few systems, for example, collect a sampling and lay them out in front of you to look for patterns, similarities, and contradictions across the reports. Big data is only as good as the questions we ask and the insights we have. Occasionally stepping back and trying to find out whether we are asking the best questions can also ensure we are not losing the analytic skills we have mentally outsourced to technology.

Over-Managing Risk

As your financial and family commitments increase, it is only natural to avoid taking steps that would put your security at risk. Gianpiero Petriglieri of INSEAD explains that big change, what he calls transformational learning, "always involves defiance—of complacency, conformity, and norms. As such, it takes courage, not just time."

That defiance—the willingness to take risks, to not follow the proscribed career path, to court seemingly irrelevant modes of thinking—can be particularly difficult in a culture that does not encourage deviation or tolerate the failure that can sometimes accompany it. Unless your financial reserves run deep, some level of caution is advisable. How much caution is too much, though, is the question. Entrepreneurs wrestle with this dilemma all the time, so understanding their thought process can help in considering the risks you face in your own career.

One entrepreneur quite familiar with risk is Brian Chesky, the founder of AirBnB. His company is an example of an entirely new business model, grounded in what is commonly called the "sharing economy," AirBnB allows residents to rent out their homes to travelers, which of course creates disruption for traditional hotels and regulatory agencies. "The most important thing I've learned how to do is learn. I've had to embrace the fact that I'm constantly going to be in uncharted waters, and I'm constantly going to be doing something I've never done before. I had to learn to get comfortable in a role of ambiguity where I had to seek out advisers and learn quickly." The more you trust your capacity to learn on the fly, the easier it is to manage risk.

The Payoff

A good education and continuing learning create a foundation for a career. To stay current requires ongoing training and development so

The tree of knowledge and the fountain of youth are one and the same.

—Lewis Lapham

that you can extend your sell-by date. By developing skills to learn on the fly, no matter what circumstances you face on the job, you will have tools for adapting and changing to meet the challenge at hand. If you are going to put yourself in the path of learning, then learn.

Learning on the fly, combined with being open, are the foundational practices because they are about how you learn and think. In the next chapter, we'll cover how to be open. How you learn and think sets the stage for expanding your network of people who can lead you to extraordinary experiences, so that even when times are tough, you can bounce forward into increasing success.

When we are learning, it can feel awkward. To break through to new levels of performance requires us to take on the risk of looking foolish while we learn new skills and stretch to a new self. Here is a tool to assess whether you might be avoiding risk at the expense of an opportunity to learn. Rate yourself on each item, with 1 being strongly disagree and 7 being strongly agree. Add your scores together, then divide by 4 to get your average your score.

Avoidance Orientation	Strongly Disagree Strongly Agree						
	1	2	3	4	5	6	7
I would avoid taking on a new task if there was a chance I would appear rather incompetent to others	1	2	3	4	5	6	7
Avoiding a show of low ability is more important to me than learning a new skill	1	2	3	4	5	6	7
I'm concerned about taking on a task at work if my performance would reveal that I had low ability	1	2	3	4	5	6	7
I avoid situations at work where I might perform poorly	1	2	3	4	5	6	7

Table excerpted from: Don VandeWalle, "Development and Validation of a Work Domain Goal Orientation Instrument", *Educational and Psychological Measurement*, December 1, 1997. The instrument has three components, and this is part three. We elected not to use the second part for this book.

In this assessment, lower scores are better. The higher your score, the more likely you are avoiding stretching. Is your work environment one that discourages risk? Can you increase your opportunities for learning and avoid complacency?

Stretch Summary

- To avoid becoming obsolete, you must learn on the fly. Most learning happens while we are doing work.
- Developing expertise can take years and requires focus and choice.
- The strategies for learning on the fly include:
  - *Adopt a growth mindset.* We approach our ability to learn either assuming we are born with a fixed set of capabilities or that our potential is unknown because we can grow throughout our lives.
  - *Mindfully observe.* Being intentionally aware and present helps to learn in the moment.
  - *Cultivate curiosity.* Search engines cannot do it all. We need to be curious in order to ask the right questions.
  - *Set aside time to reflect.* Connecting the dots between experiences through reflection helps learning become permanent.
  - *Know when to unlearn.* Life is constantly changing. We have to adapt by unlearning and relearning if we want to avoid becoming obsolete.
- Avoid learning traps so you don't get stuck in your career
  - Confusing competence with confidence
  - Unintentionally de-skilling
  - Over-managing risk

What Organizations and Managers Can Do

Our emphasis in this book is to provide advice to individuals to help them stretch to their potential and to be prepared for tomorrow's workplace. Forward-thinking organizations can provide an environment that makes it easier for their employees to learn on the job and to fulfill their potential. Formal training programs are both expensive and take time away from the job, but enabling employees to learn at work does not need to be an elaborate program or expensive investment. From our research and interviews, we have selected a few exceptional examples of how organizations and leaders can foster a growth and learning culture for employees.

Create On-Boarding Success Maps for All Transitions

Many organizations have new hire on-boarding programs, but once you are assimilated, transitions from there on are often a sink-or-swim proposition. As one result, the failure rate in new roles can be as high as 40 percent, so providing guidance through the initial few months avoids disruption and the costly hemorrhaging of new hires.

Instead of thinking of on-boarding as a practice for new-hires to the organization, help employees consider all the new things they will need to learn and know in any new role. When Andi Litz was promoted at General Electric, she said that reaching out to someone who had just held the job was beneficial. She immediately contacted the person she was replacing there. "Since he had just left the job for another position at GE," she says, "he was really helpful. We exchanged lots of phone calls, text messages, and instant messages. I'd be on a big call with people from all over the place, and I could IM him to get quick insight on anything that came up in the discussion."

Good on-boarding or transition plans can encourage learning on the job by defining early on what the employee will need to learn, from whom they can learn it, and then encouraging those connections.

Define Expected Capabilities

Most organizations have some set of employee competencies that help define the broad expectations of work. These can be especially valuable when trying to define a set of shared values by which people will agree to operate around, and they can range from very specific ("I will not use bcc on emails") to the very broad ("Don't be a jerk").

In our view, trying to catalog all the competencies for every job in an organization is a pointless task. The rapid change in work requirements outdates the detailed competencies, skills, and knowledge before they are even published. To avoid that, job analysts will often make them broad to allow a longer shelf life, but then they are less meaningful.

Job descriptions should only be the starting point. Nothing can replace the value of a solid conversation with the manager about what is expected on the job. Organizations can help by providing examples to managers of what should be covered in performance and development conversations. Managers should then be prepared to discuss what expertise looks like in very specific ways and with meaningful examples.

Curate Learning Options for Employees

Sometimes too much choice is a bad thing. Online corporate education partners can have training catalogs with thousands of courses, and if training departments simply import those catalogs without pruning or sorting them, the courses can sit on the virtual shelf with no takers.

LinkedIn helps their own employees sift through their ample corporate learning offerings by giving them a variety of lens with which to cull resources. Not only do they have their training or knowledge resources sorted by functional categories and topic areas, but they also use a tool to ask employees, "How would you like to transform?" Through a series of questions, the system refines suggestions for the employee. For example, if employees know they want to become more expert in their profession rather than become a manager, they are presented with a list of potential expertise areas from which they can choose. As they drill into the specific expertise area, a limited set of curated items are available, including online courses, downloadable books, links to TED talks, articles, Lynda.com training resources, or executive videos.

"Everyone at LinkedIn is so busy," says Kelly Palmer, chief learning officer, "they can't spend hours or even minutes trying to find content relevant to them. When we curate it for them, we have looked for the best of what we think will be relevant to them here at LinkedIn. They don't have to sort through the good, the bad, and the ugly. We do that for them to make learning easy and fast."

Sitting behind the curated list for employees are literally thousands of options, which Kelly's team has sorted through to find the most relevant based on role, learning need, topic, and so forth. An obvious requirement for an organization to be able to provide this curated content to employees is access to corporate subscriptions or custom-developed content.

Provide Ample Access to Education and On-Demand Resources

Vinolia Singh is the kind of person whose energy zings across the wire all the way from her office in Johannesburg, South Africa. Her employer, MultiChoice, the leading pay TV provider, has recognized that same energy and potential through supporting her and other high potentials with access to a bountiful set of resources. For example, for select high potentials, MultiChoice sponsors a study scholarship to obtain an MBA, all expenses paid.

Another resource is called Books 24X7, an online library of thousands of books that employees can access at any time from any place. When Vinolia decided to add a master's degree to her two undergraduate degrees, the access to the online library was an enormous time-saver.

"The program had a full dissertation requirement," she said, "and I needed dozens of citations for the 100-page-plus paper. I walked into a physical library to start my research, and I looked down all those aisles and was daunted by the amount of time it would take to find what I needed. Then I realized I could use the online library my company provides, and indeed I was able to do all my research through Books 24X7. I graduated summa cum laude and was chosen to produce a white paper based on my dissertation, all without stepping foot into a physical library. As the mom of two children, it also definitely helped with work-life balance, because I could do research from home."

The investment in Vinolia's development paid off. She has continued to be promoted at MultiChoice and now reports directly to the CEO as the group executive of HR.

Solving complex problems requires an inquiring mind and the willingness to experiment one's way to fresh solutions.

—**Daniel H. Pink**

3 BE OPEN

When he was initially passed over for a promotion to vice president, Chris James was extremely frustrated. The person who got the job came from outside the group, so Chris had to train him to run the business. If that wasn't enough, a few months later an executive was brought in to replace his new boss, and Chris felt he had to repeat the process. He felt stalled in his career progression.

A Welshman working in the United States, Chris comes across as a younger, more slender version of a butler on an English period drama. His rather formal persona at work belied a wicked sense of humor that he reserved for informal occasions, and his peers rarely got to see the fun side of him.

The new executive heard that Chris had been the real go-to person in the organization, so she gave him a new position reporting directly to her. For the next six months, she and Chris worked closely negotiating a complex, global reorganization, gaining buy-in from other functions, transferring budgets, and redefining the scope of the group. His new boss gave Chris so much feedback during the project that Chris said, "I've had more feedback in this six months than in my entire career combined."

The feedback wasn't always easy to take. "When you object to an idea immediately, it comes across as not willing to change," she once told him.

"But I embrace change," he protested. "Look at my career going around the world and in taking on this role."

"Other people don't feel you give their ideas a fair hearing, like the proposal we heard today. They were only a few slides in and you started telling them why it wouldn't work. It's the first thing you say that people are responding to, versus your overall view."

And so the feedback sessions would go. Given a new lens to think about how people viewed him, and open to the feedback from his boss, he started making small shifts. At the end of the project, he was placed in a key role with a much larger set of teams reporting to him. Watching him work with his team at an operational review, his boss told him, "I can't believe the difference in you over the last two years. Your team loves you, you're rocking the results, and you all seem to have so much fun."

"I had an insight." Chris said. "Being a leader is not about me. It's about them. I listen to them more. I take feedback from them. That has made all the difference." Chris practiced giving his team feedback in the open and honest way he had been coached. He also attended and was certified as a trainer in *Crucial Conversations*, which helped significantly in his leadership and coaching skills. Within another year, he was given an even larger role, has since been a vice president in two different companies and is now president of a company. His shifted thinking, openness to feedback, and willingness to change relaunched his career with a revived trajectory.

The Importance of Being Open

Being open is a key practice of people who successfully manage their careers, not only because they can adjust behaviors for better results but also because they are able to recognize opportunities when they come along, no matter how seemingly small at the time. Like the game "Chutes and Ladders," the person who is open recognizes when a path will yield a career shortcut.

Those career shortcuts can come about by being open to a whole host of factors. For example, adjusting your style to fit to a corporate culture can help you achieve recognition much earlier. Adjusting your style appropriately requires carefully observing the culture and responding to feedback. Or you may need to be open to letting go of a path you've invested in heavily in favor of a new opportunity, such as learning new processes or tools, even though you're an expert in the old tools.

As the first Stretch Imperative tells us, it's all on you, so you must be able to consider many possibilities to progress in your career. You don't want to become stuck in a view of the world that limits your possibilities, even if that worldview has been successful in the past. Success has a downside. As Bill Gates said, "Success is a lousy teacher. It seduces smart people into thinking they can't lose." What worked for you in the past may not continue to work for you in the future, especially in such a rapidly changing world.

Marshall Goldsmith, author and executive coach, calls this phenomenon the "success delusion." When you are continuously reinforced by promotions, positive reviews, and praise, you can delude yourself into believing that you have arrived. What could others who aren't as successful possibly have to teach you? That is, until the day you fail or find yourself obsolete. To avoid that day, and to improve the path you are on now, we offer some ideas on how to shift your thinking in small ways every day, and sometimes in big ways, to keep yourself open.

Are You Closing Doors to Your Future?

The easy decisions are not always the best decisions in the long run. Five years out of college, Audrey landed in a great company, much to the delight of her parents. She started an MBA, funded by the company, and sat down with one of her professors to get some career advice. As she talked through her engineering history, her professor said, "It sounds to me like you have had one year of experience, repeated five times." Audrey was stunned, but as she thought about it, she realized she was getting deeper in understanding the company's processes and tools, but she was not being set up to grow beyond the group she was in. By sitting and waiting for the company to take action to develop her, Audrey was closing doors to her future.

On the other hand, Manny seemed to deliberately slam doors. Convinced that his view of the world was the right view, he rejected evidence to the contrary. He readily told each of his bosses what they could be doing better in their jobs, even though he hadn't built a trust relationship to offer that advice. At three companies in a row, he was in the first wave of layoffs. Blaming it on the economy and bad bosses, he failed to see how he had behaved his way down a path that limited his options for the future.

Accept Uncertainty

Ron Wayne had several reasons for selling his interest in a side project. It was about to become a full-time endeavor, demanding far more time than he had to give. His day job at a gaming company was solid and brought in a reasonable paycheck; leaving that job would represent a certain level of financial risk. And perhaps most significantly, another side project had cost him his investment, leaving him feeling burned.

His two co-founders had a view of how they wanted to change the world, but it didn't match his own. "It just wasn't the working environment I saw for myself," he said. So twelve days after the company was formally founded, he sold his 10 percent of the company for $800. Later, once the company was gaining traction and had interested funders, he set aside any claims to the future of the company for another $1,500.

Today Ron would be one of the richest men in the world if he had decided to hold on to any part of his ownership. His partners were Steve Jobs and Steve Wozniak. The company was Apple Computer, for which he drew the first logo and wrote the first manual. Apple is now the most valuable company on the planet.

We hope your career decisions won't yield such drastically unfortunate outcomes down the line. Realizing what might be possible before you make key decisions can help minimize missing big opportunities. We're not saying he should have been able to see the future and quit his job, but from his public interviews, it seems once he made up his mind, that was it. He was done with the decision and, when he still had the chance to get back in, he took a small financial incentive just to sever the option. Did he consider how long he would have had to incur the financial risk of quitting his day job at Atari? Could less exhaustive work hours be negotiated post-launch? Would his voice and view of the world have enhanced the company further? We will never know how his life or how Apple would have been different.

Being open to embracing uncertainty while considering potential risk and discomfort could well be essential to achieving your potential. Preparing for a changing future requires that you allow yourself to be open to options you may have rejected in the past or to approaches you find uncomfortable at first. Career growth demands adaptation.

Stretch Strategies to Be Open

Elisa was asked by a search firm to interview for a job that did not particularly appeal to her. The fact that she felt behind on an important project compounded her initial reaction. On the face of it, she would have declined the opportunity simply because of the time and energy commitment to the interview process. However, after giving it a second thought, she realized there were a number of other factors to consider.

Be Open Stretch Strategies

1. Consider yourself a lean startup

2. Develop drone abilities

3. Creatively disrupt yourself

4. Test your assumptions

5. Seek feedback

6. See opportunity everywhere

7. Choose best, not necessarily first

The search firm was prestigious and typically represented some of the best jobs in the market. The opportunity she would have been missing out on was building a relationship with the search firm. By doing well in the interview, even if the job was not right for her, she would be making connections that might well be useful in the future. She also knew that she usually learned something while interviewing that would prove useful to her back on the job. Quite possibly there was more to the job than she already knew.

After reconsideration, she decided to accept the interview invitation. Her original sense that the job was not right for her proved to be true, but it did establish important connections that have yielded other opportunities for her since then.

Sometimes it's difficult to know whether an opportunity is a sidetrack or not. Of course, we can't anticipate the future or know all the pros and cons, but we can apply a thoughtful process to help us know whether we're truly making the right call.

The following strategies can help you recognize when there might be opportunities to develop, career shortcuts to take, or new options to open your career journey.

Consider Yourself a Lean Startup

Walk into the doors of any venture capitalist on Sand Hill Road in Palo Alto, California, and you will hear a common vocabulary.

"When will your MVP be ready?"

"Is that a vanity metric?"

"I think you need to make a pivot."

MVP stands for Minimum Viable Product. A vanity metric measures activity, instead of customer engagement results. Pivot or persevere is a disciplined decision point. Should you course correct on a product—pivot—or continue down the same path and persevere?

The origin of this common language comes from *The Lean Startup*, by Eric Ries. Every business, product, or service can be a startup, according to Ries. And we argue, so are you.

The appeal of the lean startup is both speed and a data-driven approach to understanding what customers will buy. If you have ever clicked on a website button to find a message of "coming soon," you're probably part of a lean startup data-gathering experiment. Rather than building the product you clicked on, the company is trying to find out whether, if they build it, will you be likely to buy it? Your click lets them know the answer is likely yes.

Successful entrepreneurs start with an idea and adjust as they learn what people respond to. If instead they become convinced their idea is what is right for the world in spite of whether customers will buy it, they are on the path to failure. The least successful entrepreneurs are the ones who never test new ideas, and instead remain steadfast on their current track. An example of a job hunting vanity metric might be only measuring how many résumés you've sent out. What really matters is whether you receive responses and then an interview. Volume matters, but results matter more.

A career, just like a company, is made up of a lifetime of both big and small decisions. Some of those are clear: "Should I take this job or that job?" Others are not so clear, because we don't even imagine the possibilities or alternatives. Sometimes we are just in a groove that is working well enough, and moving out of that groove is daunting. The groove might be so comfortable that an opportunity is staring you in the face, and you simply fail to see it.

Thinking of yourself as if you were a lean startup means that you generate and engage the ideas of where you want your career to go, put some of them into play, and test whether those ideas are working. Adapt accordingly. If you think you want to make a career switch and go back to law school, don't start by applying to law school. Instead, gain insight into the jobs you would be most likely to find by shadowing or interviewing a practicing attorney. Don't make a huge commitment from both a time and financial perspective only to regret it down the line. "I like to joke that I'm a Jewish kid who didn't like blood so I couldn't go to medical school, so I went to law school," says Casey Berman, a former attorney. "I spent more time thinking about my iPhone purchase than a degree that was expensive and took three years out of my twenties."

If you adopt a lean startup approach, then you multiply greatly the number of decisions you will be making, because every commitment requires testing to see whether it is working. But just like Silicon Valley startups, by doing your due diligence, you are increasing the odds that your time and money will pay off.

STRETCH BREAK

STRETCH 3.1

Taking even short amounts of time to consider the impact of your decisions can alter the outcome. Here are some questions to consider as you face everyday choices in your career:

- ☐ What opportunities am I potentially missing out on if I choose this path?

- ☐ Will I make significant progress in skills, experience, connections, or pay if I make this choice?

- ☐ In testing out whether this new path is right for me, what smaller steps can I take first, such as information interviewing, shadowing, or reviewing online sites such as Glassdoor.com?

- ☐ What did I learn about the last few choices I've made that I should consider now?

- ☐ Who has gone down this path before who can advise me on what to consider?

Like lean startups, the rapid cycling between ideas, implementation, testing, learning, and adapting is the most effective approach. You don't want to give your career choices almost no thought, like Casey, but you also don't want to be stuck in indecision. People who are slow to decide are ineffective. In a startup, speed is everything in order to seize opportunities. Faced with limitless opportunities, indecisive people can drift and lose identity. Seeking identity in a world where who we are is no longer rigidly defined by what we do, by our place in society, or by the institutions around us is part of the post-modern identity crisis. Am I a futurist or a corporate minion? Am I a blogger or a marketing free agent?

Rather than make a big choice and a long-term commitment, test out small moves like lean startups do, and adapt as the identity fits and as you reach your goals. The good news is that in today's world, you can pursue multiple approaches at once instead of wasting years like Casey did.

Develop Drone Abilities

In spite of all the controversy around drones, there are some useful analogies that can help you to remain open to job and career development opportunities. You may be a person who tends to see the big picture and operate at a high level, or you may build the big picture by aggregating the details. Rotating between the two views can help achieve the most comprehensive understanding of options and possibilities.

Rosabeth Moss Kanter, author and Harvard professor, calls this zooming in and zooming out. Every decision lies in a broader context. No matter how tempting a promotion may seem, if you step back to a higher level and look at, for example, your industry, is it in trouble? Would taking the promotion make you feel obligated to the company at a time when you may have more options if you left your industry?

Sherry had just such a career "pivot or persevere" point. Adopting different views helped her be more open to the possibilities and potential difficulties she faced. Sherry had worked for three years in the largest division of her company. When a position opened up in corporate headquarters over a thousand miles away, the manager in that area encouraged her to apply.

In a zoom in mode, some of the factors Sherry considered were:

✓ Will my job level change?

✓ Will I make more money?

✓ How disruptive would a move be to my family?

✓ Will I like my new boss and colleagues?

✓ Will projects I'm working on now be left in the lurch?

✓ Will I fit in at corporate?

✓ Will I be seen as committed to the company if I don't take the job?

Now imagine having a drone's ability to zoom out to a broader view and reconsider the same opportunity. Sherry might also consider:

✓ Would this be a stepping-stone job to a much bigger opportunity?

✓ Would the skills I'll develop in this role help me achieve my career goals? How?

✓ Will I have an opportunity to build a stronger network of contacts that will serve me well over the life of my career?

✓ How could a relocation help my family build experiences, opportunities, and bonds that will last them a lifetime?

✓ What does the company's future look like, and will a corporate position be a good place to build my future?

✓ Where are my industry and global business headed, and if I take this job, will I increase my ability to compete in the future?

✓ In what ways is society or public policy changing that might affect me in this job in the future?

All the questions were important to her, so it was not a matter of which was the right one to ask. Rather, it was beneficial to think of the decision openly using different viewpoints. She worked her way through the details of whether and how a move could work and realized there were more options.

Her family was open to the idea of the move and she could imagine taking a new role, so in zoom-in mode, a change was possible. Zooming out, she realized that the company she worked for was largely based in the United States. Additionally, much of its revenue was reliant on large contracts with the government. Convinced that the future of her field and her industry was in the global markets, she realized the corporate role would not give her the experience she would need to stay relevant in the future.

Before she made a final decision, she decided to explore other options. When a recruiter approached her about a role with another company, she pursued it, landed the job, relocated her family, and was able to make significant progress in her career within a short time. Five years later, she was in a senior executive role in yet another Fortune 200 company, well beyond her expectations when she was offered that first move to corporate.

Even if you are not considering a location or role change, thinking about your current role with both high-level (zoom out) and detailed viewpoints (zoom in) can help you advance in your career. How does the work you do connect to other departments? How does your job deliver value to customers, even if you are not in daily contact with them? By understanding this bigger picture, you may make decisions each day just a little differently because you understand the flow and consequences of your actions.

Employees in our survey placed a high priority on getting to know more about their company overall and having access to the big picture. High performers know the power of the big picture and train themselves to seek it out. Big picture thinkers are better able to identify when and how to collaborate with others. People who can step away from the details of their work to see the big picture also demonstrate more creativity in their roles because they can make connections others can't, and have been shown to be happier. Be sure to handle the details of your job, but remember to adopt a drone's viewpoint and zoom out once in a while as well.

Creatively Disrupt Yourself

From architect to CEO of one of the world's most iconic performance sports equipment brands is not a typical career path, but then nothing is typical about Colin Baden of Oakley. Sports superstars from PGA tour player Bubba Watson to Lin "Super" Dan, two-time Chinese Olympian and professional badminton star, swear by Oakley products.

The motorcycle sitting prominently in front of Colin's desk is the first clue he's not your average executive. Then there are the stories of his epic company pranks: he once arranged for a fire truck to douse employees in the company auditorium when he got wind of their plans to assault him with water guns. For a CEO, or any role for that matter, he is missing the conventionality gene. So does the headquarters building he designed: a tank serves as a lawn ornament, and the facade seems pulled from a *Blade Runner* post-apocalyptic set.

So it's not surprising when Colin says, "I like to have a new adventure every day. If there's not one, the first thing everyone should do when they wake up in the morning is ask: 'Who am I gonna mess with today?'" And even if you're the playful, I-welcome-disruption sort, you have to wonder what it's like to be on the opposite end of Colin's mission of the day.

Of course, it's also interesting to think about what it takes to create a culture and management team that drives the innovation Oakley has demonstrated in the marketplace. That very willingness to "mess with" the status quo may be what keeps the company changing so that change isn't forced upon it. The economist Joseph Schumpeter argued that the only way for organizations to survive was through continuous destruction of existing products, practices, and structures with updates relevant to the age. Out with the old, in with the new. Disrupt or be disrupted.

Colin met the founder of Oakley, James Jannard, while working on a residential architectural project for him. Oakley began to seek Colin's design expertise for company image and design, and eventually he joined them as director of the design group. Once in the company, his creativity and design skills helped shape a direction for the company, and he progressed to president. How easy it would have been to stay comfortable with his architectural skills and expertise rather than pursue new opportunities. Yet, he chose a new adventure, away from architecture and in a corporate setting, with uncertain outcomes. He was willing to mess with himself, not just others. The same can be said for our personal lives. You must first be open to leaving behind an invested path in order to embrace the new.

Test Your Assumptions

The more successful you become in any field, the more important it is to watch out for narrowed thinking and limitations in viewpoint. Heather experienced this with a mentor at one point. Jerry was a person she admired for his finesse in navigating office politics, so she sought advice from him on how to approach getting buy-in for new equipment that would fall in a capital improvement budget category. "Oh, I've tried to get that one through before," Jerry said. "They will never approve it."

Disappointed, Heather started to gather her laptop and head back to her office to reconsider her approach. As an afterthought, she asked Jerry, "When was the last time you tried to get it through, and why did they object?"

"Oh," Jerry pondered. "It must have been about seven years ago." Heather realized then that her mentor was stuck with a set of rules that served him well in the past, but perhaps weren't applicable to the present. She suggested to Jerry that if they approached it another way, even though some of the approvers were the same, changing conditions might lead to a different outcome. Eventually her project was approved. Although she continued to use Jerry as a trusted advisor, she realized she needed to test his advice against today's environment, and not just through his lens of the past.

The people who do the best job of minimizing the risk of becoming obsolete use a few techniques to keep themselves open to change in their environments—something Jerry missed. Here are some mental techniques to determine whether you need to test your assumptions:

Listen to Novices. Once you are on the path to success, your own experiences reinforce a tendency to sort new pieces of information in ways that fit with your established rules. The rules work, and new evidence confirms your rules are right. Or are they? Indeed, it may be that your powers of observation are attuned to evidence that supports your view, a handicap to openness called "confirmation bias." If you see a person driving way under the speed limit, and then pass the person only to see that, as you suspected, it's a an elderly person, you might begin to believe that all elderly people are slow drivers. You fail to notice the octogenarians speeding past you.

People who are novices have not yet established their biases, and what rules they do have won't be identical to yours. Think of the fortunes that have been made by people who dared to enter a field with little experience despite the experts claiming it couldn't or shouldn't be done. In 1977 Digital Equipment Corporation CEO Ken Olson could see no reason why someone would need a personal computer in his home, while newcomers Bill Gates and Paul Allen were already two years into designing software to make personal computers a useful reality.

Consider practices such as finding a reverse mentor, especially if you have been in a field longer than ten years or in one where there is rapid change. Offer a mutually beneficial relationship, where you ask the person to mentor you in the latest developments in the field, how people in their demographic are making market decisions, or the use of the latest social tools to keep a pulse on the market. In exchange, help that person make connections to useful people or resources, or offer advice and feedback. Another trick to understand the novice point of view is to hang out online in the same places they do. Most organizations now have private social collaboration sites where newcomers can get to know each other and ask questions. The questions the newcomers ask can be a rich source of data to cause you to view the world differently. Or peruse online resources rich with many different viewpoints, such as TED talks. Even their discussion forums are filled with meaningful ideas.

Assume Anyone Who Disagrees Is Partially Right.   Consider how debate teams work in high school. The teams are given a topic, and prepare a good argument. The opposing team presents its argument, and each team provides a rebuttal, aimed for a winning resolution. Unfortunately, those skills won't work as well in creating a sustainable career because the approach assumes there is one right, winning side to an argument, and one wrong, losing side.

What if, instead, you were to assume that everyone who disagrees with you has some valid points? Perhaps you've just made a killer Power-Point presentation pitching a new project to the executive team, but one person in the room objects to the cost. You suspect it is because the person is concerned about budget being siphoned from his or her project to yours. Instead of defending your position, can you step into that person's shoes and translate the person's concerns into ones others might share to open up the discussion? For example, say: "That is a concern I have considered as well, and I suspect others in the room have, too. The ROI you see on slide 18 is, I think, very compelling, and we start to earn back the investment within the fiscal year. What do others think?" What would they be given points for in their arguments? Listen and consider what key points are being raised. Are there issues that indicate you should modify your position in any way?

The answer for a problem you have could be just a few cubicles away, but not widely known. Are there people around you with whom you disagree on most points out of hand, but who still could be seen as resources in considering a situation from a different angle? We tend to avoid working with people who are jerks, even if they are very capable. Can you overcome your aversion to someone in search of the best solution for you and your organization?

Hedge Your Bets. Good corporate financial investment practices typically include a hedging strategy to guard against fluctuations in currency. Likewise, think of a hedging strategy in your career as insurance in case the path you have chosen is wrong.

Malcolm was doing exceptionally well in his career as a safety expert and had been relocated to the United States as part of a high-potential development plan. Once there, he began to suspect the rumors of the company being for sale were for real as delegates of UFOs (unidentified future owners) walked through the building. Not wanting to be seen as disloyal or self-focused, he chose to ignore the signs and focus on his new role. Three months later, he found himself with a repatriation offer and a separation package. His loyalty resulted in great disruption to his family with a second relocation within months of the first and a job search to boot.

Loyalty and long-term commitment are good attributes, and ones our research survey with Oxford Economics told us are some of the most highly valued by executives around the world. However, Malcolm could have benefitted from a hedge plan, because in this case, he was wrong about mutual loyalty, and the costs to his family and his career were extremely high. Since he was new to a role, he didn't have as many powerful connections to help protect him during buy-out decisions. A hedge strategy could have included conversations with his old boss to discuss "what if" scenarios before the decision to move on was made. He knew there was a strong possibility the company was for sale, so talking openly with his manager early on and developing a plan could have helped him to know what to expect and whether he wanted to stick around for it. Or he might have elected to begin reestablishing his connections and network as soon as the rumors were flying. Testing his marketability by reaching out to a few search firms would also have been a hedging strategy.

STRETCH BREAK

STRETCH 3.2

When should you consider a hedging strategy? If you answer yes to any of these questions, no matter how comfortable you are in your current role, you might consider hedging your bets:

☐ Does my boss seem to be more distant and unavailable, suggesting I'm losing favor? Or that he is on his way out, thus destabilizing my department?

☐ Does my function overlap heavily with others, making it possible for an efficiency expert to eliminate roles?

☐ Has my company been negatively reviewed by analysts or taken a beating in the stock market?

☐ Is emerging technology likely to affect my type of work? My company? My industry?

☐ Are there global or social trends that could affect my industry or company?

Seek Feedback

The higher you go in an organization and the more successful you become, the less likely it is that people will voluntarily offer you feedback. You will receive less feedback, and it may well be so diffused that it's unrecognizable or unhelpful. The search for genuine feedback becomes more and more your own responsibility over the course of a career, so it's good to start early. You cannot rely on it to be handed to you wrapped up as a gift, as feedback is sometimes called, prettily packaged and perfectly delivered. Later, in our chapter on Experiences, we will give you tips on how to give others good feedback as part of your own development, but first you must learn how to be gracious at receiving feedback.

Mark was a brilliant strategist, ready with a quick response to almost any relevant question. After graduation from Harvard, he had worked for one of the world's leading management consulting firms before taking a strategy role inside a company. His office lights were often the last turned off at night as he pored over data and reports, seeking trends that might affect the company's plans.

Eager to make an impression and succeed in his first corporate role, Mark worked hard and received lots of positive feedback. It was loud and easy to hear:

"Brilliant insight."

"Incredible staff work."

"Superb analysis."

The accolades boosted his efforts and he doubled-down on providing more of the same. However, he missed the subtlety in some of the feedback when his team player performance ratings weren't as high as his other marks. What Mark didn't know was that there was feedback of a different nature also circulating:

"Doesn't value the opinions of others."

"Fails to collaborate."

"Doesn't listen well."

Sensing that he wasn't fitting in, he talked to a colleague who also had a tendency to work late. Over a few Chinese takeout dinners, his colleague gently offered Mark advice on how to gain acceptance by those around him. "When Beth wants to collaborate with you, don't be so quick to dismiss the opportunity. She might be seeing a way your projects connect that you don't." And, "If you haven't gotten feedback from Bob lately, go and ask for a critique on your decks." What Mark had formerly dismissed out of hand as office politics, his colleague helped him see as part of bringing people along with him and a necessary attribute to get work done.

According to Columbia University neuroscientist Kevin Ochsner, people only apply the feedback they are given 30 percent of the time. What happens to the other 70 percent? Perhaps people have simply decided to ignore it, or perhaps they simply don't remember it. Therefore, when you are receiving feedback, it's best to switch to a listening and recording mode, so that you can write down both the positive feedback you receive along with the critical information. It's important not to react to criticism. Instead, try taking a reflective stance and thank the person giving the criticism. Let him know that you will reflect on what was said.

As researchers of vulnerability understand, our self-confidence takes a plunge when we feel we are being criticized. Since politicians and their families are objects of constant criticism, their experience and advice can be relevant to career professionals who are open to feedback. "Grow skin like a rhinoceros," was the advice of First Lady Eleanor Roosevelt. Through the challenging years of her husband's presidency, she became renown for listening to feedback while deflecting personal criticism.

Listening to feedback is not only in person when so much of our communication is digital. Sometimes you'll receive feedback in an email, and your natural reaction is to send off a defensive reply. Step back and consider whether a phone call response is better. If not possible, be sure to acknowledge the feedback with something like, "Good insight."

To make it likely that you will receive the feedback you need, one of the most important things you must do is create an environment that is safe for the person to give the feedback. Think about the last time someone asked you for feedback. Likely you delivered a partial truth and started softly, just in case the request was a gambit for ego stroking and not for genuine feedback. Remember that, and make the giver of feedback welcome.

Whether you are the boss asking for feedback from employees, or an employee sitting in front of your boss, here are a few suggestions on how you can ask for feedback in a way that creates some psychological distance and safety while getting you the advice you need.

☐ Ask for feedback in a way that feels non-personal. An example is: "If you could imagine the perfect person doing the perfect job in the role I'm in, what do you think they might be doing differently than I am?" Or "Alice is known as someone who collaborates well with other departments. What do you think are some of her secrets? If you were me, which ones would you focus on?"

☐ Admit to needing improvement and setting feedback in that context. "By the end of the presentation, I could tell I had lost the audience, or at least they weren't as engaged as I would have liked. What two or three pieces of advice do you have for me that you think would have made the presentation better?"

☐ Ask open-ended but specific questions. Instead of, "What do I need to do to lead my own project here?" ask, "What's a reasonable time frame to be able to lead my own project, and what are the most important capabilities I need to acquire first?"

☐ Watch your verbal and non-verbal reactions. Givers of feedback will usually be finely attuned to your reactions, and the moment you send any signal that you are uncomfortable or resistant to their opinions, they will begin to back off. Remain reflective, ask clarifying questions to show your interest, and deliberately slow your pace to show that you are carefully considering their views.

You can safely assume that you are receiving less than 10 percent of the feedback you need to help you tune your career. Your job is to go get the other 90 percent and do something with it. Don't limit from whom you receive feedback. At one major entertainment company, the executives always asked Virginia, the receptionist, what she had noticed about the candidate. Every behavior counts, so if a candidate interrupted Virginia when she was on a call, that was an indicator he would be equally rude on the job. Or when the candidate held the elevator door open for the mail attendant pushing a cart, Virginia reported that small kindness as well. Showing respect for the opinion of everyone around you can go a long way. What if you approached the receptionist and asked, "I'm here for a job interview, and you probably see a lot of candidates. Any advice on what makes for great fit here?" You might be remembered for that curiosity and respect.

See Opportunity Everywhere

Looking at the man collecting glass bottles from the trash in the central Los Angeles alley, you would never have guessed what lay in front of him. What lay behind for John Paul DeJoria was a string of jobs starting from newspaper boy when he was ten, and hard, door-to-door selling through his teens. Unable to get the funds together for school, he skipped college and soon after found himself a homeless single dad hustling between gigs as a janitor, selling life insurance, or doing whatever he could to pay the bills.

He accidentally discovered the passion that would change his life working yet another job in the hair products industry. However, he lost that job and faced a second brief round of homelessness. Back in a sales position and off the street, he looked around for entrepreneurial opportunities. John Paul knew from his prior experience that the hair products industry was solid and could use a new market player focused on high-quality ingredients. He approached one of his close friends, a well-known local hair stylist, with an idea, and together they developed products and a company on such a slim budget their logo had to be in black and white.

Now it was his early door-to-door selling experience that helped John Paul persist. Accustomed to 30 to 40 rejections before a sale, John Paul and his friend scrimped through two frugal years during which quitting was a daily temptation. Then their sales took a jump and a humble beginning became a global brand with over 90 products. John Paul DeJoria's partner was Paul Mitchell. John Paul not only was a founder for Paul Mitchell Hair Products, but he has also since successfully founded Patron, a best-selling, high-end tequila.

His story provides a number of insights. John Paul was able to keep himself open to the opportunities that were in front of him while using his skills from the past. He had built core skills in selling, including facing repeated rejection. He understood the industry well enough to know where there was room for a new competitor. Most importantly, he figured out what additional skills were needed to help his idea succeed. He developed a key partnership with someone who shared his vision and then launched the company.

Finding opportunity does not have to mean starting up a new company. Sometimes we just have to reframe how we are looking at a situation. Dana was nominated for a promotion to a senior manager role, but she was worried that another candidate might have the edge. She discussed her concerns with her mentor, saying, "If I don't get the job, I will have to leave the company because that job won't open up again for years."

"You're thinking about this completely wrong," he said. "Jobs are fluid. You need to find where the company has an issue or problem and figure out how you can best solve that problem. If you show how you can add value, your career will follow." Dana did receive the promotion, but her mentor's advice prompted her to pitch an idea to the company president around a culture change initiative. She was placed in charge of a company-wide change effort, which eventually led to a career shift far beyond the job she once had worried so much about getting.

Both John Paul and Dana became open to ideas beyond the obvious and most immediate choices. In what ways have you framed your options by your current job or by a job you want? If you reframed to consider options that more fully leveraged your talents, what would those options look like? What would a different version of you do in the situation, and why can't that be you now?

Choose Best, Not Necessarily First

People who continue to learn and grow across their careers also tend to have an outlook that they are a work in process, an experiment underway. The creative design process does not usually have only one right answer or one right approach. Dick Boland learned that first-hand when it came to designing a building.

Boland, a business professor, was working on the design of a new business school for Case Western Reserve University with Frank Gehry, the famed architect of the Guggenheim Museum in Bilbao and the Walt Disney Concert Hall. Because of cost overruns and funding limitations, the square footage needed to be trimmed by 4,000 feet. Boland worked with Gehry and his design team over two intense days to finally fit all the faculty requirements into the space. He reviewed the revised blueprints with the architect, content they had found a solution.

The project lead from the architectural firm acknowledged the solution would work, and then tore up the blueprints in front of Boland.

"What are you doing?" Boland asked with alarm.

"Now that we know we can make the building work, let's figure how we should make the building work," the architect said. Boland later acknowledged he was right, because their first solution focused largely on recreating in the new building the same spaces that had been in the old building. When they were able to let go of "this is the way things are done," they were able to come up with entirely new ways of thinking about the use of space.

The same creative design approach can be used to think about architecting a career. The first choice and the first path might work, but might also leave opportunity on the table. Greg's last employer was facing increasing competition from overseas manufacturers. He was a numbers guy, working as a financial controller, and from his view, the company's numbers weren't going to work. In his estimation, it was only a matter of time before they moved or sold the company, so he elected to take a voluntary exit package. One week later, a bank too big to fail did in fact fail, a front-end sign of a coming global recession. What he thought would be a pretty straightforward job search became far more daunting.

To his relief, Greg was offered a job almost immediately and he was tempted to take it. However, when he stepped back to view the big picture, he felt he could do better. If he had one offer, he figured he would get more, and there seemed to be ample temporary work available. The access to abundant temporary work gave him options. For the next year, and with a little travel and location flexibility, he did contract-based work for a variety of employers. With the economy in an uncertain condition, companies were inclined to offer temporary or contract work instead of permanent jobs. This way he was able to test a few types of roles and places to live. His last contract position seemed to be a good fit, so he renewed his contract for another year. The employer, Apple, offered him a full-time permanent position, with a much better offer than that first job offer two years prior.

Greg's experience is a preview of the way many people will work in the future. Executives from around the world resoundingly told us they intend to use more contingent, contract, and "flex" workers. Being willing to be flexible, to forego the contract in favor of the opportunity, might make you all the more desirable to hiring departments. Their company can test you out, even as you're testing them for a fit, and all the while, you are broadening your skillset and, more importantly, your network.

Greg's decision to not take the first, immediately secure choice paid off for him in the long run. Every time you have a career choice in front of you, ask yourself, "What am I potentially giving up if I take this option?"

Every day is a choice to continue the path you are on, and there are likely more options than you are considering at any given moment. At the end of her first year out of college, a Millennial we know who we'll call Traci had eleven 1099s to report for her income taxes. Her mother lamented, "It's not supposed to be like this."

"But, Mom," Traci retorted, "how am I supposed to know what I like?"

How are you exploring what you like? And are you weighing too heavily safety and security when you might be in a position where exploration will benefit you more? Even if you are committed to your employer, are there ways you can explore options other than the role you are in? When you do have new opportunities placed on your doorstep, step back and consider whether this is the best that you think will come your way.

You Are Not on Your Own

We started this part of the book with the first Stretch Imperative "It's all on you." In reality, you are never alone. All but the most reclusive of people have others they can rely on to help along the way.

The practices we've discussed in this section can help you from taking the long way around the career game of "Chutes and Ladders." Learning on the fly and developing the skills to be open can help you find those shortcuts.

Still, you can take steps to increase your options through building stronger networks and gathering a broader set of experiences— strategies we'll discuss in the next section.

Stretch Summary

- Careers are like the game of "Chutes and Ladders." You need to recognize when shortcuts might be available. That takes being open.
- Strategies for being open include:
  - *Consider yourself a lean startup.* Make sure you measure what matters.
  - *Develop drone abilities.* For big career decisions, consider the details as well as the big picture.
  - *Creatively disrupt yourself.* Look for ways to throw yourself out of any ruts you might be in.
  - *Test your assumptions.* The better you are in your job, the easier it is to overlook signs that you are becoming outdated. You can beat this by listening to novices, assuming people you disagree with are partially right, and hedging your bets.
  - *Seek feedback.* You're not receiving the feedback you need, guaranteed. Go out and find it, but make it safe for people to give you that feedback.
  - *See opportunity everywhere.* Even in the most desperate of situations, there is hope.
  - *Choose best, not necessarily first, when it comes to options.* Rarely is the first opportunity the best opportunity, so take a step back when you are ready to make a career shift.

What Organizations and Managers Can Do

It's important that organizations support employees in remaining open to all their career options and to the feedback that will help them grow. The good news is that some of the most effective strategies that follow are not expensive or time-consuming. Simple cultural choices and management practices have yielded big financial results for organizations. One such company is Zappos, which is so focused on culture as competitive advantage that it has published a book on delivering happiness. If organizations want employees to be open, they can learn from how others have employed simple solutions to yield big change.

Create a Development Culture

Robert Kegan and his colleagues have spent hundreds of hours observing organizations that they refer to as Deliberately Developmental Organizations (DDOs). One of those is Decurion, a privately held company operating businesses such as ArcLight Cinemas, Pacific Cinemas, and Hollybrook Senior Living. However, to define Decurion by its businesses is a great disservice. When you land on their main home page, this is how they begin the description of who they are: "Decurion provides places for people to flourish." That central purpose is shown in practices such as weekly conversations between managers about employees and what job assignments will allow them to grow, public competency boards where everyone can see who has developed new capabilities, and talent assessments as part of the business review that include promotion-ready candidates.

Measure Whether Managers Are Giving Feedback

How do you know whether managers are giving feedback? The easiest way to find out is to ask the people who work for them. Too often the only time an employee receives feedback is in a rushed annual performance appraisal.

Frustrated with the performance management system and the lack of more constant engagement, the Human Resources group at Oakley decided that the most important part of the annual review was the conversation between the manager and the employee. Inspired by positive-oriented psychology methodology and insights from brain science, they decided to abandon the annual form and replace it with a simple survey. Every quarter they ask the employees only one question: "Have you had a meaningful performance or career-related discussion with your boss in the last 90 days? Yes or No." The CEO, the very same Colin Baden discussed earlier, reviews the results of the survey and holds managers accountable for ensuring that these discussions are happening. Creating an expectation and measuring that managers are providing routine feedback on employee performance and development in an ongoing way, not annually as some organizations do, helps ensure that the conversations happen and result in meaningful performance advancement.

Provide Training on How Your Organization Operates

To help people develop drone capabilities—the ability to zoom in and zoom out—having access to training on how the organization operates can really help. People who understand the strategy and bigger picture of their organization make fewer errors, are more productive, and are more satisfied. While many corporate learning catalogs contain programs such as "Finance for Non-Financial Managers" and courses on an organization's products, these are building blocks but not adequate for helping people understand how the organization operates. Without a customized program that explains how the different parts of the organization interface and deliver value to its customers, employees narrow their focus to what they can see and understand, often at the expense of collaboration, mission support, and intra-organization development. If you want more collaboration across your organization, train your employees on how the organization fits together via a custom-developed program.

Increase Manager's Coaching: Managing Ratio

According to Tim Gallwey, author of books on the mental mastery of sports such as golf and tennis, "Coaching is unlocking a person's potential to maximize their own performance. It is helping them to learn, rather than teaching them." Or, as applied to the business world, coaching is not managing, which is about compelling people to fulfill the manager's goal about what to do. Instead, coaching is helping employees to achieve all they are capable of doing and being. The best managers—and, indeed, the teams that go on to greatness—are the ones who understand this important distinction.

Claudio discovered this in working with Sofia, a product manager. Sofia was an experienced product manager. Responsible for defining the specs for new products, her job involved frequent interaction with engineers inside the company and consumers outside the company. Claudio knew that everyone liked working with Sofia, but he felt she needed to push the limits a little more on innovation—not just accommodate everyone's wishes. He decided it would be better to coach her rather than manage her performance. When he sat down with her, he focused the discussion on her goals and where she wanted to develop. Once she said that she wanted increasing responsibilities in product management, he could then point out how the people who had achieved the next level had track records of innovation. That opened the door to address some development options for Sofia.

What is a good balance for coaching versus managing techniques? Each manager and group will be different, but 80 percent coaching and 20 percent managing seems achievable for most managers. That coaching can be not only on individual performance, but on helping employees understand how their work and actions fit into the big picture.

Understanding the difference between coaching and managing and learning how to incorporate it into the company culture can be achieved via a good leadership training course, and as top leadership models these behaviors, managers will follow suit. Heads of human resources can help by serving as coaches to the executive team as well. When an entire company decides to embrace this kind of culture, the benefits are boundless.

Part 3: You Need Options

Chapter 4: Build a Diverse Network

Chapter 5: Be Greedy About Experiences

One size doesn't fit all when it comes to preparing for tomorrow, which is why you need options. In this section we explore the key practices to build a diverse network and the importance of experiences.

I see now how much I've given up over the years by keeping my work focus so central and my circle so narrow.

—Tony Schwartz

4 BUILD A DIVERSE NETWORK

Zach Altneu has been a natural rebel his whole life. In high school, at the same time he was excelling as editor of his school newspaper and yearbook, he also managed to get expelled for writing underground articles critical of the Benedictine monks who were his teachers. His future career would be one in an industry that didn't yet exist when he was born in 1977—writing software and building websites.

His first job was at a marketing company, where he readily admitted to working six days a week and eighteen hours a day, with a couple of all-nighters every week. His devotion and commitment came easily because he was determined to become good enough at web design that he could implement successful solutions for his clients. Zach's other focus was on mastery of his software development skills. Networking was the last thing on his mind. It wasn't long before he became the lead programmer at the company. Soon after, the head sales guy approached him about joining forces and starting their own company. Zach's future as an entrepreneur was sealed: a rebel with a cause.

As a young entrepreneur Zach relied on his family for advice. Both his maternal and paternal grandparents had been entrepreneurs.

In conversations with his grandparents, they urged him not to get pigeonholed into the technical side of the business (writing code and building websites). Despite all the energy he'd spent developing technical expertise, they told him over and over that sales was the most important skill he could learn.

As he and his partner were looking for clients, they discovered a branch of a large software solutions company in their community. The company was in need of a website that was dynamic, with sophisticated visual content, using interactive software unique for the late 1990s. Despite the fact that Zach had no experience in these new techniques, he was undeterred. His only problem was how to get in the door.

His grandparents' words echoed in his ears: "It's about who you know." Zach knew he had to establish credibility with this new company to land the contract. So he started exploring and examining his contacts, and finally found a friend of a friend that was an old buddy of the decision-maker at the software solutions company. Zach asked his friend's friend if he'd like to partner in pitching the company for their business.

When they walked into the meeting it was like a homecoming. His friend's friend was able to establish an instant rapport. As Zach recalls, "None of the normal questions, like, 'Who have you done this for?' and 'What's your portfolio of work?' were ever asked." They landed the deal. Looking back over his career, Zach continues to enjoy his relationships with clients, and counts his ability to foster relationships as a key part of his success along with his commitment to solving problems for clients.

Zach didn't use the term "networking" to describe his search for the right connection to help him land new clients. He was simply focusing on relationship building to help him form new and necessary contacts. He probably didn't realize that this interpersonal skill would prove to be so crucial in the future of his business.

We have always lived and worked in networks. Kin networks go back to the beginning of time. The Greeks established networks of villages for trade purposes. The Romans were the first to require that your family and work networks be recorded in an official census. The British Empire was the first to use its colonies and trade partners as a communications network. Now, in the digital age of technological and social media advancements, there are no limits on how far our networks can reach.

Today, we live hyper-connected lives. Personal relationships, professional expectations and interactions, Facebook friends, Instagram, text messages, Twitter feeds, email, and new mobile platforms all compete for our attention. We live in a time of perpetual engagement with endless resources to stay connected to our networks.

Having a vibrant, diverse network will be one of your most important resources in seeking opportunities in your job and in being prepared for job changes and job searches. In our research, we found that the reward of an ever-expanding network is powerful and often transformational. That is why developing a diverse network is one of the practices that address our second Stretch Imperative: You need options. Networks facilitate collaboration on the job, assist in meeting your overall career goals, and provide support in celebrating life's successes and rebounding from its disappointments.

What Is a Network?

Kayla graduated from college into a dismal job market, the aftermath of the 2008 recession. Her frustrating job search yielded only part-time service industry jobs and hundreds of unanswered job inquiry emails. On top of that, in the few opportunities when she made it through multiple interviewing rounds, even those entry-level jobs were going to over-qualified candidates. Finally, after two years of searching, she landed her first full-time job. As you would expect, she was anxious to make a good impression with her boss and colleagues.

When her boss invited her to an upcoming company-wide after-work happy hour networking event, Kayla tried hard to avoid the voice inside her head chanting, "I hate networking events." She swore that every networking event she had ever attended was full of low-level employees who had no power, money, or leverage at their companies. Why meet them? Still, Kayla pushed aside her natural distaste and the voices in her head, and accepted.

Heading into the evening with low expectations, she was surprised to meet so many interesting new people.

The next morning, her boss assigned her responsibility for a team project—the first team she would lead. He told her that it was going to be an opportunity for her to build a network at the company and help her career. Just a few weeks later, a problem developed with one of their customers and she was asked to solve it. She knew that a quick resolution would make a big difference to the customer. As she sat in her cubicle thinking about what to do next, she realized that a colleague she'd met at the networking event had mentioned working with the same customer. A couple quick emails later, answer in hand, she was really glad they had connected at the happy hour. Not only did she have a new idea on how to proceed with the customer, but she was also building a great friendship. Kayla's new network connection came alive at the moment she reached out for help.

Exchanging business cards may seem an exercise in futility, because in that moment we don't see the potential for how this person might fit into our network. In fact, some exchanges never lead to any further interaction. That's okay. We don't invest in networking when we have a limited view of what it is really about. On the surface, the act of networking is merely an exchange of information and contacts for professional or social purposes. The give and take of using people and helping people to advance our mutual goals is what makes a network come alive.

Networks are not the same as networking. Networks are the various groups with whom we are associated, while networking implies that we are using our networks in a deliberate way to further our personal or professional goals.

Zach and Kayla's stories remind us that your network can be a powerful resource. The mantra "It's not what you know but who you know" is all too true when it comes to getting an interview or providing critical access to information. What a difference it would make if, instead of focusing only on the number of contacts, we were forming a community of support for our future. Who wouldn't want an interconnected group of people who can help us land jobs, find new business, solve a problem, or support us in times of crisis?

STRETCH BREAK

STRETCH 4.1

What is the quality and functionality of your network? Here are some questions to consider as you build your network:

- ☐ What's your estimate for the number of contacts in your network?
- ☐ How many contacts do you think you need?
- ☐ Make a list of all the databases or social sites where you keep contact information. Can you consolidate it all in one place?
- ☐ How are you using the people in your network? Do they help you tap into new ideas? Connect to people in different worlds? Help you work collaboratively?
- ☐ What's lacking?

The Two Networks Everyone Has

You already have at least two different types of networks in your life: personal and professional. Personal networks are populated with family and friends, people you see often and people who care for you deeply. You might think of those in your personal network as the people you know who would be willing to go to the mat for you. You could call them at 3:00 a.m. and they would answer the phone. The relationships used primarily for support and friendship make up your personal network.

Many networks that are primarily personal contain a number of close ties. Close or strong ties are usually defined as family and friends and could include your spouse, life partner, close family members, and even distant relatives that you might see frequently. Other strong ties include friendships, primarily those that are non-work related but could include your closest work friends (or perhaps the platonic bond of a "work spouse"), friends from school or your place of worship. All together these groups make up the close tie component of your personal network.

Most people also have a number of "loose tie" or "weak tie" networks. Perhaps you are a member of an alumni association from the college or university you attended. Maybe you have a group of acquaintances or friends who have moved away but you still keep in touch regularly via holiday messages or occasional Facebook comments. Or you might have an even looser group of people you used to work with or met at conferences and are in your address book or online social network. Non-reciprocal relationships don't count; following your favorite actor or comedian's Twitter feed isn't going to be helpful to you in this regard. These looser collections of networks—especially the ones including business associates—are what form the foundation of your professional network.

Think about those two basic networks in your own life. Who is in your strong personal close tie network? Who is in your professional loose tie network? Now we'd like to pose a question: If you were searching for a job today, which kind of network would you think would best serve you in finding a job?

A. Close Tie

B. Loose Tie

If you answered A. Close Tie, the strong personal network that would do anything for you, you are among the majority who answered this question. It's natural to think that those closest to us would have our best interests at heart. After all, friends don't let friends fail. If you selected this answer, most likely you have a strong group of close friends and family that you depend on and who depend on you. However, when looking for a job, the broader and looser your network, the more successful your search. Our close ties often share our same networks of contacts—they know who you know.

If you answered B. Loose Tie, you may already know how powerful a wide net of loose tie contacts can be. At the least, it gives us the opportunity to connect to friends of friends or acquaintances who in turn can provide a bridge to other contacts.

But loose tie networks are more powerful than that. Since many of these contacts are less directly tied to you, they are less concerned with mitigating risk on your behalf.

"Do you know what the odds are for a first-time business to succeed?"

"Entrepreneurial ventures aren't safe places to work—better to get a job at an established company."

"No one makes any money in that industry!"

These comments are made by lots of good friends and family. They only wish the best for us, but may end up discouraging us from stretching beyond anything that isn't guaranteed.

Because they care for us so deeply, the people closest to us don't want to see us fail. But sometimes we just need the freedom to explore new options and risk failure.

In his landmark work, *The Strength of Weak Ties*, Stanford sociologist Mark Granovetter studied people who were searching for jobs to find out what role their social networks played in landing one. He found that people who used loose tie connections had greater success in job searches, experienced greater levels of job satisfaction, and made more money. Since loose tie contacts are a bit more removed, they see the world a little differently and can evaluate risk with a more objective view.

Maybe no one in your close circle of friends and family started a company before or worked in a high-risk venture or quit a good paying job. But in the outer reaches of your network, someone surely has. Connecting with them will help you gain the confidence to take a little more risk. They might provide that valuable insight you need to make that risk a success or offer other connections to people who could be helpful. They might help you recognize an entrepreneurial opportunity and perhaps even help you raise money for your venture.

We all need to have both personal and professional networks. As you can see in Figure 4.1, both are important. Both play a critical role in our success, happiness, and careers. However, it's your loose tie network that has the best potential for helping you access new opportunities.

FIG 4.1 Loose Ties—Close Ties

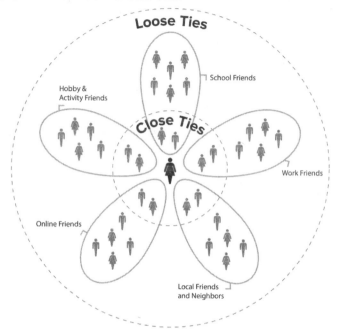

Why Do Diverse Networks Matter?

Without exception, everyone we have interviewed agrees that they have both personal and professional networks. We are sure that's true for you, too. Now let's super-charge your networks by intentionally building in some diversity.

A diverse network should include people of different ages, genders, power, and influence. Building connections to more powerful people in your organization or community provides a great source for professional and leadership development and effective bridges to other networks. Staying connected to younger people can help you to stay current on new technologies and provide a bridge to outside social networks.

Networks that are geographically diverse can help you expand your reach into new markets. And networks that are diverse in connections to peers, direct reports, and supervisors expand the opportunities for cross-functional success. Finally, you'll want a network that has people from different jobs and industry types to help you keep abreast of best practices.

"What's so important about diversity in our networks?" This isn't hard to answer. As Nathaniel Koloc, the co-founder of ReWork, says, "Diverse networks are everything. They're the best asset you can develop for your career." Networks that are made up of the same kinds of people limit who we can influence and who we can turn to for help. Over time, our beliefs, experiences, and connections become more and more similar. As a result, our ability to reach and connect with dissimilar people becomes limited. Yet those dissimilar people can make the greatest difference in the expansion of our business.

There are other not-so-obvious reasons to build diverse networks. Nathaniel says, "It's not rocket science: if you genuinely help people they will help you back." ReWork, a recruiting platform powered by Millennials looking for jobs with a social or environmental impact, landed their first retained search customer because one of their early employees happened to know someone who worked for a prestigious philanthropic consulting firm in Seattle. That loose tie relationship yielded a contract that helped put the company on the map.

When it comes to job searches or promotions, your network is the means by which you can reach for introductions and information. Building diversity into your networks prepares you to anticipate change and make sure you have the resources to stay relevant at work. It's your personal system to access when you need to understand changes in your field of work or industry. Consider it a testing ground of people who have different perspectives that you can tap into when you want to test out a new idea or refine how you will pitch an idea to others.

Or perhaps your next major business idea may come from this network. Barbara was launched into her first entrepreneurial venture at the suggestion of a client. The client served special needs students and needed a transportation provider to take students from a new group home community to various schools. Barbara saw the need as well and knew other providers would not be readily interested in the idea.

As Nathaniel and Barbara experienced, diverse networks are simply everything. Your goal should be to build a diverse network, with people like you and unlike you.

STRETCH BREAK

STRETCH 4.2

Let's circle back to the quality and functionality of your network. How diverse is it? When you answer the questions below, think about the biggest segments of your network:

☐ Do they look like you?

☐ Think like you?

☐ Same age as you?

☐ Do they have similar beliefs to yours?

☐ Are they your high school friends or your college roommates?

☐ Are they your work colleagues?

☐ Are they your direct reports and/or your bosses?

☐ Are they your customers, outside vendors, and suppliers?

☐ Are they mostly located near you?

If you answered yes to a few of these, consider how you can increase the diversity of your network.

The Magic Is in the Mix

Close tie networks might be more inclined to stop you from taking any risks, whereas loose tie networks hold the knowledge and resources to make those risks pay off. However, true power comes from a union of the two.

Kickstarter is a great example of how you can leverage the strength of both close and loose tie networks. Through their web presence, Kickstarter provides the largest virtual funding platform for creative projects. Entrepreneurs and inventors like Helen Volkov Behn, the founder of Spand-Ice, use the site to connect to investors, many of whom they haven't met before.

Helen spent years in physical therapy because her hypermobile spine meant that she was often pulling muscles in her back and legs. After years of medication and physical therapy, she discovered that the best way to manage the muscle inflammation was through icing and heating. As Helen explains, the only difficulty was that "no one can spend the whole day alternating between 20 minutes of icing and heating." Helen developed a clothing line that would integrate heating and cooling so that you could do it inconspicuously and on-the-go.

In preparation for launching her Kickstarter campaign, she compiled contacts through social media sources like Facebook, Twitter, Google+, Pinterest, and LinkedIn and supplemented those contacts with entrepreneurial networks in her local community. In the end, her campaign went live to approximately 1,000 contacts. In addition, Kickstarter featured her campaign, allowing her to attract funding from complete strangers who happened to be in the Kickstarter network.

Kickstarter sets a deadline to reach your funding goal; if you miss that deadline you walk away with nothing, so it's important to prepare your network in advance. Just a week away from the close of Helen's Kickstarter campaign, she was still $8,000 short of her goal of $30,000, so she supplemented her online efforts with in-person events and special pleas to her close tie network to act as bridges to their networks.

Helen told us her biggest surprise and aha moment was how important loose ties were to the success of her campaign. She estimates that 50 percent of her goal was met by close friends and family and the rest was thanks to loose ties. She says, "The goal would have been impossible to reach without those loose ties."

Can You Get to Kevin Bacon?

Our loose ties are also far more likely to be bridges to people important for us to know. Zach, our rebel entrepreneur whose story started off our chapter, found that a friend of a friend was the key connection in helping him land a new business account. Even though Zach's grandparents' advice was important in the launch of his business, it was his ability to tap into his loose ties network that delivered success. Since our network needs change over time, it's crucial that we think broadly about what connections we might need. When you are in a job search, you will want your network to be rich with connections to others. Or, if you're launching a business as Helen did, you will want lots of connections that can provide access to resources.

Before social media there was the "Six Degrees of Kevin Bacon" game: connect any actor to a film featuring Kevin Bacon within six films (Elizabeth Perkins starred in *Big*, which co-starred Tom Hanks, who was in *Apollo 13* with Kevin Bacon. Done!). Or there is the famous study done by psychologist Stanley Milgram. In 1967, Milgram wanted to see how many degrees were between any random person in Nebraska and a Massachusetts stockbroker he knew. He asked 200 Nebraskans to mail a letter to someone they knew personally who might in turn know the stockbroker. On average it took only six different stops before the letter showed up at the stockbroker's address.

Social network theorists use degree-of-separation to refer to individuals who can be reached within your network. Today, the degrees of separation are getting smaller and contacts are just a click away. A recent study discovered that any Facebook member with a Friends circle of 300 or more is less than five degrees of separation from everyone else on Facebook. And, when you look at the United States alone, the degree of separation is just three contacts.

According to Reid Hoffman in his book, *The Start-Up of You*, when it comes to using your loose tie network for professional purposes, he argues for leveraging those who are only three degrees of separation from you. As he explains, three degrees is the optimum number because when you're introduced to a second- or third-degree connection, at least one person in the introduction chain personally knows the origin of the connection request. Those third-degree connections exponentially expand your network, which is why LinkedIn uses the tagline, "Your network is bigger than you think."

Obviously, the wider your diverse network, the fewer steps it is to connecting to someone. But what if there is a specific someone who can make a significant difference in your future, and you want to reach out to her? Then you need to be able to identify the connections. Online services like LinkedIn can be highly effective—we see everyone our network knows, allowing us the opportunity to treat them as connections.

And trust us—we're all going to need this kind of help in a future where there will be an average of eleven job changes between our first job and our last. Every one of those job changes will use your network in some way, whether it is to find a job, find a referral, or support you as you transition. When jobs are fluid, your network is more permanent than your job.

Strategies to Build a Diverse Network

Social networks are accelerating the pace of networking. Almost every conversation now includes someone updating you based on information he picked up from a Facebook or other social platform post. Ever since Facebook became a verb, researchers have been studying the impact of our online lives. According to Pew Research Center, adults on Facebook average over 300 friends. Modern social encounters involving new people often result in a request that you friend them. Everyone today knows the power of a social network presence, and many organizations hire people whose sole job is to keep feeding that presence online.

Build a Diverse Network Stretch Strategies

1. Groom a Clan

2. Build for Depth

3. Bridge for Breadth

4. Adjust Constantly

5. Scratch a Back

6. Strive for Five to Thrive

Social networks are powerful tools that can help us develop, maintain, and expand our contacts. However, the number one complaint of most social media users is that people share too much. Avoiding this narcissistic tendency is wise if you have blended your personal and professional networks.

According to Pew, more than two-thirds of American adults and more than 80 percent of Millennials consistently create content on social media. That's a lot of information and can lead to a downside. Prolonged time online can increase our working hours and lower productivity, leaving a feeling of blurred boundaries between our online lives and our professional and personal lives. Then there's the whole exposure to trolls and negative people who can exhaust our energy and leave us wondering about our shared humanity. Curating our network carefully is important to help avoid these downsides.

You may feel the temptation to accept every friend or connection request that comes your way in an arms race for the biggest network. While social networks are important, remember that loose tie networks are never going to replace your "lifeline" friends. We are more interconnected than we ever thought possible, but sometimes, even with thousands of contacts, there is no one to call.

Having the largest number of followers or contacts is not necessarily a sign of network strength. The secret is to find the right balance for your career goals between online social networks and off-line relationships, perhaps by using some of the following strategies.

Groom a Clan

As we've fallen into the habit of gathering friends and contacts, many people think that just accepting every request to connect can help build their networks. In our research, we've found that most people fall into one of two categories: those who embrace saying yes to all requests and those who will only accept connections to and from people they know. As it turns out, in most cases, quality matters more than quantity. If you are likely to have dozens of vendors contacting you to try to sell to you, then a more selective approach might make sense; but in an example of "the more the merrier," if you are in sales, knowing as many people as possible might be a better strategy.

Not only is the quality of your closest network ties important, but so is having the right size network. Robin Dunbar, who studies evolutionary psychology at the University of Oxford, has developed a theory called "Dunbar's Number" that suggest we can only meaningfully track about 150 contacts. His work relies on an understanding of the connection between brain size and ideal group size, known as social brain hypothesis.

With smaller brains, chimps cannot sustain a social group larger than 50 because of how much time grooming consumes. He found that, as the group size increased, the grooming became more stressful. With less time devoted to each member of the group, it became harder to keep track of who would come to their aid. This created an upper limit on the size of the chimp's social group.

Fortunately, your human brain can handle more contacts than a chimp's can. How much grooming do your contacts need? As our networks grow larger they require more time to manage, but do not necessarily add more value to our networks. One high maintenance friend might deplete us of the energy for 20 other contacts, but perhaps the support that one person provides at this stage of your life is essential for your mental health. If you find yourself devoting an inordinate amount of time interacting with your networks, but aren't seeing a return on that time investment, you might be ready to downsize. If you spend no time at all maintaining these relationships, now is an ideal time to think about expanding. In either case, understanding what you want your network to do for you can help you determine its ideal size and make-up.

That might mean a network of 15 people, 50 people, 150 people or 1,000. However, know that relationships are very susceptible to decay if we don't invest time in them. According to Dunbar, failure to spend time with a friend for over a year reduces the quality of that friendship by a third. Take time to think realistically about both the purpose of your network and your capacity for grooming as you set the size and demographics for your network.

STRETCH 4.3

When you think about your current network, you might now have a goal or two in mind. Perhaps you would like to build a bigger network, or one that is more powerful or more geographically diverse. Maybe you need to let some relationships fade out while building tighter connections with new people. Once you've reflected on how you want to shift your network, write a goal statement below.

GOAL STATEMENT: In the near future, I want my network to:

_____

_____

_____

Build for Depth

Now that you have a goal about the purpose, size, and type of network you need, how should you go about creating that network? In personal interviews with award-winning people we conducted for our doctoral research, we discovered two distinct and broad categories for expanding networks. We call those that construct relationships one at a time "building approaches." The other category of strategies was more diffused and included more sets of connections, so we called those "bridging approaches." Different situations may call for different approaches. You will also want to pick approaches that suit your personality and appeal. So for example, if you are an enthusiastic extrovert who is comfortable juggling hundreds of connections, an extensive weak tie network might be right for you. Introverts might prefer a smaller network more dependent on close-tie contacts.

The Building Strategies include four approaches that are highly focused actions, concentrating on individuals and incremental, deep, relationship-oriented growth. If you are an introvert or cringe deeply at the idea of reaching out to strangers, these may be right for you. Likewise, if you see yourself in a relatively stable environment, where relationships tend to extend over time, these could be right for you, too. You may find that you are already using many of these strategies or approaches. Or you may like to select behavioral approaches from both categories, depending on your own personal style.

Knowing. This strategy is based on the premise to know yourself first and build relationships with people who will value what you bring to the table. With a primary focus on introspection, this strategy allows you to make the selection of which groups and organizations to join. Since you are choosing events or activities that are personal interests, this could be a successful method for creating self-confidence in building your network before employing other strategies. People who use this strategy often build personal relationships with other members of clubs and organizations in ways that have a mentoring quality. They often give affirmations like this comment from Lori, a bank manager: "She just cheered me on, so I always had this person who was in my camp."

Persisting. For people with an abundance of confidence, a strategy to consider is good old-fashioned persistence. Karie once hired an internal candidate because he showed up at her office nearly every day to try to convince her he was the right candidate. The persistence he showed as a candidate ended up being a good fit to a job that required constant follow-up with administrators.

People in sales might rely on a state of mind that allows for persistent pursuit to identify and get to know people. In this strategy, there are no perceived boundaries, no people are unreachable, and gatekeepers are temporary roadblocks. Since this strategy's focus is on a targeted person and often has a specific desired outcome, it can work well for those who like building relationships.

Trish, an entrepreneur with a budding business told us, "I keep my face in front of people and then just keep knocking on their doors." Or, as Carl, a line manager for a regional manufacturing company, says, "I would sort of muscle my way into the office of the general manager." If you are using this strategy, it helps if you think of yourself as someone with a tough skin who enjoys the challenge of persisting until you are successful.

Performing.   Choose this strategy if you face a highly structured, hierarchical environment where there are unwritten rules about reaching above your level. Performing may be the best choice if you pride yourself on a job well done and are someone who routinely asks for additional responsibility. If your goal is to get to know others in a field in which you want to improve your competence, finding others who are a step or two ahead of you can help you understand what is expected at those levels.

Choosing to perform extra work duties will help your colleagues recognize your contributions. Some might feel threatened, it's true, but those higher-ups who value competence tend to open their networks to people based on competence, or at least a demonstration of eagerness to learn. In National Guard flight instructor Tina's words, "No matter who it is, if people do the job, then people will get to know them." Bill, a software developer, shared, "When you know somebody that's a self-starter or a top performer, you're going to pick that person to take to the next step."

When Terry Lundgren, CEO of Macy's became frustrated in an earlier job and started to think about leaving, recruiter Gene Ross gave him this advice: "You're not going to do this forever. There's a finite amount of time you're going to be doing this. Do this really, really well. And if you do this really, really well, everybody will see that, and they'll move you onto the next thing."

Growing.   Are you one of those people who connects to people in a soulful way, over time, or not at all? This strategy might be for you.

Developing relationships one at a time was the key to this strategy. This works for those with a preference to focus their energy on getting to know people and their stories fairly deeply right from the start. The relationship can be with people like themselves as well as with people who are very different.

Martin, an account executive, said, "I have a tremendous gift of remembering people's names and their stories. When you tell me your life story, I really remember, and the thing is, I really care. I think that sincerity validates people." Since account executives need to sustain relationships with clients over a long period of time, this is a perfect approach for Martin.

Bridge for Breadth

The bridging approaches are more diffused and include more than one linkage to network connections, with the effect of having a less immediate return. The upside is that they have the potential of reaching a broader, more diverse set of contacts. They are the natural breeding ground for extroverts, but introverts can benefit from these strategies as well.

Brokering. Do you think of yourself as a matchmaker of sorts at work? The brokering strategy might be for you. This is a good strategy for linking people to each other and their needs as a way of expanding your network. People will remember that you did them a favor by connecting them, and their goodwill may help you some day.

Often referred to as people brokers or connectors, the ones who use this strategy really enjoy knowing a lot of people. They have the ability to act as a bridge in introducing people to others in their networks and in a network analysis, would typically be a power hub. No problem is too big, as long as they know someone with a solution. Linda, a 20-year veteran HR specialist, said it best: "I think the greatest thing is when you need something and know someone who can help. It's not about loving a big network, it's about solving people's problems."

Connecting. Think of this strategy as leaping from one network point to another. Rather than being the broker, how can you connect to a broker or connector? Emphasizing knowledge and information, this approach helps you to shortcut building relationships one at a time by tapping into a power broker. To make a distant connection, sometimes the fastest way is to build a relationship between you and the other person is through a connector.

Nina, the CEO of a non-profit, shares, "I started doing a lot of fundraising. As it turns out, there is a winery up the valley that's owned by a woman who shares an interest of mine. But how do I get to know her, and how do I get six cases of wine from her for this fundraiser?

Then I found out that one of our donors plays golf with her regularly. I don't play golf, but they do. That's it!" Nina used her connection to leverage a quick route for an introduction.

Joining.   At some level, we all need to use a joining strategy, whether it's attending professional meetings or social events. For many, a huge part of networking is attending events and supporting non-profit causes. So make the most of the causes you are passionate about. Since you are probably already attending these events, just do what you do naturally, and the networking opportunities will fall into place.

Becoming involved in community organizations is a great way to connect with people already in your network and to meet new people with whom you already share an interest. You might consider joining business associations, professional societies, your local Chamber of Commerce, service organizations like Rotary International, charity events, civic and community associations, Meetup.com, church choirs, book clubs, the soup kitchen—the list goes on. It's easy to then make the transition to connecting outside of events. The advantage of this approach is that you create connections that may be singular in focus to start, but can spread beyond the original purpose. For example, you find your spinning class friend also wants to get better at public speaking, so with the other's support, you sign up for a class.

Ed, a budding entrepreneur who was new to his city, said, "I just joined everything I could to make new connections." Or as Taylor expressed, "You know, I got involved with doing this and that, and that's basically what launched all of my career success."

Sowing.   Sometimes you just have to play a numbers game. This strategy appeals to a wide range of individuals, but especially those who want a large network just in case. Relying on constant inter-actions, this approach is directly opposite to the building strategy of growing by getting to know one person at a time. Although this approach appears to be unfocused, those using this strategy like the idea of being open to a broad group of people and acquainting others with themselves, often without a specific purpose in mind.

Mindy, a marketing executive in the financial services industry, put it this way: "It's being out there. You have to be out there to meet people. You have to be out there in a lot of different places." Or as Jack, who owns a multi-location car dealership, told us, "It was also very important to me after I purchased the business to be 'out and about,' as they say. You just have to get out there and meet as many people as you can." Serendipity happens when you use this strategy. Table 4.1 provides an overview of the strategies.

Table 4.1 Personal Networking Strategies

BUILDING STRATEGIES	BRIDGING STRATEGIES
Knowing—exhibits introspection: getting to know yourself and what you can do before employing other strategies	Brokering—matchmakers, links people to each other and their needs; a people broker
Persisting—uses persistent, un-bounded pursuit and chutzpah to get to know people	Connecting—develops relationships with people through others
Performing—achieves recognition through accepting multiple leadership opportunities	Joining—participates in many organizations and activities
Growing—builds close, focused relationships one at a time	Sowing—uses constant interaction with many others, a scattergun approach

Adjust Constantly

Just building a network is not enough. Our experience and research have shown a need for dynamic, adaptive networks that can shift over time because our relationships with our relationships change. The colleagues you saw every day at work change when you change organizations. Although your hometown stays constant, when you move, the proximity to your relationships change and new relationships are formed. When you change to a new role, you must also think about what and how your network needs to shift.

At INSEAD, Herminia Ibarra led a research study looking at managers moving into bigger leadership positions. They found that, in general, managers needed to reorient their networks to be more externally focused and aimed with future goals in mind. Many of the new managers already understood the importance of network relationships to meet routine objectives such as sales quotas. However, to work at the new strategic level required a shift in networking. Managers had to broker information from one portion of their networks to another to achieve results. Inevitably, those moving into leadership positions discovered that a different network composition was needed.

It helps to be proactive in order to avoid spending all of your time maintaining past contacts. Taking time at several points in the year to assess your network diversity can help maintain a forward-focused network. As your need for information changes, make sure that your network is future-focused, populated with people who challenge you to think more broadly, and can help you grow and develop.

Scratch a Back

Your network is made up of relationships. Strong relationships are built over time based on the principal of give and take. Building strong relationships requires reciprocity, and sometimes you may need to scratch the person's back first before being able to make use of that contact. Therefore, it's important that you respond when asked for assistance by those in your network.

One of the best ways to build the network you want is to understand the balance between doing for others while asking others to do for you. Keeping track of the interests of those in your network and connecting them to ideas and opportunities lets people know you are thinking of them, and the more exchanges made, the more trustworthy, dependable, and helpful you are perceived to be.

Social networks such as LinkedIn and Twitter have a number of practices that create opportunities to share with others in your network. Providing endorsements or testimonials to others in your network is a great way to keep in touch with your contacts and let others know that you are following their work and have noticed their progress. Commenting on a blog, liking a post, forwarding interesting articles, or congratulating someone on a new promotion is as easy as clicking an automatic response button. Being consistently in touch helps to ensure that your personal connections last. If you only want to network when you need something, people will remember it and shun your requests. By finding ways to practice reciprocity within your network, you can build authentic relationships that can help you when you need your network most—as in a job search.

Strive for Five to Thrive

Hang out with people better than you, and you cannot help but improve.

—Warren Buffet

The best network stretches you. While you may have hundreds of people in your network, who are the five people who can help you be a better person, especially when it comes to your work? Every time you are with them, you feel you have upped your game and are thinking a little differently. Since we can't maintain close connections to everyone in our networks, focus on the five you could groom to help you thrive. For the last fifteen years, Barbara and Karie have counted on each other as part of their own five to thrive groups.

Who can challenge you to think beyond where you are now? You need options, access to new ideas, and connections that can help you advance. Is there someone in your network you can spend more time with to help you continue to stretch, think more strategically, and introduce you to new concepts from other fields?

It's All About Options

A healthy network increases your options. And having a diverse network can give you access to experiences that can help you accomplish your goals. We will explore the importance of experiences in the next chapter. Have fun and enjoy your network.

STRETCH 4.4

Identify your five to thrive. Review your calendar or email inbox to identify the five people who inspired you or gave you new ideas in the last year. Perhaps when you spent time with them, they:

☐ Inspired you

☐ Stretched your thinking

☐ Left you feeling it's possible to change

☐ Introduced you to new knowledge in different fields

☐ Demonstrated being an expert in ways you aren't

Do you have the five who can help you stretch to explore new possibilities and become a better person? Who are those five?

1.

2.

3.

4.

5.

Are you happy with the amount of time you spend with your five? If you'd like to make adjustments to your five, make a plan to reach out to those you'd like to include. Make sure that within the next month you connect with those people, not just online but in person as well. A one-hour coffee meeting or video conference is worth dozens of emails. Commit to investing time and energy to making these relationships the five that will help you thrive.

Stretch Summary

- The second Stretch Imperative, "You need options," starts with a diverse network. As the maxim goes, "It's not what you know but who you know."
- Diverse networks help you see the future, sell your ideas, and obtain the investment and resources you need.
- Everyone has two networks, personal close and professional loose ties.
- Why diverse networks matter:
    - Friends don't let friends fail
    - Your big idea may come from your network
    - Power comes from the union of your close and loose contacts
    - Three degrees of separation gets you closer to who you need to know
- Strategies to build and adjust networks
    - *Groom a clan.* Building relationships take time, so make sure you think realistically about both the purpose of your network and your capacity for staying connected.
    - *Build for depth.* Every network needs a broader, more diverse set of contacts.
    - *Bridge for breadth.* Don't let a few degrees of separation keep you from leveraging and expanding your network.
    - *Adjust constantly.* Future-proof your network by shifting the composition as your career needs change.
    - *Scratch a back.* Look for ways to take care of those in your network so that you can count on them when you need help.
    - *Strive for five to thrive.* The best network stretches you. Make sure your network can help you become the person you know you can be.

What Organizations and Managers Can Do

When people collaborate across organizations, good things happen, whether better innovation, better sales, or better operations. Collaboration relies on people having good networks to know who they should reach out to without spending an inordinate amount of time finding the right connections. It makes sense for organizations and managers to support the development of healthy networks in their organizations. People who network amplify the performance of those around them, increasing their total performance contribution. Here are some ideas to consider.

Sponsor Mentoring and Affinity Programs

Employees told us in our survey that informal mentoring and relationships with managers were the top two ways in which they experienced the most professional development. Yet, for an activity that can bring so much satisfaction, only about half of the executives we surveyed said their organizations had a mentoring program. Having a mentor who can help navigate the political and organizational structure at work improves your employees' networking ability, interpersonal influence, social astuteness, and ultimately, their career outcomes.

The best organizational practices we have seen support and facilitate access to a diverse network of mentors. Establishing communities of practice based on common interests or function-based networks is ideal. DeMarco, a Millennial at a large financial services organization, told us how much a marketing network helped him get started and feel connected across several work groups. He said that the networks are effective because they have their own autonomy. People connect by topics and regions in affinity networks, with names like the Black Enterprise Network, Marketing Club, and Women's Intercompany Network.

To help people who have been in their careers a long time, reverse mentoring can also provide two-way benefits. Using younger talent to mentor senior executives or experienced employees on things such as social media, brand awareness, or the buying habits of Millennials creates new relationships across the organization. Inevitably, the senior person will be impressed with her mentor and offer advice and sponsorship as well.

Use Leadership Events to Do Organic Talent Management

In typical talent management reviews, HR sits down with managers to determine their views of where talent sits in the organization, conducts succession plans, and then plans development activities for the various levels. Directors attend director training, managers with other managers, and so on. The challenge with this type of talent process and development is that managers do not get to know the talent in other organizations and on different hierarchical levels than their own in a meaningful and memorable way. Bjorn Atterstam, the former group head of talent and leadership development at Prudential plc U.K., thought there had to be a better way.

In Bjorn's view, in a world characterized as VUCA—volatility, uncertainty, complexity, and ambiguity. HR cannot possibly keep up with ever-changing shifts in strategic direction, talent need, and skill requirements. The responsibility for organizational development and developing the right capabilities must lie primarily with the leaders in the organization. Although there are benefits to training people on specific levels, for Prudential, there were big advantages to mixing up people across levels in a large-scale development events.

One example of how to build the required VUCA skills and bring talent from different levels together was the design of a total immersion event staged in Hong Kong for over 100 leaders to participate in. Using professionally written scripts and actors allowed the entire group talent pool to develop a shared and collective view on how the strategy of the company could conceivably play out and how to deliver results in a complex environment. With mixed-level teams, senior leaders had an opportunity to observe and coach junior leaders. They also included external speakers with provocative and future-oriented topics, followed by roundtables of discussions, again with mixed groups.

At the end of one of these types of multi-level events, Bjorn and the Prudential talent team asked the senior-most leaders to stay an additional half-day. The experience with more junior people had just finished and the executives' impressions were fresh. The senior leaders were asked, "Now that we have had a chance to explore and discuss the strategy in a changing world, what talent are we going to need? How are you going to be ready to have the leadership team you need to succeed you? Who have you been exposed to here that we need to develop and in what way?"

The net effect was that senior leaders were far more engaged in making on-the-spot developmental assignments happen as a result of the networking and working together with real people instead of reports and profiles. This created an "organic" approach and culture of developing talent. Baseball cards are fun to trade, but networking with real company stars is even better.

Conduct Speed Networking Events

Borrowing from the speed-dating phenomenon, consider speed-networking events at work. Speed dating helps people save time and money to find romantically attractive people quickly. Why not consider the same for finding professionally useful contacts at work?

The typical approach at speed dating is to have women sit at the tables and men move from station to station. One organization we interviewed uses a variation of this to introduce potential mentors to mentees. They have those looking for mentors sit at tables while the executives move from table to table. It's a great way to meet a lot of people in a short amount of time. The next time you have a management meeting, can you invite in some up-and-coming talent and do a speed-networking session with them?

Provide Online Tools for Social Collaboration

Encouraging one-on-one meetings and coffees are the best way to ensure that people will come away feeling that they have made meaningful contacts. Leaders need to be willing to put time on their busy calendar for structured, but casual engagements—standing at someone's desk for a few minutes doesn't count. However, when that isn't geographically possible, look to social collaboration software and message boards as a way to connect people throughout the organization.

Lisa O'Donnell, vice president of Global Learning Services at Marriott International, has introduced social collaboration into some leadership development programs. The focus of guest service at Marriott is high-touch, so any training platform needed to mirror that high-touch focus.

In one of their training programs that prepare people to become hotel property leaders, they were able to quickly connect the participants using social collaboration space. The group size was 350, and participants got to know one another virtually over time by completing a simple Icebreaker prior to the live training session. Senior executives posted informal videos on the site providing information and feedback, so the networking extended not only across to peers, but up and down so that senior executives also had a chance to get to know their emerging property leaders.

Because the social engagement was high, social collaboration sites were used to also support company innovation. The executive responsible for preserving the overall brand at Marriott International used the sites to connect people across the organization in discussions of what each of the hotels many brands delivered as a lifestyle promise. Through that online conversation, people who never would have met in person were able to collaborate and innovate in a unique and new way, expanding the inclusion of people on an important topic.

The only source of knowledge is experience.
—Albert Einstein

A mind that is stretched by a new experience can never go back to its old dimensions.
—Oliver Wendell Holmes, Jr.

5 BE GREEDY ABOUT EXPERIENCES

The Tale of Two Attorneys

Julie specializes in banking policy in Washington D.C. and Jarred Taylor specializes in Internet and technology law in San Francisco. Both discovered a passion for law in two very different ways.

Julie, a Houston native, was a psychology major in college. Jarred, born and raised in Birmingham, Alabama, was a political science major. Julie thought she wanted to be a clinical psychologist until she spent a summer working at a state-funded mental institution in North Carolina. Jarred's interests, on the other hand, shifted from diplomacy to intelligence, and he even applied for a CIA internship. By the time he graduated college, he was focused on working in a legal environment so that he could test out whether he liked the law before applying to law schools.

After graduating college, Julie took a position with a major bank in New York City. Her first assignment in due diligence was, in her words, "just boring." In her second year, she angled for a split assignment that gave her experience reporting on risk for various countries

123

and doing qualitative industry analysis. "I learned a lot," she recalls, including that she liked highly regulated industries.

After two years at the bank, it was an easy call to quit. Most days were uninspiring, and she felt unsatisfied and disappointed not to be engaged with her supervisor or a plan for her career. Julie applied and was accepted for law school at the University of Michigan.

That summer Julie worked for the credit arm of an automaker in Detroit. "I liked working there because they plan that you are going to be there for a long time, so they treat you accordingly. The way their program worked, you interacted with different groups and got well-rounded experiences. It was really fun, and the people cared about each other."

Jarred stuck to his plan and followed a number of other classmates from college to Washington, D.C., testing out his interest in the law by working for two years as a paralegal. "That job was not very satisfying for me. I think it was the way the law firm was structured. The paralegals were given very discrete tasks and were removed from the actual story of the case. We really didn't know why we were doing the tasks we were assigned. In the meantime, at night and on the weekends, I started a blog called *Tropophilia* (the love of change). That's when I started realizing that there was this whole area of Internet and technology law that I found very interesting."

When Jarred saw a posting for a legal assistant position at Google, he applied. "This was 2007, so Google was a medium-sized company, but everybody was talking about it. I felt like it was a long shot since they had rejected me a year earlier. But my blog really helped. Everyone in my interviews referred to my blog. Once I was there, several attorneys recognized how interested I was in this area of law and have continued to be really great mentors."

After two years, Jarred said, it was hard to leave Google, but he knew it was time to go to law school. Getting that experience, however, was invaluable. "Every job I've had since then has been a result of working at Google. There were a lot of new legal issues for Google as they grew and regulations changed. I got to see how lawyers dealt with really difficult concepts and legal issues."

Although Julie and Jarred's career journeys followed different directions, looking back, they both say that having lots of diverse experiences in the workplace and on side projects altered their career paths and helped them stretch. Today, they are both successful attorneys who have learned as much from the good experiences as from the bad.

The Experience Catch 22

Experiences are the ways in which we obtain knowledge and skills. That's why anyone searching for a first job understands the conundrum that "You can't get a job without experience, and you can't get experience without a job." When you have the opportunity to see or feel something, it has an effect on you that goes beyond what you can learn through observation. Take Russian winters. Were you to experience a Russian winter, you'd know what it feels like to breathe in air that is so cold it makes your lungs burn and your fingers tingle. Having the direct experience benefits your practical knowledge of Russian winters. Bringing up that shared experience could be the one factor that differentiates you when you are trying to close a sales deal with a Russian client.

Whether you are launching your career, considering a career shift, or simply wanting to stay relevant where you are, it's important to have a plan to manage and acquire a variety of experiences. Being able to answer the question: "What kind of experiences have prepared you for this role?" with practical and tangible examples can provide you with surprising leverage and desirability. That's why we advise you to be greedy about experiences.

The word "greedy" is almost never used in a positive context. However, when it comes to experiences, the best way to future-proof yourself is to be voracious in seeking out as many opportunities as you can. Experiences are the most effective way to learn new skills, reinforce what you know, and help you build on your strengths. People who have developed a repertoire of skills throughout their career know that this is a gradual and continuous process. It takes practice and repetition.

For example, once you have experienced the anxieties of presenting in front of groups, you understand the value of having well-developed strategies that help you feel confident. You learn that, even when a big deal is on the cusp of falling apart, you have to keep a level head and keep everyone talking until the deal is finished. Career experiences like these teach us how to push toward a goal without letting emotions muddle the conversation. They help us see that, even when you aren't in the middle of an enormous opportunity, you can still gain experiences on a daily basis.

One manager we know has experimented with over 20 different ways to run meetings and now uses a rotating system of his favorites to keep meetings interesting and productive. People who are developmentally engaged look for new chances to stretch and capitalize on experiences, even when they don't seem particularly relevant to their current role. When Jenny's manager was on medical leave, she volunteered to do a pitch for one of their clients, even though she served in a financial role and wasn't interested in the sales side of the company. She said it helped her to understand more about the business and their clients.

While repetition aids in building expertise, when it comes to experience, you will want to seek out diversity to stretch to the next level. You must acquire new experiences and not just repeat the same ones over and over again. One of the benefits of diversifying your experiences is test-driving a career, as Julie did before law school with her summer employment at the state mental hospital. Another benefit of diverse experiences is that they can help you to become more well rounded, as Julie discovered during her time working at the automaker, when her internship provided an opportunity for her to work in different departments. A third benefit is that they are a great way to help you expand your skillset, especially when the experiences are a bit outside your comfort zone, as they were for Jarred at Google.

No Two People Are the Same

Nothing ever becomes real 'til it is experienced.

—John Keats

Rarely do two people recount the same opinions, even when they have had the same experiences. Consider restaurant reviews as an example. How many times have you consulted an app for feedback or recommendations, only to discover vastly conflicting opinions? One customer responds with a five-star review, raving that the service was outstanding and the food presentation creative and delectable, while another gives it two stars and cites inattentive service, pretentious presentation and disappointment with the quality of the food.

There can be any variety of reasons for the vast differences we record for the same experience. Perhaps expectations were different. One customer might be a consultant in a large city with a vibrant mix of restaurants, eat out five nights a week and have acquired a very demanding palate. Another reviewer is stretched thin with three young children and hasn't eaten out in four months—anything that wasn't macaroni and cheese would thrill her.

Two people, given the same experiences, might not each gain the same growth of knowledge and capability. You must get the right experiences for you. We construct a narrative of who we are based on our experience. Therefore, the more experiences you can gain, the more options you'll have to expand your own personal narrative.

Obviously, you should think about how to get more experiences in the job that you are in, but why not expand your thinking to pursue other developmental experiences? The more varied you can make your experiences, the greater the likelihood of developing a broad set of skills. Stepping outside your comfort zone into new situations that call for untested abilities is a great way to boost your confidence and discover new capabilities. How often do you put yourself in the unknown or the uncomfortable? If you don't feel in over your head at least three to four times a year, you are not aiming high enough. You are not stretching.

Boost Your Skill Set

I had no choice but to grow with it. And that meant developing my leadership and management skills often on the fly.

—Bill Strickland

If you are always one of the first to volunteer for new assignments, your enthusiasm will guarantee that you have no shortage of work. If that's the case, then it's important to be strategic and deliberate in setting goals for what experiences to go after. Instead of focusing on fixing weaknesses, try focusing on your strengths as a way to build mastery. By becoming the go-to person for certain expertises in your organization, you will distinguish yourself, not just on your team but to others as well. Then when you want to advance you will have a number of powerful advocates with great stories to share about your work. Better still, people who focus on building on their strengths are six times more likely to be engaged in their jobs and three times more likely to report having an excellent quality of life.

Set realistic goals when boosting your skill set. When Barbara stepped into her position as college president, she inherited a strategic plan that had 81 goals. It wasn't surprising that no one could remember the goals or be excited by the plan-it lacked focus. Reconfiguring the plan into five goals made it actionable and memorable. This way she was able to build her team's skill set at a manageable pace, and engage the college community in working together to achieve their goals.

Strategies for Being Greedy About Experiences

Experience is what you get when you didn't get what you wanted. And experience is often the most valuable thing you have to offer.

—Randy Pausch

Our natural default is to work on things that interest us. That may not be the best strategy. Instead, think strategically, both in terms of the number of experiences you'd like to acquire and the timeframe in which you hope to accomplish them. Don't just let experiences happen to you, but choose the experiences that benefit you the most.

Approach Work with a Development Stance

As a first step, let's go back to the skills you said you wanted to acquire in Chapter 2. Now consider what might be the best way to acquire experiences to match those skills. Part of the challenge with learning at work is that we already feel overwhelmed with what we have to achieve. The average salaried worker puts in 49 hours a week at the job and can still feel behind. According to researchers at Harvard, we can approach our work from one of three stances: completion, performance, or development. The stance we take will affect how much we learn in any given situation.

> **Be Greedy About Experiences Stretch Strategies**
>
> 1. Approach work with a development stance
>
> 2. Get global
>
> 3. Find a need, solve a problem
>
> 4. Stretch your limits
>
> 5. Gift feedback
>
> 6. Look sideways
>
> 7. Stay educated

In the *completion stance*, our primary goal is to get the task or job done. We need simply to get it off our to-do list and not look for any additional challenge. If any learning happens, it is somewhat accidental.

The stakes in a *performance stance* are little higher. Here you care more about high-quality results and may push yourself with new challenges. Surmounting these challenges leads to learning, even though it may not have been a conscious goal.

In a *development stance*, you care about getting the task done really well and using what you learn to do even better work in the future.

As an example, let's assume you have been put in charge of chairing a meeting. In a completion stance, you would use the standing agenda or formats by which meetings are routinely run in your organization, or maybe even less. You just want to get the meeting off your to-do list.

In a performance stance, you might consider how to make the meeting more efficient and meaningful for everyone in the room and consider some ways to run the meeting differently than others have done. Because you have applied some thought on how to conduct the meeting better, you will have a better opportunity to learn something new.

In the third stance—development—you might do a little research to find ways to have effective meetings, talk to people who are known for running great meetings, and be more attentive at other meetings about the processes people are using that work or do not work for effective meetings. Maybe you would take an online course or sign up for a MOOC (massively open online course) on how to run effective meetings. With or without the formal training, taking this stance will allow you to learn more from the experience.

If you are new to a content area or task and have decided to take a development stance, having some guidance can really accelerate your performance. In a study of software engineers, a simple 15-minute discussion with a more experienced developer about the task helped improve performance significantly. Can you seek out people who can help guide you, especially if you promise to use only 15 minutes of their time?

Of course it isn't possible to approach all our work with a development stance. On the other hand, if you are approaching all your work with a completion stance, you are unlikely to be learning on the fly and gaining real value from the experience. Your risk of slowly losing ground in your field increases. The key is to find a balance.

S T R E T C H   B R E A K

STRETCH

5.1

Think about your overall goals and assignments at work. List the major projects and tasks you are working on at the moment. Next consider each project's potential for helping you develop skills that you wish to focus on improving. List the skills in the second column. Then decide which approach you will take on each of your current projects: completion(C), performance(P), or development(D).

MY PROJECTS	SKILLS I CAN DEVELOP	MY DEVELOPMENT STANCE		
		C	P	D
1.				
2.				
3.				

This framework will allow you to determine your effectiveness in each stance for various experiences. Try asking yourself: "How important is it to develop expertise for this task?" Only one or two projects should be using a development stance. Now think about how to develop a plan to go about obtaining the experiences you need.

Get Global

A job or assignment abroad can give your career a big boost. People often make the mistake of thinking that, with all the virtual opportunities available at work, they can gain all the work experiences they want without leaving home. That's not true. In today's globalized economy, international experience will differentiate you.

Charlene was fortunate to be the fifth person hired into a start-up company that developed sales leads for emergent markets in Europe, India, and Southeast Asia. Her boss, the founder, required everyone to be willing to travel. She says, "It just wasn't an option not to travel to Europe, India, and Japan." The founder's advice to all of his hires was to learn to enjoy business travel by making sure that you take time to play alongside the local people you are visiting, rather than observing the culture from afar.

Airline flight crews have a name for their colleagues who just go straight to the hotel, slam the door and click the lock shut, ordering room service. They are called "slam-clickers." Don't be a slam-clicker. Experience the hospitality of having dinner in your local host's home or favorite restaurant, or gather some fellow travelers and explore the sights. Post pictures to social media; you might be surprised how many people respond to your adventures.

Understanding culture and community in different countries is one of the benefits you can get from global experiences. You could also gain language skills and an opportunity to demonstrate that you can manage a multicultural, multilingual working environment while producing great work. Succeeding despite being outside your comfort zone lets organizations know that you are adaptable.

In a competitive job market, you may well find that expanding your horizons and gaining work experience abroad will help you reap the rewards later in your career. Dan Black, Ernst & Young's director of campus recruiting for the Americas, says applicants who have served in the Peace Corps or worked overseas in an internship have a leg up on everyone else. He says, "Our clients are demanding more of us these days; they want diversity of thought and diversity of values."

Overseas experience can help you to advance more quickly. Since there are a limited number of candidates with international experience, your chances are better to win plum assignments.

STRETCH BREAK

STRETCH 5.2

While the best global experience is to spend time working overseas, there are a number of things you can do to boost your global awareness:

☐ Study the world news and find out how global events may affect your industry. Make a habit of reading from at least three continents, whether newspapers or Twitter feeds.

☐ Boost your social capital by building your network of people from different cultures.

☐ Practice ways to feel comfortable in new environments. Seek out new cuisines—the more exotic the better—or attend cultural festivals, music or theater shows, or author readings; take a class about a foreign land; learn a second or third language.

☐ Volunteer to host international students from your local schools so that you can get to know their customs.

☐ Vacation abroad. A number of opportunities exist to volunteer your time abroad, or there are ways to travel relatively inexpensively. We know Millennials who travel abroad regularly to work with nongovernmental organizations and use social media sites such as GoFundMe.com to raise funds for their experiences.

☐ Seek out opportunities at work to travel or ask for assignments abroad.

Find a Need—Solve a Problem

When you begin with the mantra of "find a need—solve a problem," you declare to those around you that you care deeply about the organization and are willing to help in any way possible. As long as organizations have needs, they will always be searching for people passionate about solving problems. If you can help identify or provide better, faster, and smarter ways to solve problems, you are bound to gain many valuable experiences and probably some champions for your efforts.

Now look around your organization for problems that you can solve. Is there some issue that everyone knows is a problem, but no one wants to fix? People jump at the opportunity to fix the fun, sexy problems, but the dirty ones, not so much. Can you tackle some grunt work that no one wants to do and establish yourself as a problem-solver? Are your team's documents and resources scattered across dozens of sites and sitting on individual hard drives so that time is wasted trying to find things? Can you organize it in an easy-to-maintain fashion? Or is the remote team struggling to deliver work in a timely fashion, and you've heard of a terrific new app that could help? Do you think your company should be slicing their big data in ways no one has thought of yet? Speak up.

Vivek Gupta, CEO of Zenzar Technologies, says, "I like to tell people try and do as much as you can within the confines of what your company can offer. Raise your hand if somebody says, 'Is anyone willing to take this job?' Take it. Be visible. Be seen. If you've got a good idea, don't keep it to yourself."

Alexandra Ames, 28, exemplifies how to create your own job. With a graduate degree in international relations and limited job prospects in her field, Alexandra spent a number of years working in public relations for a New York financial services company. Eventually, she felt burnt out by the endless communication demands of the 2008 financial meltdown and quit her job for a period of self-reflection. She realized she wanted to work for an organization that would be a fit for her existing skills, along with her love of the outdoors and her passion for conservation. She found just such an organization in the Lewa Wildlife Conservancy in Kenya. She knew that she could increase Lewa's effectiveness in achieving their mission if they had someone like her in an international role.

The problem was that the job she wanted didn't exist. She created a network of supporters within Lewa, people she met through her loose ties networks in London and California. Eventually, she convinced them to let her build an international marketing and development role, which she then assumed. She now works from London, with regular trips to Kenya. She has also acquired a few unexpected skills, such as driving through herds of elephants, rapidly changing tires, and picking up some Swahili.

Stretch Your Limits

Perhaps the blues rock band The Doors were onto something in the 1970s when they sang, "You gotta try everything once. You better build up your endurance. Well variety is the spice of life." While the variety The Doors embraced created plenty of trouble, in the context of work experiences, stretching the limits of your skills is something you should try regularly.

If you know you can manage your department, could you manage two departments? What skills would you need to make that stretch possible? Maybe you'd want to consider developing more effective people skills or expand on your team-building skills?

Stretching your limits doesn't always mean an upward step, as Lori Goler demonstrated. When Lori was looking to leave eBay, she called Sheryl Sandberg at Facebook and asked, "What is your biggest problem, and how can I solve it?" Lori's deep expertise in marketing at eBay was not a skill fit for Facebook at the time. Instead, Sheryl hired Lori to address Facebook's biggest problem—recruiting. Because Lori was willing to drop down a level to learn a new function and let go of her seniority status at eBay, she gained new skills and a successful career, rebooting her sell-by date.

A commonly held maxim among recruiters is that if you are successful at what you are doing now, you can stretch to triple your responsibilities. For example, if you manage a budget of $1 million, you can stretch to handle a budget of $3 million. The big dilemma, of course, is how far to stretch. What percentage of the criteria in a job description do you feel you need to meet in order to apply for it? If you're a man, you likely answer about 50 percent. If you're a woman, you probably answer 100 percent. Perhaps there's especially room for women to stretch their limits a little more.

Allyson was given a challenging assignment that she feared put her in over her head. When she told her manager, the manager advised her, "Do it scared." She had to step outside her comfort zone.

Another consideration is how many areas you might be stretching in at the same time. For example, it might not be wise, even if you land it, to take a job in both a new industry and a new functional area with increased responsibilities. In Lori's story above, she changed functional areas, downgraded a level, and stayed in technology. Stretch, but don't try to be Elastigirl.

Here's the opposite of stretching. When we asked our friend Howard whether he ever considered volunteering for an assignment at work, he said, "Heck no; if you volunteer for extra work, then the next thing you know you have problems to solve. And if you do that successfully, then they are going to ask you to take on other assignments." While Howard was successful in limiting his responsibilities at work, he was also limiting his potential to develop expertise and demonstrate value for his company.

Gift Feedback

Complex human exchanges are increasing. If you are uncomfortable with giving and receiving feedback, it's time to pursue those experiences until you have the kind of soft skills that are in demand. The expectations to stay connected and communicate feedback constantly will require greater sophistication and skill.

It doesn't take a Dilbert cartoon strip to recognize the team member who is always late for staff meetings, never remembers to silence her mobile phone, and is the first person to interrupt a presentation with an off-topic question. How many times have you wondered why someone doesn't tell her how to be a better professional? No matter where you work, there will be difficult people. That is why it is important not only to receive feedback, as discussed in Chapter 3, but also to learn how to give feedback.

Developing confidence in our interpersonal skills is one of the most challenging issues we have to navigate at work. Giving feedback is a necessary part of growing as a professional and receiving what you need in return. The more practice you have at giving feedback, the easier it will be for you to deal with difficult situations with both your direct reports and your boss. Feeling safe when giving feedback requires trust. In order to develop trust, people on your team or in your organization must get to know one another and feel comfortable talking about their emotions.

Many of us don't want to hurt our colleagues' feelings, or perhaps we are terrified by what others might say about us, so we remain silent, refusing to express an opinion. But if you can approach giving feedback with humility, there is a good likelihood it will be taken with appreciation.

People say over and over that they don't receive the feedback they need, so consider making it one of your goals to give it. Remember, feedback is only applied 30 percent of the time, so don't be disillusioned when people don't seem to take your advice straightaway. You might need to try more than one approach to have the desired impact.

S T R E T C H   B R E A K

STRETCH 5.3

Since it is important to provide feedback to managers as well as to colleagues and direct reports, think about how you can alter your approach for different situations. It might be addressing how your new boss's tales of "In my last job we did it this way" is dampening your team's spirit. Or it might be letting your peers know that arriving at meetings on time is essential. Here are some tips to practice as you become comfortable gifting feedback:

☐ To focus your thoughts, try writing out a script of what you are going to say in advance of the meeting.

☐ Create a shared goal that you can agree on, and aim your feedback toward that shared goal.

☐ Shift the conversation to get others on the team to join in with advice on how they would handle the situation.

☐ Make sure the feedback you gift is done confidentially and in private to the person or the team.

☐ Focus on being positive and specific.

Look Sideways

A terrific way to try out new experiences is to volunteer inside your organization but outside your normal goals—"looking sideways." If you want experience in sales, ask whether you can help with lead generation calls. If you want marketing experience, volunteer to be a part of your company's social media team or take part in a focus group rolling out a new product. Be specific about the skills you want to acquire and the time that you can devote to the experience.

Also looking sideways: short bursts of volunteering outside the organization can also help you build or maintain bridges to people in your network, as well as develop experience. If you haven't been able to gain sales experience at work, consider volunteering with a non-profit to make annual fund calls. Be specific about the time frame and consider asking for a reference or an endorsement for your skills in return for your efforts. You might even get a title to use that you can add to your résumé or online profile.

If you are a freelancer, you'll find plenty of company. According to the software company Intuit, by 2020 more than 40 percent of the U.S. workforce will be freelancers. That's more than 60 million people. However, when you are a freelancer, the expectation is that you already have plenty of expertise. An aspiring developer, George was changing fields and knew it might be difficult as a newbie to land his first clients. When he responded to a request for a software developer assignment, he volunteered to work with no compensation until he started to deliver value. In the end, he volunteered his time for three months before he started landing paid assignments.

Sofia, also a freelancer, had just launched her own social media consultancy and wanted to grow her client base. She discovered that volunteering with non-profits to help them build their social media profiles also helped build her client base. She was able to obtain referrals and recommendations and testimonials that helped expand her network and enhance her reputation.

The opportunities for project-based work are exploding as technology and mobility become intertwined. Make sure you take the opportunity to try something that you'll be proud to include on your résumé.

There are two special categories of looking sideways that we think warrant close attention: sidepreneurship and sabbaticals.

Try Sidepreneurship. After interviewing for two years and mining her network to land a job for a top ten global ad agency, Samantha was stunned when the internal culture wasn't what she'd been led to expect. She'd reached out to her network and asked a lot of questions of those who had worked at the agency and done plenty of research on the agency's website and blogs to get a sense of the culture. She'd just left a job at a small agency that was heavily creative and now found herself tied to a desk slogging through layers of bureaucracy on a client account. It was impossible to see the impact of her efforts. Samantha gave notice after only six months at her new agency.

Through the ups and downs of ad agency life, Samantha had maintained a freelance digital media consulting practice. Free of the unsatisfying job, she was now able to leverage her consulting practice into full-time work. A year and a half later, she's thrilled with the flexibility and impact she provides for her clients as an entrepreneur.

Starting a business on the side can be a great way to develop different skills and earn extra income. A banker we know has a photography business on the side. Another colleague who is a chief financial officer sells financial modeling software. Jarred, whose story started this chapter, still maintains his blog separate from his job as an attorney.

Whether it's to feed your passion, provide creative release, or explore the potential to launch your own venture, sidepreneurship is a good way to test drive opportunities.

Seek Sabbaticals. Andy Claiborne had over a decade of experience at the same location of his high-tech company and was feeling uninspired in his career. He had considered some startup opportunities, but with a family to support and one child with a serious illness, he didn't feel it would be wise to take too much risk. Then a local startup approached him and asked him to consider working part-time and weekends to get the company going.

Working for a startup was a completely new experience for Andy compared to working for a huge, established corporation. As a software engineer, he had the opportunity to practice new ways of developing software and to deliver code to customers. Working with a small team, he gained more management experience and felt the pressure of deadlines personally.

As the need for his time increased at the startup, he decided to take advantage of the company's sabbatical program and work part-time at both jobs for six months. What he didn't anticipate was the degree to which the things he was learning at the startup would make a difference back in his group at the large company. At the end of the six months, the startup was not yet gaining customer traction, so he went back to the large company full-time. However, his experience in the startup was instrumental in rejuvenating his career.

"I am really rocking it now," he said. "The startup experience helped me think of new ways to approach my work. My boss and team were open to those ideas, and we implemented many of them. It's made me feel more grateful to the company because they gave me the opportunity to take a part-time sabbatical, listened to new ways of working, and reintegrated my new skills into the business. Pleasantly, it's given me opportunities for new roles and some major promotions."

Although you may not have the same opportunity to take a sabbatical as Andy, keeping your day job while pursuing an entrepreneurial opportunity is feasible for most people. Do you have an idea you've always wanted to pursue? Do you have friends you could enroll to make that idea come to life? Or can you join an existing startup and gain some experience? Any new startup is looking for talent, and if you're willing to work for a share of the equity, you're likely to find opportunity waiting. It could pay off as a full-time job and new career, but it could also be a powerful way to develop new skills and network for the future.

STRETCH

5.4

"Looking sideways" is a great way to extend what you do professionally. Consider these options for side projects or to tap into sidepreneurship opportunities:

- ☐ Volunteer for a non-profit to get experiences different from your current work.

- ☐ Give a brown-bag talk on a topic or ideas you yourself would like to learn more about.

- ☐ Ask for a short-term assignment that's outside your area of expertise.

- ☐ Give consulting a try. If you could consult on any topic, what would it be?

- ☐ Tap into your creative passion by opening an Etsy store or leveraging your local "I made it" market.

- ☐ Volunteer to serve as a mentor. By offering to mentor others who are starting businesses or need tactical help, you will have an opportunity to share your expertise and see the benefits in action.

- ☐ Team with a startup accelerator or incubator to volunteer or get exposure to entrepreneurial opportunities in your area.

- ☐ Work with your employer or other like-minded professionals to host a "hack-a-thon" and build or improve a software-based product or process.

- ☐ Express yourself. Tap into your other interests and consider starting a creative project where you learn additional skills. If you love music, start a band and learn all the marketing and business aspects while enjoying your passion. Or learn blogging skills by writing about food or your favorite city.

- ☐ Extend your presentation and teaching skills as an adjunct at your local college.

Stay Educated

Considering that your authors met in graduate school, it's probably understandable that we would be advocates for the experience of education. If we were honest, however, we would admit that we both spent several years on the fence before we took the plunge to enroll in graduate school. Deciding whether to go back to school is difficult, particularly if you are going to have to step out of the workforce. However, if you select a part-time or a low-residency program, as we did, juggling work, families, and school can be stressful but manageable.

Studies show that people with more education enjoy lower unemployment rates and earn more money over their careers. Education is the ultimate value equation: invest in yourself and your future and it pays off. As with all investments, it's important to know your goals before you start. Is an additional degree important to advance in your career? Or do you need additional education in order to change fields? In some fields, pursuing a graduate degree isn't required, but in others like education and healthcare, it is mandatory.

A graduate degree made a difference for Zari, the manager for a specialty giftware manufacturer. When the owner decided to move the manufacturing function offshore, Zari, along with the rest of the workforce, was laid off. Thanks to funding from the U.S. Trade Adjustment Assistance program and the diligence of her unemployment counselor, Zari discovered that she was eligible to substitute some of her unemployment benefits for graduate school tuition. While the benefits didn't cover the entire cost, when combined with a scholarship, it was possible for her to graduate with minimal loans. Graduating with a degree in non-profit management, Zari is now the statewide director for a workforce development program. She's achieved her income goals and is saving for retirement. She says going back to school changed her life. In her words: "It's made everything else possible."

If you are no longer learning on the job, or want to change fields entirely, going back to school could help enhance your employability. This is especially true if you are in a field that is changing rapidly and higher credentialing is important just to keep your knowledge current or remain professionally licensed. While some enjoy school for the pure joy of learning and are willing to finance that passion, pursuing education is easier to take advantage of if your employer supports professional development through tuition reimbursement. Increasingly, there are lower-cost educational options to consider.

Today, there are also many other informal opportunities for additional educational skill enhancement. TED talks, MOOCs, online or blended learning courses offered through colleges and universities, certifications by professional societies or books written by the best experts in their fields are all readily available.

Outside of workplace interests, it's easy to take advantage of educational alternatives by attending lecture series or by joining or starting a new club or team. There are even travel opportunities through which you can earn continuing education units toward certain professional licenses.

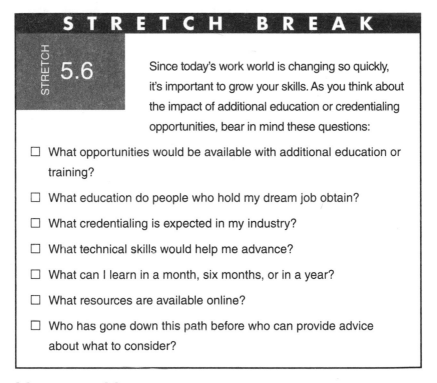

STRETCH BREAK

STRETCH **5.6**

Since today's work world is changing so quickly, it's important to grow your skills. As you think about the impact of additional education or credentialing opportunities, bear in mind these questions:

☐ What opportunities would be available with additional education or training?

☐ What education do people who hold my dream job obtain?

☐ What credentialing is expected in my industry?

☐ What technical skills would help me advance?

☐ What can I learn in a month, six months, or in a year?

☐ What resources are available online?

☐ Who has gone down this path before who can provide advice about what to consider?

Managers Matter

In our survey, when we asked the question: "In what way have you experienced the most professional development?" the number one response was: "My relationship with my manager." Our professional relationships with managers and bosses can have a significant impact on our work experience. A great boss can inspire and guide us to stretch and try new things—or treat us well but neglect developing us. And a bad boss can have us watching the clock all day and learning bad habits. There are lessons of experience to be gained in any situation, even the bad ones, and we can learn to make the most out of any situation.

Is Your Good Boss Holding You Back?

Being loyal to someone who has your back and makes life comfortable at work is easy. When your boss shows an understanding for your challenges at home and at work, you are bound to feel a sense of loyalty. Being loyal increases our sense of belonging and safety.

Robert had a great relationship with his boss. His boss had seen him through a difficult divorce. His boss always understood and never judged him when he wanted to leave work early to pick his kids up from school or attend their sporting events. As the years went by, Robert began to feel frustrated with his increased work duties without commensurate increases in compensation. Then he'd look back to those years of support and feel that it was only fair that he should do more than his share when the company entered difficult times. It seemed his industry, commercial industrial supply sales, was going through massive changes.

Robert knew his days were numbered when the company was acquired. Although his boss never directly asked him to stay, he was the employee who posted the "For Sale" sign outside the warehouse.

Unemployed and looking to the future, Robert now saw how his understanding boss and his own loyalty had left him scrambling with a résumé that showed minimal career progression over 22 years at the same company. When we become too comfortable or let our good feelings of loyalty keep us from applying a critical eye to our employability, work is easy, work is good, but it's not challenging. We don't stretch.

If you aren't getting a range of experiences and seeing the results in your skill development, is it an illusion that you are working for a good boss? Good bosses are talent developers and career makers. They help you to develop skills that ensure your employability and value to the company. Good bosses don't just stretch you; they change you.

If you allow your boss only to give you positive feedback and reinforce keeping you in a position that inhibits promotions, you are complicit in your lack of growth. The only way to resolve the loyalty dilemma is to know how to ask for the feedback you need from others and your boss and to know when it's time to move on. To continue to grow, you must get in over your head once in a while. Make sure your boss is helping you do that.

STRETCH BREAK

STRETCH **5.7**

How can you determine the quality of your manager relationship? Here are some questions you might consider:

☐ Are you receiving regular feedback from your boss?

☐ Does that feedback include helping you find ways to stretch?

☐ Are you routinely assigned to projects that develop your skills?

☐ Has your job description changed in several years compared to your peers?

☐ Has the job you do changed in educational and/or technological requirements?

☐ Have you had the opportunity to gain additional training or education?

☐ When was your last promotion? Was it on track with company standards?

☐ Are your peers promoted more than you are?

☐ Have you created and discussed a career plan at your company with your boss?

Making Lemonade from a Bad Boss

We all know bad bosses. We are fascinated by the biographies they write. We flock to movies about them. We even love to give them nicknames. One of the most notorious was Chainsaw Al, otherwise known as Albert Dunlap, author of *Mean Business*, superstar turnaround artist and professional downsizer. His ruthless methods led to thousands of firings and a swath of demeaned and demoralized employees in his wake. Fortunately, his sell-by date expired when he was ruined by a massive accounting scandal at Sunbeam-Oster and was banned for life from serving on the board of any publicly traded company.

In *The Devil Wears Prada*, fashion magazine editor Miranda Priestly (Meryl Streep) abuses her subordinates endlessly. Many reviewers believe that Anna Wintour, editor-in-chief of *Vogue* magazine is the inspiration for Priestly's character. Priestly's grueling schedule, constant belittling of her assistant, and demeaning requests for unreasonable, purely personal chores created a revolving door of assistants. Why was she tolerated at all? Quite simply, because it guaranteed the next job; any assistant who survived her abuse launched their career thanks to Priestly's brilliant and tough reputation. If you survived working for her, you would thrive in any other workplace.

Bad bosses are everywhere. A simple scan of *The New York Times'* *Workologist* columns finds no shortage of advice for those working for bully bosses. "Speaking up"—calling your boss out on the bad behavior—seems the first line of advice, but is the experience of working for a bad boss worth it?

That depends

Can you justify working for a bad boss? Sheryl Sandberg says yes, as long as you know the tradeoff and can stay focused on what you will take away from the experience. Engaging with a bad boss who is a genius and can teach you lots is different than the gut-wrenching dread of an abusive boss. If there isn't an upside, it's best to avoid or leave a bad boss.

Bad bosses often motivate us to seek a change rather than settle for intolerable situations. Acknowledging the toxic situation can be the perfect opportunity to reassess how you define success and what you want out of your career and company culture. Seeking alternative solutions both inside and outside your organization can give you time to interview and test out new jobs. For Samantha, the unhealthy culture at the ad agency helped push her to become an entrepreneur, using the contacts she had nurtured over the years into a successful consulting practice.

You also might confront your boss directly and try to develop a plan to improve the relationship. Just remember that people don't change unless they want to, so don't try to change your boss. Finding something that is satisfying about your work can be a good way to stay positive while you wait out changes in leadership.

A non-profit CEO we know had a challenging board chair prone to micromanaging. After hours and hours of conversation with her, she knew that the chair wasn't going to change. But, rather than leave the organization, which would require her to leave the community to find an equivalent job, she decided to wait out the board chair's term. Instead of trying to change what she couldn't, she spent a year working with internal managers to develop new programs that excited and engaged her until the board chair's term was up. She made lemonade from the bad experience and gained a better relationship with her team. When the new board chair started, she was able to establish a more functional partnership and continue doing the work she loved.

Unless you are exiting the organization, it is critical that you approach the situation with caution. Don't engage others in gossip because you never know what will be passed back to the boss. Bad bosses foster negative behaviors and nasty environments that reduce trust and increase unhealthy competition.

Completing your assignments on time and participating in meetings lets everyone know that you haven't checked out. Make sure you maintain your professionalism and sense of humor. If your bad boss chronically erodes your aspirations, you have a choice. Exit. Find a job somewhere else in the organization or take this as an opportunity to move elsewhere. In the end, you will be better equipped to recognize a good boss, especially when one day that good boss is you.

Evaluate Your Options

The combination of an aggressive approach to seeking experiences and making the most of the good and bad in any work environment is in your hands. With every experience you gather, be sure to gain as much from it as possible. Stretch to get the experiences you need to acquire new skills, work on anything that is holding you back, and improve on that sweet spot at the edge of your abilities. Don't wait for experiences to come to you. Make it your choice.

Now that you have lots of options from your diverse network and you've had plenty of experiences to boost your skills, you have dreams to realize.

 **Stretch Summary**

- Gain the experiences you need to acquire new skills and master others. Learn by doing.
- You need options, which is why it's important to get the right experiences.
- Boost your skill set by focusing on your strengths.
- The strategies for being greedy about obtaining experiences include:
  - *Approach work with a development stance.* Enhance what you learn at work by approaching assignments in one of three ways: completion—when you just want to get it done; performance— when the stakes are higher; or development—when you want to take your skills to the next level.
  - *Get global.* To expand your career options, consider an assignment abroad.
  - *Find a need—solve a problem.* Everyone loves a problem-solver.
  - *Stretch your limits.* Try everything once, even if it means "doing it scared."
  - *Gift feedback.* Universally, people say they don't get the feedback they need; do your part by learning how to give feedback.
  - *Look sideways.* Instead of waiting for experiences to come to you, look sideways to sidepreneurship or sabbaticals to gain broader experience.
  - *Stay educated.* Education is the ultimate value equation. Invest in yourself and your future.
- Managers matter
  - Is your good boss holding you back?
  - Make lemonade from a bad boss.

What Organizations and Managers Can Do

Encouraging employees to seek out a wide range of experiences can often be seen as the individual responsibility of managers and not a responsibility within the organization. In truth, it's a product of the organization's culture. Deliberate effort and encouragement can create space for people to be open to new ideas and experimentation, yielding big results for organization while helping to ensure retention and maximum performance as jobs shift and change.

Measure Intra-Organizational Experience

If you measure it, you value it. Organizations with a deliberate focus on up-skilling establish a valuable culture for employees. The best way to encourage people to put their hands up and volunteer for new opportunities within your organization is to actively expose employees to those opportunities. Helping people gain a broader set of experiences across the organization is an investment in tenure and merit. Specific performance management programs that measure participation as part of a regular series of reviews are more likely to reap rewards. Once managers and employees know it's measured, they are more likely to take risks and put their hands up to try new experiences.

Measure your leaders' track record on developing and moving talent. Do you have leaders who desperately hold on to every person in fear of losing budget for a replacement? Check to see whether your leaders have a net record of importing or exporting talent, and reward those who take the time and risk to be talent exporters.

Give Employees Customer Experience

What if everyone in the organization could understand the customer experience by being in a front-line position at some point? At the Canadian telecommunication company, TELUS, they can. Closer to the Customer (C2C) gives non-customer-facing employees a short experience away from their regular jobs to shadow other people. For example, a person in accounts receivable might shadow a store manager. Team members find insights into the customer experience that can help them make more informed decisions down the road, and they are exposed to other parts of TELUS.

The extraordinary aspect to C2C is the scale at which it operates. In any given year, up to 5,000 employees receive an invitation to participate in either a company-wide or team-specific C2C event. "You observe everything and get a real live experience, almost like being on *Undercover Boss*," says Dan Pontefract, chief envisioner. "People blog about it and share pictures on Habitat Photo, our online photo-sharing network. Our employee engagement scores have gone up dramatically, partially due to this experience." Paul Bleier, a Business Solutions Consultant at TELUS, said after his experience, "For me, the really nice thing is it made me want to get out in the field more."

Offer Sabbaticals

The opportunity to take a career break usually conjures up visions of academics on extended absences to write books or research the next scientific breakthrough. But companies like HP, 3M, and Google understand that employees have a variety of interests and encourage creative exploration. These include part-time sabbaticals or unpaid leave, which can rejuvenate innovation. In one such case, those now ubiquitous 3M Post-it Notes came about on a sabbatical when chemist Art Fry was frustrated with trying to mark places in his hymnal. Mini-sabbaticals of less than a month can allow employees to do volunteer work, travel, seek training, or offer palliative care. Time off is a powerful antidote to job fatigue.

Sponsor Mid-Life Internships

Internships are not just for college students. The British bank Barclays announced a mature workers program designed for those who have been out of the workforce for at least two years and want to return. Barclays is not alone, as Goldman Sachs, J.P. Morgan Chase, Credit Suisse, MetLife, and Morgan Stanley all have programs to return workers back to the ranks after career breaks. Unlike unpaid college internships, older interns receive salaries and can provide an opportunity for companies to test prospective employees before committing. The head of the apprenticeship program at Barclays remarks: "We see real benefit in employing a workforce . . . who have had previous careers and greater life experiences . . . and are able to really understand and support our customers."

Reward Career Makers

The most significant way to build engagement in the workplace is through the relationships employees have with their managers and supervisors. Organizations that reward and develop interpersonal skills at the supervisor and manager level achieve lower levels of turnover and higher levels of employee job satisfaction. People work hardest for people who care about them and will work with them to improve performance. Training and coaching people as they move into supervisory roles can help new managers in turn develop the next level of employees.

Donna Morris, Adobe's senior vice president for People and Places, says that her company provides for "check-ins," during which managers provide employees targeted coaching and advice. Managers aren't asked to record their interactions but simply to help employees with their growth and development plans. The goal is to give people information in real time rather than months after the teachable moments have passed. As part of the implementation, managers were trained in giving and receiving feedback and other challenging scenarios through role playing and lectures.

Create a Job Rotation or Fellowship Program

Embrace the mantra "Experiences are the spice of life." At software company SAP, any manager has the option of defining fellowship opportunities. Encouraging managers to collaborate with other departments to define those opportunities is a great way to facilitate training across the company. Job descriptions are then posted to SAP's internal eRecruiting system. Before applying for the six-month fellowships, employees review their interest, development goals, and fit with their existing managers. An added benefit for employees is feedback from managers participating in each rotation—people they otherwise wouldn't have a chance to interact with. Frequently, the fellowships include an international component, giving people an opportunity to develop their global skills as well.

Part 4: You Have Dreams

Chapter 6: Bounce Forward

In today's workplace, work is no longer a place, but a thing. In order to realize your career dreams and create a path to the future, we'll explore ways to not just bounce back but also to bounce forward.

It is impossible to live without failing at something,
unless you live so cautiously that you might as well not
have lived at all—in which case, you fail by default.
—J.K. Rowling

6 BOUNCE FORWARD

Mario Capecchi's parents were American-born poet Lucy Ramberg and Luciano Capecchi, an officer in the Italian Airforce. They were living in the Italian Alps near the German border when World War II broke out. Mario's father was reported missing in action while manning an anti-aircraft gun in the Western Desert campaign. His mother was ordered to one of the notoriously dehumanizing concentration camps established at Hitler's direction. She became a political prisoner punished for belonging to an anti-Fascist group. Knowing she was in danger, Mario's mother sold her belongings and made plans with a peasant family near Bolzano, Italy, to take care of her son.

After a single year, the money was exhausted and the family was unable to care for him. Mario recalls: "They didn't have the resources to keep me and maintain their own family. So I went on the streets." At four-and-a-half years old, he was left to fend for himself on the streets of northern Italy for the next four years, living in various orphanages and roving through towns with gangs of other homeless children, stealing food from carts while others distracted the vendors. It was a nearly feral lifestyle. He almost died of malnutrition. He recalls: "Just surviving from day to day pretty much occupies your mind."

Eventually, his little gang landed in a hospital, with conditions only slightly better. To ensure that the children didn't run away, they were not given any clothing. He survived on a daily bowl of chicory coffee and a small crust of bread.

His mother was liberated from the concentration camps by U.S. troops in 1945, and she searched for Mario for a year before finding him at the hospital near Bologna. He was feverish and malnourished. She showed up on his ninth birthday, carrying a Tyrolean outfit for him, complete with a small cap with a feather. He still has the cap. She took him to Rome, where he had his first bath in six years.

In 1946, Capecchi's uncle sent his mother money so they could immigrate to the United States. They moved to Pennsylvania, where Capecchi attended school for the first time. He earned a bachelor's degree in chemistry and physics from Antioch College in 1961 and a doctorate in biophysics from Harvard University in 1967.

In a remarkable example of bouncing forward, sixty years later, in 2007, Mario Capecchi—illiterate at nine years old—was awarded the Nobel Prize for Medicine. He had discovered a method to breed a mouse missing a specific gene, known as a "knockout mouse," which through genetic engineering has a gene that can be turned off.

Don't Bounce Back—Bounce Forward

Bouncing Forward is a key practice of people who have the ability to overcome even the most extreme hardships. Rarely do people do this alone, as nearly every great story of overcoming obstacles includes relying on their close ties to help them through dark times. Yet people who bounce forward have an inner compass that never falters. Success seeks them out. They have aspirations and the willpower to remain focused on the future and use their networks to keep them motivated.

At any moment many of us are dealing with insecurities and uncertainties. Mounting performance pressures in the workplace, radical changes in the global business world, plus strained economic forecasts mean we need to figure out how to thrive and not simply survive. It's not just about having the mental stamina to bounce back but about moving forward—bouncing forward.

Figuring out how to bounce forward assures that you aren't simply surviving career challenges but prospering to tell the tale, as Capecchi demonstrates. Simply surviving setbacks brings greater risk of not being able to reach your career goals. Self-doubt sneaks in. Not surprisingly this makes it harder to stay focused on your dreams.

Beyond having a good support system, bouncing forward is a multi-faceted, deliberate and dynamic mix consisting of:

1. *Grit:* perseverance and commitment (passion) for long-term goals

2. *Resilience:* ability to adapt and recover quickly from difficulties

3. *Motivation:* the drive to initiate and maintain goal-oriented behaviors

All aspects of these three fundamentals are important to cultivate. The interdependent relationship among grit, resilience, and motivation are amplified when you combine them. In addition, having someone who believes in you is the super glue that holds all of these elements together. No doubt, this is why, sixty years later, Capecchi is still holding onto the felt cap his mother gave him when they were reunited.

How do you respond to losses and setbacks? What kind of problem-solving techniques do you depend on when you find yourself in rough situations? In moments when you've had to confront life-altering challenges, what have you taken away from that experience? Finding effective ways to deal with our emotions and fears builds stamina amid a changing world without turning us into naïve optimists. We all have dreams, and we've all had setbacks on the way to those dreams; what we need are the right motivational strategies to bounce forward and make them a reality.

Silver Linings

Experience is not what happens to a man; it is what a man does with what happens to him.

—Aldous Huxley

Alan Horn was still celebrating a successful run as the film chief at Warner Brothers in the 2000s when he was pushed into retirement. He was told he was too old, too out of touch. He could have retired; instead he became chairman of Walt Disney Studios. Disney's pipeline is now overflowing with blockbusters.

In a groundbreaking moment in early 2011, Jill Abramson became the first female executive editor in *The New York Times* 160-year history. She was prepared, skills-wise. And she knew a lot about how to gather her reserve for new challenges. In 2007, she was run over by a truck while crossing the street in Times Square. She had to learn to walk again, an experience she said gave her an amazing insight into what you can make yourself do and how you can heal from profound injury.

She needed those reserves of resilience when she was publicly fired from the *Times* in 2014. Just two years earlier, Abramson was ranked number five on the Forbes list of most powerful women. Abramson felt being hit by a truck was far worse than the top brass at the *Times* firing her. Of going from the highest to the lowest point in her career in only a few years, she said, "You can recover from most experiences."

That includes recovering from rejection. After both Twitter and Facebook turned him down for employment, Brian Acton co-founded Whatsapp. In an interesting twist, Whatsapp become Facebook's largest acquisition to date when it was acquired for $19 billion. Acton netted over 40 million shares of stock in Facebook, a 20 percent interest in the company.

Experiences like these show us that career failures can become a springboard to success if you respond in the right way. The common thread in each of these stories is that, despite a setback, resilient people don't get stuck in shame, grief, or blame. They keep going.

Part of human nature is to go through a period of shock, denial, and self-doubt after a job loss or career setback. Getting stuck in feelings of anger is easy. Instead, consider the abilities, attributes, and attitudes found in highly resilient people. They focus on what they can learn from the experience.

Andrew Zolli and Anne Marie Healy detail in their book *Resilience* that those who are "psychologically resilient" can certainly feel great sadness after a loss, but are able to move on, even adapt and grow without becoming stuck in grief or blame. In exploring what makes people resilient, they identified personality traits like optimism and confidence. People who had personal belief systems rooted in ego-resiliency, defined as the capacity to overcome adversity, did better at reappraising and regulating their emotions. Simply, they had enough control over their feelings that they could focus on the silver lining and bounce not only back, but forward to the next step.

Pursue Mastery

Failure is the condiment that gives success its flavor.

—Truman Capote

Increasing pressures and uncertainty in the workplace tell us that if you haven't already experienced a career setback you should anticipate one at some point. Setbacks come in many varieties. Frequently they are outside your control. Failures, false starts, disruptions, missed opportunities, and the workday blahs are only the beginning. None of us seek out failure, but those of us who embrace the experience often triumph.

Carol Dweck, the psychology professor at Stanford University whose theory on mindsets we discussed in Chapter 2, would say that our beliefs about our abilities and ourselves determine how we interpret our experiences. Psychologists who study motivation and achievement tell us that our beliefs also shape what we can achieve. Abramson's ability to learn to walk after a devastating accident taught her not to set boundaries on what she could accomplish. Surviving years living on the street shaped Capecchi's world-view as a medical researcher decades before he won the Nobel Prize.

According to Dweck, people hold two different views on their own abilities: fixed or growth. Your view of your abilities determines how you approach setbacks and failures. Those who held a helpless view believe abilities are a fixed trait—a person can only have so much. Dweck calls this a fixed mindset. Failures and setbacks undermine the self-confidence of those with this mindset because they attribute errors to a lack of ability, which they feel powerless to change.

On the other hand, people with a growth mindset think abilities can be developed through hard work and education. They enjoy challenges. There is no limit on mastery for this group. They embrace learning and consistently see potential to develop new skills.

Dramatic, catastrophic events reach deep into our personal resolve and become life-changing, but what about the small failures we experience over the course of our careers? What we learn from those setbacks is equally important. For example, look at Steven Spielberg. He seemed destined to be a filmmaker after he shot his first movie at age 12, fulfilling the requirements for a Boy Scout badge. But his first big commercial film, *Jaws*, left him traumatized. He was convinced that because of *Jaws*, his film career was over. No one had ever taken a film 100 days over schedule and blown the budget as badly as he had. He said he had full-blown panic attacks because he knew he had made so many mistakes. Eventually, he acknowledged that there were things that he didn't do well, particularly managing budgets and people.

Putting aside his ego and despite the fact that in the end *Jaws* was a massive box office success, he took a position reporting to George Lucas. Lucas was known for staying on budget and maintaining a disciplined schedule. A mentor was just what Spielberg needed on the road to becoming one of the greatest directors of all time.

Spielberg didn't interpret his failures in managing budgets and people as the end of the world. Once he acknowledged what skills he needed to master, he came up with a plan for how to get those skills by securing a mentor. He went for mastery rather than giving up.

People with a growth mindset are confronted by failure the same as anyone, but those failures only encourage them to seek advice or try a different strategy—to overcome and move forward.

Fits and Starts

These two mindsets lead down two very different paths. As people who've had several false starts in their careers can testify, jobs that sound great can fizzle out, lead you nowhere or, even worse, become dead ends. On the other hand, there are those who thrive on challenges.

The late comedian Joan Rivers once famously said, "I had a lot of false starts." When she began her career, female performers were expected to conform to certain norms. As Rivers explained, "When I started it was a very difficult thing for a woman to be fairly good-looking and funny; it just was not accepted." When interviewed for the PBS comedy series *Make 'Em Laugh*, she said, "You were either funny-looking, and then you could do jokes—that was the tradition I came out of—or you were attractive and you were a singer." Rivers had to break through the conventions of the day.

Not many of us have Rivers' chutzpah to break through and create opportunities not only for herself, but also for a future generation of female comedians. Slipping into a pattern of false starts is easy. Finding any job can take priority over finding the right job, leaving you stranded in a bad job or neglecting the steps that will take your career to a higher level. Next time you are tempted to set aside your dreams, just remember one of Rivers' favorite pieces of advice: "Love the process." Skip the shame and resist the urge to brood over failures. Angst and rumination are just part of the process of growth.

Finding Meaning in the Commotion

Career disruptions can be anything that changes the course of our daily routines. Life-enhancing events, like the birth of a child or the offer to move overseas for a job, interrupt the order of our daily habits. Disruptions beyond our control, such as the company being acquired or economic downturns, make us feel vulnerable and anxious.

Between disruptions and workplace shifts, it's not uncommon to hear complaints of feeling overwhelmed by all we have to manage, making it difficult to know what to prioritize. Many companies are exploring the impacts of living in a VUCA environment. VUCA, a term borrowed from the military, stands for volatility, uncertainty, complexity and ambiguity. To put it another way, we are living in crazy and intense times.

The resulting stress has led many of us to seek meaning in all the commotion. Looking for meaning in work has often been singled out as the mantra of the Millennial generation. Whether it is Boomers, Generation X, or Millennials, our research shows *everyone* is redefining how they think about success at work. A challenging economic cycle has created a shift in thinking about careers. Success has been redefined as less about accumulating status and more about finding meaning in our careers. In a recent Career Advisory Board Report, nearly three-quarters of the young adults surveyed said they agreed, "Meaningful work was among the three most important factors defining career success."

STRETCH BREAK

STRETCH 6.1

Rising above the noise in your company or industry, what meaning do you find in your work? Here are some questions to consider:

☐ What meaning-oriented goals do I want my career to fulfill?

☐ In what ways do my current job and company align with those goals?

☐ What stresses me out at work?

☐ What energizes me?

☐ What can I do to create more personal value?

☐ What can I do to decrease those aspects of work that create the most stress?

☐ How would my family or friends answer these questions?

By adopting a way of thinking that focuses on meaning or the broader purpose their work enables, we become more engaged and are less likely to leave our current positions. The Shift Index validates this way of thinking. Developed by Deloitte's Center for the Edge, its purpose is to help executives understand and take advantage of long-term forces of change shaping the U.S. economy. The Shift Index tracks 25 metrics about technological and political developments, information, and talent and their impacts on performance. In their search for the kinds of traits that will excel in this new uncertainty, they believe that individuals with the "passion of an explorer" will be the most resilient.

These passionate explorers have three attributes:

- Commitment to having a lasting impact on their industry or function;
- Actively seeking out challenges to improve performance; and
- An ability to build trust-based relationships.

Connecting your work to a larger purpose can help you stay engaged at those times when work feels overwhelming. Identifying the meaning you find in your work is a good way to shift your approach away from the commotion and stress to the big picture of what your job does for you and others.

The One That Got Away

Another type of setback is missed opportunities. The interview that didn't turn out as you'd hoped. The introduction you worked for months to connect to . . . and then you dropped the ball and never closed the loop. The investment opportunity you passed up that now is worth millions. Missed opportunities can cause us to look backward and dwell on what could have been instead of on what can be. We all know the feeling when you relive the events of a meeting or an interview in your mind and the outcome in your mind is different from the experience. Small scale or large, lamenting the past seems to be hard-wired into humanity.

Martin Seligman, author of *Flourish* and guru on positive psychology, points to athletic coaches for inspiration. He observed one coach who developed a character strengths exercise to debrief his team following games. During the debriefing sessions, team members reviewed the game's successes and challenges by discussing the character strengths used or not used throughout the game. Team members then identified in themselves, teammates, and coaches examples where the strengths like team work, patience, and fortitude were called upon. Additionally, they identified missed opportunities for using various strengths. The idea was that by identifying the missed opportunities they would increase awareness of future opportunities to use strengths.

Adam, a freelance social media strategist, told us that, although he maintains an active presence on LinkedIn, he admits that he often forgets to check his LinkedIn inbox. Inevitably, weeks later he'll discover messages about potential work. Those opportunities were missed, but rather than linger and lament, Adam figured out a way to rebound: he put a prompt in his calendar to check in, and now he has a few new clients. Whether the size of your missed opportunity is a state championship or a project assignment, making the most of it means recognizing what the mistake was and working to fix it in the future.

The Workday Blues

Perhaps the most common workplace issue comes from the most motivated of employees. Maybe you are the person with that burning passion to do well. You come in early, are the last to leave, and haven't taken off a day or weekend since you started. While you'd planned to scale back after you got the promotion or when the project was finished, you never did. Consequently, it's five or ten or fifteen years later and you are burned out.

Face it. You are a workaholic, or perhaps this sounds like someone you know. No desire to hang out with friends much less expand your network. Permanently stressed. No longer performing at your best. And it's become a chronic situation.

Exhaustion, frustration, lack of energy, and sleep deprivation are all signs that more demands and less resources have gotten the best of you. In order to overcome the blahs, consider the following advice from Manfred Kets De Vries at INSEAD: take relaxation seriously, cultivate a rich non-work life, and consider unplugging.

Setbacks at work can take their toll. Let's explore the three psychological components of bouncing forward. We hope you will find bouncing forward to be even better than bouncing back.

The Recipe for Springing Back

Don't cry because it's over, smile because it happened.

—Unknown

Don't just bounce back. Adopt an attitude whereby you accept that work is going to stretch your capabilities to the limit and that you have the ability to not just cope but also flourish. Bouncing forward to the future requires that we cultivate ways to manage the inexorably accelerating pace of change. We need more than just the internal resources to recover quickly from setbacks. Patience, along with the ability to anticipate the future, helps us to maintain momentum. Developing this kind of energy force keeps us from feeling devastated or judging ourselves too harshly when setbacks occur.

In order to persevere in the pursuit of your dreams, it's optimum to have a reflexive ability to recover from setbacks while having the stamina to keep going in good times and bad. However, in order to be prepared for the future, you will need an understanding of grit, resilience, and motivation and the ways in which they combine to create the multiplier effect you need to succeed.

Grit

Extraordinary achievement, as psychologist Martin Seligman describes it, is very rare. He found that, while bell-shaped or normal distributions held true for ordinary things like school grades and height, they totally failed in describing achievement. When measuring achievement of top performers in a wide range of fields, those considered geniuses far outdistanced excellent performers, and left above-average in the dust. The only way to achieve true genius in a field is to dedicate to the mastery of it.

This is the underlying rationale for grit: a never-yielding commitment to self-discipline. As Seligman explains, the more time you spend on the task, the more all those hours multiply your progress.

Angela Lee Duckworth is a graduate of the highly competitive Ph.D. program in psychology at The University of Pennsylvania, where Seligman is a professor. Duckworth discovered that the more education a person has, the more grit they have as well. It's impossible to tell whether education results in the mental fortitude seen in grit or if, as a result of failures, people with grit use learning as a response to overcome a challenge. What is also of interest is her discovery that older people have more grit than younger people.

As Heraclitus of Ephesus, the pre-Socratic Greek philosopher, said several millennia ago, "The only thing that is constant is change." In general, the older we are the more willing we are to accept that the world changes. As we age, experience teaches us that change is inevitable. Heraclitus also said, "No man ever steps in the same river twice, for it's not the same river and he's not the same man." The upshot is that experiencing changes prepares us for more change, and we learn that different isn't better or worse, but just different. Our endurance for staying the course can increase even as the challenges and changes keep coming, or as new ideas distract us.

Fostering grit is about developing that endurance. Not to be confused with motivation, which is merely the willingness to do something; grit is the *determination to do whatever it takes over time*. Your grittiness increases achievement by acting as a multiplier of skills and knowledge, at the same time increasing skills and knowledge, which results in increased chances of success.

Resilience

A champion is someone who gets up when he can't.

—Jack Dempsey

Ask anyone to tell you a story of survival and you are bound to hear heart-rending tales of wars and disasters, untimely deaths, acts of courage, incurable illnesses, and the strength of the human spirit. In the words of Henry Wadsworth Longfellow, "Into each life some rain must fall." Longfellow assured us that we all would experience adversity. How people respond to adversity has fed literary traditions throughout time, because, while there is no one standard response, there is a definite archetype of a hero. The hero's most defining trait? Resilience.

Why are some people resilient and others not?

Harvard journalist Diane Coutu says resilience is "one of the great puzzles of human nature." Coutu explored how Holocaust victims were able to develop a "plastic shield"—an inner psychological space that protected them from the intrusions of abuse. Combined with an ability to form attachments to others and maintain some semblance of a sense of humor, they were able to hold onto a critical sense of perspective. Coutu reports that resilience is not just genetic, as people can become more resilient over their lifetimes.

Of the many stories we have shared, perhaps the one that best exemplifies the incredible importance of resiliency is Melody Gardot. Her life story inspires us with the ways in which optimism, hardiness, a positive view of the future, and the ability to make the best of a situation can be used to master extreme resiliency challenges.

Melody's difficulties began when she was hit by an SUV that had ignored a red traffic light and smashed into her while she rode her bicycle. Her pelvis was broken in two places and she received serious head and spinal injuries. Her injuries were severe and left her unable to sit up for more than 10 minutes at a time. She was confined to lying flat on her back in her hospital bed for a year.

Melody suffers acute sensitivity to light and sound because of the neural injuries, requiring her to wear dark sunglasses and sound-dampening devices at all times. She had to relearn simple tasks such as brushing her teeth and walking. The accident resulted in both long- and short-term memory problems and difficulty with her sense of time.

Her doctor suggested that she consider using music as a kind of recovery therapy. She had played the piano before the accident, but since she now couldn't sit comfortably at the piano, she picked up the guitar, and the focus of her music making evolved. She found jazz.

Now a professional musician with a full-length album called *Worrisome Heart*, she uses her resiliency as a springboard for her musical success. Melody's lyrics tell her story: "Some lessons we learn the hard way. Some lessons don't come easy, and that's the price we have to pay." Through it all she hasn't forgotten her good fortune. Melody says, "I forgot a lot of things, but I don't forget that."

Melody Gardot's unswerving ability to look forward and embrace new realities is consistent with what we heard from others when they told us stories of overcoming adversity. Above all, they didn't perceive their situations as misfortunes. They accepted hard times with a steady hand. Rather than feeling despair, they accepted the new normal and looked for ways to make the best of it.

Looking back at Melody's story, you can see that she does not specifically say "Life is meaningful" or "I'm going to make the best of this situation," but rather she shows us in her recovery her ability to make meaning out of a difficult time. She epitomizes resilience.

She never looks back to blame the driver of the vehicle that hit her. She is not a victim. Rather, had it not been for the accident, she might never have discovered her true passion in life.

Resilient people invest a lot of effort in what Coutu calls an uncanny ability to improvise in seeking solutions. They understand that, when searching for answers in difficult situations, the more realistically they grasped the true situation, the more quickly they were able to move into a problem-solving mode.

Motivation

What motivated you to read this book? Chances are the first answer that pops into your mind is not about money. We'd speculate that the more likely answer is your intrinsic desire to be better at what you do. You are reading this for yourself, not for others. Sure, you want to be more employable. But even more than that, you want to be the best you can be.

Many companies are still focused on compensation as a primary motivator. However, extensive research substantiates that money is not the answer. Ironically, financial incentives can actually have a negative impact on intrinsic motivation, when tasks are especially interesting or enjoyable. The consequence is that rewards may help you accomplish the things you don't enjoy doing but for the things you love, intrinsic motivation is a stronger predictor in inspiring performance. Money matters, but it's not all about money for most of us.

You might think of what defines your motivation as what gets you up in the morning or the things that keep you going at work, even when progress is difficult. Perhaps you like the community-building aspects of your job or knowing that it has an impact on society, or maybe you are becoming better at something that matters to you. These factors take the focus off money.

In our research and experience, tapping into our intrinsic motivation provides grounding between resilience and grit. Your self-directed desire or intrinsic motivation is the compass that keeps you looking forward to tomorrow.

What does a person who is intrinsically motivated look like? Perhaps like Jack Ma, one of the most successful entrepreneurs on the planet. His e-commerce company, Alibaba, attracts 100 million shoppers a day. He is now the richest person in China. But before he started Alibaba, he often had to call on his inner reserves. His frustrations and setbacks included failing his college entrance exams three times. He applied to the police academy and was told "You're no good." He applied for 30 different jobs and was rejected for every one. He says the most discouraging was when Kentucky Fried Chicken opened in his hometown in China, and of the 24 people who applied for jobs, 23 were accepted. He was not.

When he started Alibaba, there were more obstacles. No bank would work with him to process payments. But Ma was determined to succeed, so he started Alipay, his own online payment system. Many people told him that "this is the stupidest idea you've ever had." Today over 800 million people use Alipay, which transfers payments in different currencies between international buyers and sellers.

How did Ma do it? We'd say it was the combination of grit, resilience, and intrinsic motivation. He exhibited a tremendous determination that wasn't swayed when someone called his ideas stupid. His drive, combined with enthusiasm and ambition, helped him find new goals to strive for until he finally found success.

To facilitate your own intrinsic motivation, consider the five sources of meaning for humans at work: the impact of your work on society, the customer, the company, the team, and "me." According to McKinsey, connecting to one or more of these five sources of meaning can help you tap into your enthusiasm.

Mental Strategies to Help You Bounce Forward

Bounce Forward Stretch Strategies

1. Renounce

2. Pounce

3. Trounce

4. Announce

5. Denounce the small stuff

Now that you've learned the three fundamental components of bouncing forward, it's time to consider the practical strategies to deploy them. The very heart of bouncing forward is acknowledging that jobs are fluid and not perfect. But that doesn't mean that you can't have more happy days at work. Cindi Leive, editor in chief of *Glamour* magazine, says, "The idea that your job is going to make your heart sing on a daily basis is just not true." Some days are going to inevitably test your spirit. But, as Leive notes, "You can aim for a pretty good heart-singing-to-bummed-out ratio." Your grit, motivation, and determination can see you through. Here are some mental strategies that can help you persevere toward more happy days at work.

Renounce

Brian Ray, an assistant professor at the University of Nebraska, has received many letters of rejection from scholarly and literary journals for his research papers and short stories. He's learned more from rejection letters than from the acceptances, he says. Some ideas need time to marinate, some spoil, and some aren't that great to begin with, Ray has learned. Now he's the author of two novels. Ray says his trick is always to be working on an article or a book. Keep on practicing.

Getting comfortable with feedback is a skill we can all benefit from. As we discussed in Chapters 3 and 5, if you aren't receiving feedback at work, ask for it. And when you hear something you don't like, use it as an opportunity to bounce forward. Renounce the fixed mindset that you always have to be right or in control. Instead, adopt a growth mindset where you learn as much from failure and feedback as you do from success.

Pounce

In his breakthrough book *The Resiliency Advantage*, Al Siebert advocates adopting a curiosity habit. First, he asks, "How do you react to surprising incidents?" Do you hunker down and try to stay the course, or do you wonder what's going on, look for answers about cause and effect? Curious people ask a lot of questions, which is a great way to gather information and stage the best action for the best outcome—*pouncing*.

Fred Rogers, host of the popular long-running public television show *Mister Rogers' Neighborhood*, said: "Discovering the truth about ourselves is a lifetime's work, but it's worth the effort." Mr. Rogers' curiosity was apparent to all because he never stopped asking questions. He seemed to perpetually possess the spirit of a three-year-old who peppers his parents with the question "Why?" over and over again.

When opportunities present themselves, be curious and pounce.

STRETCH BREAK

STRETCH 6.2

The next time you are dealing with an unexpected challenge or a new opportunity, think about these questions adapted from *The Resiliency Advantage*:

☐ What is the situation?

☐ Does the situation require any action? What would be the impact if you took action?

☐ What are the important facts?

☐ How are others responding? Or not responding?

☐ What are others not seeing? How can you bring them along?

Staying curious will help you to pounce because you'll have discovered the right solution to the problem.

Trounce

There are those who come through and win in the end and then there are those who lead "wire-to-wire." The term wire-to-wire originated in horse racing when races started and ended with a wire across the track. Wire-to-wire winners distinguish themselves by leading the way—*trouncing* the competition—with their excellence the entire time.

The road to trouncing isn't being a wire-to-wire leader every time out of the gate. Most of us are still developing our winning strategy or rebounding from our last unspectacular finish. One key to preserving and prevailing in pursuit of our excellence is to never stop trying. Geno Auriemma, women's basketball coach at the University of Connecticut, tells his players: "We have to make sure that we forget about the last shot and keep shooting." As any basketball player knows, you can't score if you aren't shooting. For this coach, trouncing his competition is about consistency of numbers. They may lose some games, but in the end, his players will out-shoot their rivals.

Setting the stage for winning comes from practice and repetition. Just like basketball players, we can't expect to score if we aren't prepared to shoot. Being prepared to shoot comes from a relentless commitment to practice. Not just practicing before games, but practicing every day. Not just weekdays, but every day. Not just this year, but year in and year out.

Max Levchin's successful online payment company PayPal wasn't his first. As the co-founder tells it: "The very first company I started failed with a great bang. The second one failed a little bit less, but still failed. The third one, you know, proper failed, but it was kind of okay. I recovered quickly. Number four almost didn't fail. It still didn't really feel great, but it did okay. Number five was PayPal." It seems that all that practice paid off.

Announce

Anyone who has trained for a marathon knows that you don't go out on the first day of training and run 26 miles. Jeff Galloway, author of *Marathon: You Can Do It*, has helped over 200,000 people, including Barbara, train for the Marine Corps Marathon. He suggests you start with a few miles at a time, interspersing walking and running to build stamina, and as Barbara discovered, it gets easier to run further distances. Instead of thinking of your career as an epic marathon to be run at one time, try working in sprints, as in taking on a special project that will add depth to your skills.

Many of us become focused on the finish line of retirement. We are hoping to get there as soon as possible. Often, by the time we reach the finish line, we are exhausted, too drained to pursue our post-career bucket list. Sprinters also have a finish line in mind, but their strategy is to focus and work hard through the sprints while taking time to rest and recover in between, thereby building their endurance for the next sprint. They know when to be working and when to be resting. Once you've committed to the sprint, then announce your intentions to others.

Announcing your intentions to others can help you find the motivation you need to stay focused on your goals. Enroll a few people directly in your sprint goals, perhaps from your "five to thrive" from Chapter 4. When you announce a goal, people will jump in to help you and keep you on track. In a sense, joining a group like Weight Watchers is an "announce" strategy.

Announcing can have other benefits. Don was chronically late to meetings and his manager mentioned it on a performance review. He decided to fix it, but six months later, in a peer review, people mentioned he was always late to meetings. "That's not fair," he thought, because he knew for a fact he hadn't been late in at least six months. So at the next few meetings, when he walked in to a team meeting, he'd announce his arrival cheerfully with something like: "Three minutes to start time and I'm here. Wow, could have knocked off five emails in that time." He was announcing he had changed, and people noticed on the next peer review.

Denounce the Small Stuff

Most of us agree that we shouldn't sweat the small stuff. But staying motivated and connected to the big picture of how you are creating meaning in your life isn't easy. Legendary management guru and Common Cause founder John Gardner observed that people in the workforce are staler than they know and more bored than they will admit. The redundancy of the job, the lack of inspiration, and the petty frustrations have sunk them. The small stuff has won.

Consider this quote from Gardner, who has studied personal renewal for over 30 years: "Meaning is not something you stumble across, like the answer to a riddle or the prize in a treasure hunt. Meaning is something you build into your life. You build it out of your own past, out of your affections and loyalties, out of the experience of humankind as it is passed on to you, out of your own talent and understanding, out of the things you believe in, out of the things and people you love, out of the values for which you are willing to sacrifice something. You are the only one who can put them together into that unique pattern that will be your life. Let it be a life that has dignity and meaning for you."

We all need to be able to hold onto inspiration to stay motivated. Too often the first year in a job becomes the fifth and then the tenth, indistinguishable from one another. Not sweating the small stuff let's us put our focus elsewhere and think about the big picture.

STRETCH BREAK

STRETCH 6.3

Instead of marking the success of your day based on the 200 emails you answered, try thinking about these questions:

☐ Who did I help today?

☐ How did what I accomplished today help me toward my bigger goals?

☐ How am I maintaining my energy for myself?

☐ Where can I say no?

☐ Did I choose to ignore my "small stuff (gossip, complaining about the dirty refrigerator, kicking the copy machine) today?

The answers can help us remember not to sweat the small stuff.

Maintain the Faith

Most people go through life a wee bit disappointed in themselves. I think we all keep a memory of a moment when we missed someone or something, when we could have gone down another path, a happier or better or just a different path. Just because they're in the past doesn't mean you can't treasure the possibilities ... maybe we put down a marker for another time. And now's the time. Now we can do whatever we want to do.

—James Robertson, *And the Land Lay Still*

Careers are built on more than a chain of personal bests—they are built through a combination of grit, motivation, and resiliency. When you are in the midst of a setback, think to the future and your dreams. In what way might you look back at your current situation and consider it one of the best learning experiences of your life? How might you think about a situation so that, even if you were given the choice never to have faced this setback, you would still choose to go through it again?

Vice Admiral James B. Stockdale, former president of the Naval War College, ranks among the most highly decorated Navy pilots in U.S. history. Nothing defined his life as a celebrated leader as much as his experience during the Vietnam War. In September of 1965, Stockdale's fighter jet was shot down over North Vietnam. Parachuting from his disabled fighter jet, he landed with such force that it fractured his back and severely damaged his leg. He was captured and taken prisoner.

He spent nearly eight years as a prisoner of war (POW), most of it in solitary confinement. Stockdale endured tremendous physical torture and trauma, including a broken shoulder, a broken bone in his back, and a leg that was broken twice. However, he said that was peanuts in comparison to the shame he felt of breaking with his personal code of honor. He says, "Shame is a heavier burden than any physical wounds." In the midst of torture, the shame he experienced came from his internal unrealistic expectations not to break with the Military Code of Conduct.

In writing about the experience in his memoir, *In Love and War*, he says his imprisonment was the defining event of his life. In retrospect, he says he would not trade the experience because he knew it made him a better, more humble leader.

All those days in solitary confinement gave him plenty of time to think about what was happening in terms of "what is up to you" and "what is not up to you." Ultimately, he determined that the torture they were enduring was not up to them since it was not in the realm of their power or free will. This realization allowed him to assess his values and come to terms with his code of honor.

The rules that Stockdale developed and shared with his fellow prisoners while in captivity were summed up in the acronym BACK US. The code was composed of rules that took into account the reality of prison life. For example, the US stood for Unity Over Self, so that he and fellow POWs would be able to recall in the midst of interrogations never to agree to offers of leniency on your own behalf unless what was offered was offered to all of them.

Luckily, we don't need acronyms forged during wartime to remember that we can learn from our own setbacks. We can't control the fact that jobs are at risk and entire industries are in the midst of disruptive change, but we can remember to take lessons from our experiences. Those lessons can help us stay motivated through life's ups and downs.

 **Stretch Summary**

- To stay motivated through the ups and downs of a career and re-main focused on your dreams, bounce forward.
- The recipe to bouncing forward:
  - *Grit:* perseverance and commitment
  - *Resilience:* ability to adapt and recover quickly from difficulties
  - *Motivation:* the drive to initiate and maintain your goal orientation
- Just do it. Strive for your success through curiosity and self-management.
- Embrace these setbacks as opportunities for growth so you don't become stuck in your career:
  - Failure
  - False Starts
  - Career Disruptions
  - Missed Opportunities
- Use these mental strategies for Bouncing Forward:
  - *Renounce.* Rejection can be a great teacher.
  - *Pounce.* Stay curious and ask a lot of questions.
  - *Trounce.* Practice makes perfect. Never stop trying, even if you don't succeed at first.
  - *Announce.* Enlist support by letting others know your goals.
  - *Denounce the small stuff.* Stay focused on the big picture to avoid the trap of sweating the small stuff.
- Stay motivated by holding onto inspiration and meaning at work.

What Organizations and Managers Can Do

We seldom visit the periphery of our knowledge and competence — the region where transformational learning happens — without feeling threatened, exposed, or ashamed. (That is why when we meet a friendly, forgiving face out there — which makes learning easier — we cherish it. We call that a mentor.) People like failure only in inspirational speeches. In real life we endure it, at best, and come to value it only if and when its lessons become clear. Workplace pressures and norms just turn our instinct to steer clear of failure into a habit.

—Gianpiero Petriglieri

Fortunately, some of the most effective strategies that organizations use to support career resiliency can also have great potential to improve employee engagement, commitment to mission, and job satisfaction. There are other ancillary engagement benefits, such as fostering collaboration and building cultural change capability. Some of the best practices do not require huge investments but are simply accomplished by fostering transparency and adopting new management practices.

Change Your Focus from Employment to Employability

Motorola once tracked that for every dollar invested in education, they received $33 in employee return on investment (ROI). Employees are frustrated when they find that they lack the skills to be promoted to the next-level job. Instead of depending on outplacement programs, consider supporting the development of skill enhancement, job satisfaction enhancement, and productivity benefit programs. Investing in employability helps your employees become career resilient.

Many organizations such as Deloitte, Lockheed Martin, and McKinsey maintain employee alumni associations. Think of your employees the way that colleges and universities think of their graduates: treat your employees like trusted alumni of your organization, which encourages them to be advocates of the organization and work experience. The benefits will create good will and positive buzz, enhancing your recruitment efforts.

If you have a limited budget, think about providing an annual benchmarking and tracking of skill attainment event. The annual valuing of skill enhancement is an intangible benefit that lets your employees know you care about their futures. Or ask employees on your climate survey whether they believe they are prepared for the future of work.

Connect Employees to Purpose

Our research discovered that employers don't truly under stand what motivates employees. Employees care more about your organization than you think they do. By creating shared goals in your strategic planning process and annual goal setting, you let employees know that you are taking their interest seriously.

Refer back to the five sources for meaning at work: impact on society, the customer, the organization, the team, and "me." While one size does not fit all, there are ways to help your employees see the connections to these sources. Finding ways to articulate your organization's impact on society connects your employees to a larger meaning of their work; tracking your impact on customers connects the meaning of work to the purpose of others. Spotlighting successful teamwork feeds our drive to bond. When employees feel proud of belonging, it creates a huge boost in motivation—and a corresponding loss of morale when institutions betray them.

Connect Beyond Compensation

While it's important that compensation track your industry's standards and be equitable within your organization, there are a number of non-compensation ways to reward your employees. Numerous studies have found that smaller, unexpected gestures are more effective than bonuses in bonding employees to mission and results.

When you can celebrate and mark accomplishments together, employees feel more connected to the organization. Gordon Bethune helped Continental Airlines become an attractive merger target for United Airlines by leading a turnaround where every employee felt a part of the excitement. When Continental made it to the Top 5 for on-time flights, Bethune sent every employee an unexpected check for $65 as recognition of what they accomplished together. The amount of the check was far less important than the recognition they had all done it together.

Foster Innovation with a Failure Wall

After spending a sizeable amount of time studying brain science, Jeff Stibel, the CEO of Dun & Bradstreet Credibility Corporation, says he learned that humans learn far more from failure than they do from success. The brain is a "failure engine." It studies mistakes and errors in order to improve on performance in the future. If our ancestors could learn to avoid poisonous plants and hungry carnivores, we can certainly learn how to create a business brain that gets smarter and smarter.

Turning that learning into action, he and his assistant snuck into the office one night and scrawled out their failures in permanent marker on a communal wall. They wanted to encourage colleagues to share their failures publicly. Once the list started growing it was easy to see that few failures were as bad as people thought. In sharing, he hoped that everyone would learn from each other's mistakes. A junior associate wrote that he had failed to include a timeline in a contract he was working on and it subsequently killed the deal. Instead of being shameful, admitting his mistake taught a lesson and brought the team closer together. They had made mistakes, too. And now others in his company could learn from them, too.

Part 5: Charting the Path Forward

Chapter 7: Stretch into Your Future

To bring it all together, we offer some insights into the future of work, the capabilities you need for the future, and the next steps to take.

Will you be a reader, a student merely, or a seer? Read your fate, see what is before you, and walk on into futurity.

—Henry David Thoreau

7 STRETCH INTO YOUR FUTURE

Sydney, March 15, 2025

Ian finishes his cup of coffee before heading into his office space. No liquids are allowed in the workspace. Climbing down some steps, he ducks under one of the six ultra-HD curved monitors that form a full circle, then climbs back up and into the chair surrounded by heavy-equipment controls. Similar pods fill the gigantic space—one even more sophisticated than NASA's control rooms. Over the top of the monitors he can see a glimpse of the bridge traversing the harbor, with clouds scudding behind it. As much as he has watched it, he doesn't notice any looping of the projection.

The lighting of the room shifts slightly to correspond to the weather outside, and if he listens very carefully, he notices the pink noise being filtered into the room. For working in a windowless room all day, he finds he never experiences the dissonance he gets when walking from a dark movie theater into broad daylight.

As he settles into his chair and places four of his fingers on the touch-pad, the screens come to life. "Good morning, Ian. Welcome back to work. I am ready and waiting for you today. Would you like to begin?"

"Good morning to you as well, Val. Everything quiet on the western front?"

It was not long ago that Ian was driving trucks nearly 1,500 kilometers outside of Perth, a 12-hour flight away, leaving his family for weeks at a time for the high-wage opportunity in the mining district. Trained as a mechanical engineer, upon graduation in 2010 he was enticed by the wages of the Australian western minefields, where drivers earned more than the lawyers and doctors in Sydney. By 2014, a few drone-operated trucks were already in position and the last truck actually driven by a human in the minefields was in 2018. He reminds himself daily how lucky he is compared to his mates, who didn't prepare to make the shift to virtual command of drone trucks. Only one other person from his original team of 25 still has a job making what he made a few years ago. The others just didn't see the shift coming.

From the comfortable seat of Val's control center, he now commands ten trucks at once, reminding him of his gaming days as a youth. He knows his situation won't go on forever. He'll need to shift out of the mining industry because future drone operators will soon be able to command twice as many trucks as he does now.

While following a thread on Reddit, he learned of a potential new project, funded by a British billionaire frustrated at the inability to readily track and recover downed jetliners. Redditors speculated the project would be to explore, map, and place sensors across the entire ocean floor using advanced drone submarines. Exploring earth's final frontier holds a strong appeal for him, and he has established a number of connections with people who are rumored to be connected to the project so he can get in early. He'll miss Val, because she has learned how he thinks and reacts to unexpected situations, but he knows the next generation command posts will be even more sophisticated. Ian has studied his field and, rather than just keep up with drone truck technology, he's ready for a new challenge. He is confident that this is the direction he'll be heading in the future.

❑❑❑

Preparing for a career tomorrow means anticipating what that future will look like and what capabilities will be needed. Ian watched the trends, used his network and stretched beyond his comfort zone to stay continuously updated and a step ahead in his field.

Change is happening faster than ever before. Back in the days when we had rotary telephones it took 75 years to acquire 50 million users. It only took 35 days to get to the same number of Angry Bird users. Who would have guessed cursive writing in the United States would be turned into an elective, as it is today for most elementary students? A child born today, for example, may never need to learn to drive, since the first driverless cars will be available soon from a number of manufacturers, including Tesla, Cadillac, and Audi.

But predicting the future is tricky business. Just a few years before Google had driverless cars on the road, one Stanford futurist predicted the complex decision making in driving ensured that no driverless cars would be available for 20 years. Change is happening not only more quickly but also less predictably. Futurists sometimes overestimate the impact of a promising direction, believing new and innovative technologies are just around the corner. Looking back at predictions from 2005 in *Scientific American,* only two in 16 medical forecasts have come to fruition.

Job trends are slightly easier to calculate, and because this is a book about the future of your career, we put special attention into synthesizing what predictions we see as most likely to have impact on jobs.

Ten Predictions for the Future of Work

What does the future mean for you? Considering both the megatrends in Chapter 1 and a scan of forecasts from futurists of every type, we have identified our ten predictions. We believe these ten already show signs of being underway and are likely to continue over the next decade. Largely, these pertain to the white-collar workforce, although some may be applicable more broadly.

Prediction 1: The Flexible Workforce Arises

In our survey, executives told us they plan to use more contract, part-time, and temporary work. People will also want to work in more flexible ways at different points in their careers or due to family/life balance preferences.

Additionally, up to 67 percent of Millennials surveyed want to work as entrepreneurs at some point in their lives, and as people work longer before retirement, it is increasingly likely that many will move between these broad categories of work over the course of their lives. Work within organizations can be thought of along a spectrum from on demand to permanent, as shown in Table 7.1.

Prediction 2: Talent Shortages Emerge

Top talent will enjoy a seller's market as Baby Boomers exit the workforce in droves and fewer workers are available to replace them. By 2030, there will be a sharp and sustained talent shortage in most developed economies.

One implication will be the need for immigration laws to loosen in order to feed the entry-level job needs. To attract top talent, organizations will offer increasingly flexible employment packages and options. Organizations that have not prepared a talent strategy for the next decade will not be able to expand into new markets for lack of talent and will find themselves at the mercy of competitive talent pricing.

Prediction 3: Organizations Become Increasingly Virtual

Brick-and-mortar operations are expensive. As markets shift, climate risks change, and labor supplies vary, organizations will seek the flexibility to adapt. Large, centralized corporate headquarters will become the exception rather than the norm. To manage complexity, organizations will increasingly use virtual teams. Economists now estimate that about 25 percent of U.S. jobs are at risk of being moved to low-wage countries. This percentage could increase as countries improve educational attainment levels and become more sophisticated in training for specific skills.

Table 7.1. Employment Categories

	ON DEMAND	CONTRACT	PERMANENT
Examples	Substitute teacher; Uber drivers; Task Rabbit; interns; start-up entrepreneurs; business of one, such as small practice CPA	Contract developers or small development teams, creatives such as actors, production teams; professional athletes; emerging businesses	Large multi-national companies, non-profits, government; established entrepreneurial ventures
Contract type and duration	Gigs on call	Pre-determined duration or deliverable; formal contract regularly renegotiated	Long-term contract, regular renegotiation of goals at least annually
Pay	Market-based commodity, typically low or highly negotiable	Skill, demonstrated success, and reputation based; ranges from minimal to astronomical pay; no set limits other than what the market will bear	Progressive on a linear timeline with organizational limits by level
Individual long-term security	Low	Low to medium	Medium to high
Development implications	Little opportunity to develop on the job; all development up to the individual	Must stay skilled on your own to get a contract. Constant emphasis on staying up-to-date and prepared for the job	Organization provides resources for development but employee is largely on their own
Loyalty obligation	Little to none; simply turn down requests	Medium; repeat customers necessary for business	High; expected to adapt life to fit culture

Multinational corporations will continue to have to design their organizations to respond to customer types, geographies, product lines, and functional areas. Any of those factors might be the major organizing scheme. For example, a company may organize primarily by country, to gain access to the latest product development expertise from engineering centers, or to provide proximity for specialists in the oil and gas industry. Teams will include more and more people not located at the global or regional headquarters.

As more and more virtualization of teams occurs, and collaboration through online technologies continues to improve, it will become less important where contributors live or when they work. Other than for manufacturing, facilities will serve as customer demonstration centers, the occasional gathering points for staff, and as the hive for joint, complex decision making.

Prediction 4: Your Biggest Job Competitor Is a Robot

Technology advances will make 50 percent of existing jobs obsolete in the next decade, while new jobs are introduced. In one extensive study, 47 percent of U.S. jobs were classified as at high risk for replacement with computerization or automation, and another 19 percent at medium risk. Factors such as pre-fabrication will affect construction jobs, 3D printing reduce manufacturing work, and robotics will supplement or replace even medical workers by delivering drugs, bed pans, and other rote tasks. Text-to-voice technology based on speech analytics will continue to improve, affecting call center employment. Any work that can be defined through a series of processes or procedures will be ripe for replacement by computers or robots.

Journalism is no exception. Reporters already use artificial intelligence tools like Quill to augment their own writing or even automatically pen routine stories. Most people are unable to tell the difference between sentences written by a human versus those written by a computer. Consider the following two opening sentences. Despite the variety of the language of sports, can you tell which one was written by a robot and which one by your authors? For the answer, see page 241.

1. "Friona fell 10 to 8 to Boys Ranch in five innings on Monday at Friona despite racking up seven hits and eight runs. Friona was led by a flawless day at the dish by Hunter Sundre, who went 2-2 against Boys Ranch pitching. Sundre singled in the third inning and tripled in the fourth inning."

2. "Boys Ranch pulled from behind to beat Friona 10-8 Saturday. Hunter Sundre of Friona continued a star performance in his two times at bat with a single in the third inning and a triple in the fourth. Altogether he stole eight bases, impressive for a game only lasting five innings."

It's not just non-technology jobs that will become obsolete. Computers are getting smarter. Many software programmers will be replaced as automation of software development becomes more prevalent and sophisticated. Bill Gates, founder of Microsoft and global philanthropist, has warned repeatedly that people, organizations, and governments are not ready for the changes ahead. "Software substitution, whether it's for drivers or waiters or nurses . . . it's progressing. . . . Technology over time will reduce demand for jobs, particularly at the lower end of skills sets. . . . I don't think people have that in their mental model." As artificial intelligence is used to augment time-consuming tasks, we will embrace having robots do the menial work we detest. Inevitably, this will lead to an increasing divide between the top and bottom earners as well as increasing the imperative that workers learn new skills to remain up-to-date.

Prediction 5: It's the End of the Career Track as We Know It

Conscientious organizations, responding to the need for employees to have career tracks, have established paths to provide guidance and motivation. Sometimes organizations have dual paths—one for management and one for individual contributors. These paths have been called career ladders, jungle gyms, or lattices.

We believe as organizations flatten, management will become an assignment or shared responsibility, not a job track. In a sense, it could be the end of management as a profession. Team performance will matter as much as individual performance, if not more. One of the main purposes of the career tracks is to provide a compensation range, rather than serving to recognize development or capability attainment. We don't see a strong future in what is really tenure recognition rather than a merit-driven approach to careers.

What will replace it? Possibly we will move more toward negotiated employment contracts, a step beyond the kind of approach many Europeans already use. Instead of outlining the broad responsibilities and rewards, these contracts would be more focused on deliverables and not have an automatic renewal pattern. Renewal indicates relevance, and the more relevant an employee's skills, the better the pay. Careers become increasingly self-directed and progress is measured by experiences, rather than a pre-determined path. Your career won't be a track or a ladder, but a journey, with diversions encouraged and rewarded.

Prediction 6: Manufacturing Re-Shores with Regional Cross-Industry Centers

Around the world, manufacturing has been chasing low-cost labor areas for almost three decades. First seen as a boon to local economies, the working conditions for employees have been problematic. Nearly 150 workers at the Foxconn plant in Wuhan, China, threatened mass suicide by climbing on the roof and threatening to jump if their pay demands were not met. In response, the Foxconn CEO announced that he intends to replace humans with a million robots, named Foxbots, at the cost of about $25,000 each to replace hundreds of thousands of workers. His move to automation may be too late, however: manufacturing is headed back to where the customers are located due to advances in manufacturing.

With the advent of 3D printing technologies, it is easy to imagine advanced manufacturing centers able to assemble anything from clothing to cars in one facility. Designers from around the world can send their assembly instructions to a regional center that can print on demand. Customers can in turn pick up their locally made products at the center, arrange drone delivery, or buy through a regional distributor. Not only is the need for manufacturing robots minimized, but cost-prohibitive and time-consuming shipping from thousands of miles away is eliminated. Consumers will also be able to print simple designs at home. Imagine being able to replace the part in your hot water heater rather than ordering and waiting a few days, also eliminating the need for manufacturers to inventory thousands of parts. All you will need is to buy and download the design and print on demand.

The impact on jobs is, of course, enormously negative for the economies that supply low-cost labor and promising for those with design or emerging manufacturing technology expertise. The total impact to the environment is also greatly reduced, making the possibility of zero-impact manufacturing companies conceivable.

Prediction 7: The Enhanced Employee Emerges

"Text Olivia and tell her I'll be 15 minutes late." Anyone with a smart phone likely has a personal assistant able to fulfill that request, whether the program is Siri, Google Now or Cortana. According to the consulting firm McKinsey, knowledge workers spend up to 60 percent of their time looking for information, responding to emails, and collaborating with others. By using social technologies, those workers can become up to 25 percent more productive.

The need for productivity gains through working harder and longer has a limit and a human toll. The solution is to enable people to work smarter, not just by saying it, but by putting smart tools and improved processes in place so that people can perform at enhanced levels. Think of it as the robot-assisted human, given superpowers through the aid of technology. Our jobs become enriched by relying on robots to do the tedious while we work on increasingly more sophisticated tasks.

As *Wired* reports: "We're on the brink of a revolution in crazy-smart digital assistants." One helpful way to consider the promise of intelligent machines is to shift from "pursuing automation to pursuing augmentation." The vision of the enhanced human is too great to sit on the shelf for long.

Prediction 8: Universities Respond to Disruption

To fill the need for people to stay continuously updated, universities will offer lifetime update subscriptions. For an annual fee or a lifetime subscription upon graduation, universities will find affordable ways to keep people not only up to speed, but also engaged with their universities for ongoing learning, library access, job placement services, study abroad and connections to other alumni. These subscriptions will include benefits such as refresher webinars covering the latest technologies or regulations, free or preferred access to online courses, curation of MOOC offerings, reduced tuition to skill credentialing courses, and access to private seminars with professors expert in their fields.

Price competition and increased operating costs have caused a conundrum that has created great stress for universities. To maintain a sustainable future for themselves, universities will need to come up with new business models. Technology will continue to be used to augment instruction, changing how faculty interact with students. Baby Boomers will be a big target market as they exit the workforce and seek learning opportunities to re-career.

For adult learners, technology provides web-based opportunities for learning at a lower cost. As soon as a widely accepted method is developed to credential non-accredited online programs, universities will be at great risk of losing market share. Already Georgia Tech, Udacity, and AT&T have worked together to make it possible to earn a master's of computer science degree for about $7,000. If universities don't help their alumni stay up-to-date, then for-profit entities will step in to fill the gap.

Prediction 9: Governments Encourage Training Investment

Because displaced workers and decreasing job security are going to put enormous pressure on societal structures, public policy will have to help hedge the economic dangers. To avoid unrest and extreme pressure on entitlement programs such as welfare or unemployment, governments will begin to encourage training or retraining programs from employers in the form of tax incentives or other policy tools. Governments will also look for ways to address the mounting costs of education and resulting student debt.

The United States is far behind other countries when it comes to total training expenditures as a percent of GDP, as shown in Figure 7.1. As more and more jobs become subject to displacement due to automation, we predict governments will establish public policy to encourage increased investment in training and human capital development.

Prediction 10: Mega-Corporations Set People and Benefits Standards Throughout the Supply Chain

The largest global organizations will set expectations for how their suppliers treat their employees, including edicts on benefits and development, thus improving the conditions for hundreds of thousands of workers. These kinds of standards have been in place for a while in places like retail and electronics manufacturing. We predict that

FIG 7.1 Labor Market Training Expenditures as a Percentage of GDP in OECD Countries, 2011

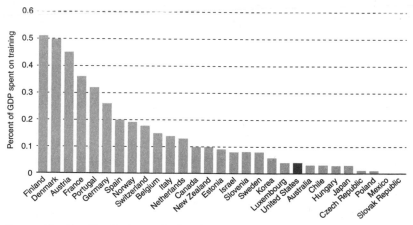

Source: The Hamilton Project at the Brookings Institution.

market pressure from industry leaders will have stronger power than government policy.

The contrast between the employees who have high pay and generous benefits working alongside the flexible workforce, who in many cases work without contracts or benefits, is growing starker. In the technology industry, average pay for employees is over $100K annually and can include Wi-Fi–enabled transportation to work, childcare, free cafeteria food, and many other benefits. But those same workers are surrounded by temporary or contingent workers, support staff, foodservice, groundskeepers, and security with far fewer perquisites, including something as basic as sick days.

The United States has had a bill requiring paid sick leave in process since 2004. The United States is the only large economy without a law in place. Frustrated with the lack of government action, large corporations like Microsoft are setting standards that must be adhered to throughout the supply chain. Microsoft required its vendors and contractors to provide 15 paid time-off days per year for vacation and sick leave. Microsoft's representative said it only made sense to ensure that contractors don't show up and infect their colleagues while sick. Studies prove that employees with paid time off are happier and more productive. Top-down employee perquisites could radically improve the quality of life for employees, no government participation required.

The Top Ten Capabilities for Tomorrow

What does it all mean for you? How do you future-proof yourself for tomorrow? To help you make a concrete plan for the capabilities you need for the workplace to come, we synthesized dozens of studies and added our expertise to identify the top ten capabilities you will need for the future.

We are convinced these capabilities will serve you well across jobs, industries, time, and geography. By capability, we mean "a collection of credentials, skills, and qualifications that demonstrate accomplishment and potential in a given area." Here are the capabilities we believe will be most in demand.

Capability 1: Functional Excellence

Tim Brown, the CEO of the design consultancy IDEO, says he likes to hire people with T-shaped skills. "T-shaped people have two kinds of characteristics, hence the use of the letter 'T' to describe them. The vertical stroke of the 'T' is a depth of skill that allows them to contribute to the creative process."

This part of the T refers to functional excellence, which, as we defined in Chapter 2, means having a set of honed skills related to a specific discipline, such as finance, architecture, social science, or software engineering. Without depth in at least one area, it's difficult to be a meaningful team member on a high-performing team. The trick is to build depth in an area that will be in demand and is not readily subject to automation soon. You want to be the go-to person for expertise in your area at work.

As you gather expertise in one functional area, consider adding others. The more options you have the better, but it is important to build depth, not just breadth, in your chosen fields.

Once you join an organization, focus as much as you can on learning one function, including the sub domains. For example, not only earn a degree in finance and start in accounts receivable, but learn treasury, financial planning and analysis, controller, risk management, and the other finance functions.

Capability 2: Emotional Intelligence

"The horizontal stroke of the "T," Brown continues, "is the disposition for collaboration across disciplines. It is composed of two things. First, empathy. It's important because it allows people to imagine the problem from another perspective—to stand in somebody else's shoes. Second, they tend to get very enthusiastic about other people's disciplines, to the point that they may actually start to practice them."

"Emotional intelligence is the ability to perceive emotions, to access and generate emotions so as to assist thought, to understand emotions and emotional knowledge, and to reflectively regulate emotions so as to promote emotional and intellectual growth," according to researchers. With emotional intelligence, you can perform better in interviews and navigate organizational politics, which are proven to be necessary for success.

Empathy is an important aspect of emotional intelligence, and enthusiasm is the drive to collaborate with others. Emotional intelligence is necessary to collaborate with others in an increasingly complex work environment. Simplification requires collaboration, and collaboration requires working with others. Nobody wants to work with a jerk.

Musical and social pioneer Lady Gaga understands the importance of learning emotional intelligence early, and believes it can be taught. Her foundation, Born This Way, "has partnered with the Yale Center for Emotional Intelligence to launch the Emotion Revolution . . . which is dedicated to building awareness of the central role emotions play in young people's learning, decision making, relationships, and achievement."

In many functional areas, education and certifications are (lazy) proxies for excellence. That is why so many companies rely on them for hiring. They haven't discovered, as Google did, that there are better ways to measure expertise and company fit. In the case of Google, this can include coding samples, but they also seek out emotional intelligence traits such as intellectual humility.

Functional excellence and emotional intelligence are a Powerball combination. Be extraordinary in the work you've chosen to do and be able to collaborate and communicate that excellence with others.

Capability 3: Personal Advocacy

You are on your own now, and will remain so. As people move from one type of employment state to another, everyone will be required to market, sell, develop, and sustain themselves. Daniel Pink, author of *Everyone Sells*, says that we must all learn how to persuade, influence, and convince others of our skills and capabilities.

By personal advocacy, we mean the ability to publicly support and promote yourself in a way that persuades others to engage with you. This includes both in-person and virtual personas, allowing you to have connections and options in many forums. The most effective personal advocacy doesn't cross the line into tedious self-promotion or become displays of virtual neon signs.

An essential building block of personal advocacy is establishing and building a personal brand. The trick is in the balance: sell yourself, keep relationships two-sided, and have fun content to share, even if it's cat videos. Some people even recruit a personal board of directors to help provide advice and mentorship.

Capability 4: Cross-Cultural Dexterity

One of Mike Ettling's enduring South African childhood memories is watching his mother harbor a black man who was running from the South African police during the period of Apartheid. She beckoned the fugitive into her home as he ran across the neighborhood backyards. That early lesson in empathy and compassion helped Mike appreciate and see cultural differences in a very different light from those who were raised in a homogenous culture.

As a result, he was open to a wide variety of options in both locations and types of jobs. Currently the president of the HR cloud business for SAP, he has rotated between entrepreneurial and corporate roles, lived on three continents, and worked in dozens of countries. He is comfortable in nearly any setting and takes to heart the idea that every situation is unique. What worked in the past might not work in a new setting, and he has the flexibility to work with and across countries, ethnicities, genders, ages, and background.

Increasingly, you will work in a globally diverse environment. How you interact with colleagues from outside your home country may need to be quite different, from being aware of different holidays to adjusting how you interface based on cultural norms. Do you know when to bow? The protocol for whom to serve first at dinner? How to present a business card? When a tweet is insensitive?

Justine Sacco found out the hard way that one insensitive tweet can blow up your life. Even though she had only 170 Twitter followers, one sarcastic and racially thoughtless tweet before she boarded a plane for a business trip to South Africa escalated into a global trending topic. By the time she landed, she was fired and her reputation in shambles.

There are a few implications for your future as you consider these demographic shifts. You can anticipate an increasingly diverse set of colleagues, even in your own country, whether it's the elderly front desk receptionist, the Gen Y software engineer celebrating his marriage to an arranged bride, or your female black manager– a Gen X MBA from Harvard. Embracing and flourishing in diversity will be a key criteria for success both now and in the near future.

Capability 5: Geek Acumen

No matter what career you have or job you are in, you are a technologist, and that means being a little bit of a geek. The phrase "I'm not really that technical" should be banned from everyone's thinking. To be ready for the future, we all must embrace at least the technologies and the enabling power of machine learning in our own fields. Otherwise, be prepared to become obsolete. As Ettling told us: "I have always tried to keep abreast with technology in my field. There's always been a geekish part of me."

Geek acumen means to keep up-to-date with emerging technologies not only in your immediate expertise area, but also in the broader domain. If you are a manufacturing and operations specialist, that means not only knowing what is emerging in additive (3D) manufacturing, but also understanding how consumer social media advances will influence how customers buy. The earlier you integrate this mentality, the easier it will be to keep up as technologies evolve and change your workplace.

Capability 6: Virtual Collaboration

Learning to work with colleagues scattered among various locations and using the tools of telecommuting will certainly be part of the future. Virtual collaboration has three components. First, it requires being able to work independently to achieve a set of shared goals. Second, you must be able to communicate and share knowledge effectively with others who are not in time or space proximity to you. Finally, people who have a capability to virtually collaborate are able to use technology-mediated communication tools.

We predict that nearly all jobs will have some component that will be done virtually. Whether that is from your home, the local coffee shop, at a customer's site, or an office, the ability to collaborate virtually prepares you with more options for flexible work. Can you initiate and host a video conference call? Do you recognize and include all virtual team members, or do some struggle to get a word in edgewise? Does everyone have access to the same software and digital processes?

Capability 7: Entrepreneurial Spirit

The entrepreneurial spirit is useful in any role. Successful entrepreneurs bring a set of skills and competencies, such as the ability to identify a niche market, financially manage a business, and build customer relationships, among others. But in this capability, we refer to a set of traits and attitudes that entrepreneurs use to help them establish and sustain a venture.

Some of the additional entrepreneurial traits that we believe enable nearly any career are initiative, passion, innovation, and the willingness to take risks. Certainly the first three are desirable to most employers and will serve you well should you choose an entrepreneurial path at some point in your career. And the willingness to take risks is essential for you to continue to stretch over the life of your career, even though it might not be at the encouragement of your employer.

Do you find meaning in your work? Do you step up to do tasks that others won't, and do you come up with new ideas? Are you willing to stretch to learn new things, even if there might be some risk of failing? Do you inspire others with your passion? If you can't muster these attitudes for your work now, what changes do you need to make to be able to do so? If you don't love your job most of the time, find one that connects to your entrepreneurial spirit.

Capability 8: Creative Problem Solving

Problem solving shows up as a competency on almost any posted job description in the world, matched only by the number of résumés claiming skills in problem solving. But yesterday's problem-solving skills are not the same as tomorrow's.

Traditional problem solving followed a fairly linear path: first identify a problem, involve others in seeking solutions, collect data and conduct analyses, search for best solutions, and, finally, make a decision. In a VUCA world, no such linearity exists save for the simplest of problems. The valued contributor of tomorrow will adapt to any situation with creative resolve and always have the ability to revisit and modify while still engaged in a methodical problem-solving process.

A creative problem-solver can use a structured path for problem solving, but is willing to continually adapt and change to the circumstances. A return to prior assumptions and conclusions as well as the grit to work around obstacles is part of creative problem solving.

Capability 9: Leadership

Organizations may be flattening with a need for fewer managers, but leadership is a different matter. Our overall research showed that employees yearn to be inspired by others, to have a vision to follow, to see meaning in their work, and to be guided with a clear pathway for making the vision come alive. These are the responsibilities of leadership, and they will remain an important capability in the future.

The "how" of leadership will shift, though. If leaders were to rely on physical visits to see everyone in the organization, they could spend all their time on airplanes traveling around the world. The new leaders must be able to collaborate and connect in real ways with employees, making social media and other technology and staff tools the delivery system for the company mission.

Leaders of tomorrow must also be able to live in a much more transparent environment, with two-way feedback. The mass email announcement, with only a trickle of ego-enhancing responses, is nearly over. Instead, it is being replaced by social media with blog posts, social comment, or videos, visible both internally and externally. Due to the two-way nature of social media, this will elicit questions, criticisms, and a higher level of transparency. Leaders will need rhinoceros skin.

Due to demographic shifts, and because organizations have done little to prepare future leaders, grooming those who aspire to leadership before the position is needed is an essential leadership trait. The workplace of tomorrow needs leader makers.

Capability 10: Stretchpertise

A favorite device of fiction writers using immortal characters is to require the occasional rejuvenation, frequently powered by stolen life, as in vampires or farmed donors. Fortunately, the ability for self-renewal in a career doesn't take such radical measures.

No one can sustain a lifetime of passion, initiative, innovation, and top performance without periods of restoration. Stretchpertise isn't about taking a week off at your favorite vacation spot. Instead, it's the professional ability to creatively restructure and repurpose in order to adjust to changing environmental demands. Stretchpertise means adapting your career to meet your own evolving personal needs and motivation. You must be able to learn on the fly, be open, create an effective network, and gather a variety of experiences. Stretchpertise is the immunization against obsolescence and requires the bounce-forward skills of grit, resilience, and motivation to aim toward longer-term goals.

The information and the strategies presented throughout this book provide you with a baseline for stretchpertise. We've given you the "know-how." As Yoda said, "Do or do not. There is no try."

STRETCH **7.1**

How prepared are you for tomorrow's capabilities? Rate yourself on each of the capabilities and then consider which you should include as part of your development planning.

	I COULD USE SIGNIFICANT DEVELOPMENT IN THIS AREA	I AM GENERALLY PREPARED IN THIS AREA	THIS IS A DISTINGUISHING STRENGTH FOR ME
Functional excellence			
Emotional intelligence			
Geek acumen			
Personal advocacy			
Cross-cultural dexterity			
Virtual collaboration			
Entrepreneurial spirit			
Creative problem solving			
Leadership			
Stretchpertise			

The Home Stretch

Throughout the book we have provided you with stretch breaks to help you start on your journey. We've given you 30 strategies to consider. Now we would like to help you launch into the next phase.

Many of the following steps were covered in the book, so you can refer back to some of the Stretch Breaks for clarification or reminders. To start now:

- **Set attainable stretch goals.** Set goals that can be accomplished in the next year, but have an eye toward your five-year dreams as well. Entrepreneurs must be able to describe their companies to potential funders in under 25 words. You should also be able to describe your goals in 25 words or less.

- **Prioritize you.** Something's got to give if you are going to have the time to achieve your goals. You have to make the time. Barbara had a major goal to write this book, but the demands of her job as a college president could easily have filled all her available time. Because she knew she needed a stop-doing list, she put a sign facing her in the office that simply said, "No." It served as a constant reminder to the side of her that did everything possible to say, "Yes." Delaying, delegating, or denying the request can help you find the time you need to prioritize your goals. No one is going to do that for you, especially if he or she has been on the receiving end of your helpful nature. It's all on you.

- **Work in sprints.** Don't imagine your career as a marathon. Instead, think of it as a series of sprints. To manage your energy over a career, it is absolutely necessary to have recharging periods, just like professional athletes who have on and off seasons. Athletes continue to train in the off-season, but not as vigorously as when they are in full-performance mode. You don't need to be in a constant stretch state; instead set some ambitious goals, complete them, and then work at a more normal pace for a period of time. Take advantage of your full vacation allowance to build the energy for your sprint periods. Employees who try to run full-speed for long periods of time burn out, are less productive, and are less successful over time.

- **Build your guild.** In Chapter 4 we gave you a strong set of strategies for how to build the network you need for a successful career. At a minimum, identify your "five to thrive," the five people who will help you achieve the world you imagine and leave you a better person. Set 20 meetings on your calendar for the next year so that you meet with each of the five people at least quarterly.

- **Enroll your resources.** Who or what do you need to fulfill your dreams? Do you need to have a conversation with your manager about your goals? (See our website at www.StretchTheBook.com for a script of an empowering, effective conversation to have with your boss.) What training resources does your company have available? Large organizations frequently have subscriptions to training or content libraries like SkillSoft, Books 24X7, or Lynda.com. Become familiar with what your company has, and don't be shy about calling your training department with specific requests for advice on what is available. If you want to continue your education, discover your corporate tuition refund policies. In addition to your five to thrive, can you line up a mentor or a set of mentors, even for just a short-term engagement?

- **Pick three strategies.** We've provided 29 strategies for career development in this book. Go back through the book, and in each of the five practices you will see a section of Strategies. Which resonated with you so that you might start now? Don't try to deploy all of them at once. Instead, pick a few—we suggest three—and incorporate them into your plan.

- **Document your plan.** Having a written plan that you can refer back to and adjust as needed will help make the plan more real, and will also help when you sit down with your boss or mentor. Visit our website at www.StretchTheBook.com for a downloadable version of a sample action plan.

- **Check in with yourself quarterly**. Did you feel in over your head this quarter? Was it job stress or the excitement of moving forward on a project? Be attentive to where you are on your development plan, and be adaptive in adjusting your path to be the right one for you at this time.

- **Appoint trigger points.** People who maintain healthy weights often use a trigger-point strategy. In their minds, they set a weight goal they won't exceed. Their ideal weight might be 130, but they set a trigger point of 140. The moment the scale hits 140, they invoke a promise to themselves to take action to rectify being off-target. A work trigger point might be, "Make a job change if I have not had the opportunity to lead a project team by July 15th, of next year." Then go to your calendar and set a reminder, "Project team lead goal achieved?"

- **Bounce forward.** You need motivation strategies or motivation resources to keep going. Reward yourself when you achieve a significant goal. Karie has a favorite champagne she only buys for significant life achievements and does not purchase at any other time. She has only had six bottles in her life, but her friends and family heartily join the celebration. That celebration helps provide the incentive to keep going, just like the crowds that cheer runners at races.

You Are Never Finished

Vijay Iyer is one of the most successful jazz performers in the world, working as both a composer and a pianist. Yet he started out thinking he had a defined career path in physics. With a physics and math degree from Yale under his belt, he then enrolled in the Ph.D. program at Berkeley. On the side, he gave musical performances. Eventually, he decided to choose a musical career. Perhaps that early dilemma shaped his thinking about the music he creates now.

"The most I can say is that it never feels finished to me—I never think I've mastered anything yet. I just think of myself as a student," he says. "I also work really hard on details and I don't mean in an obsessive way—I mean in a patient way.

"One thing that's been important to me is rethinking this notion of success. What is success? When it comes to making art, I don't know what that is," Iyer says. "I know what's genuine and I know what I want to hear. And sometimes other people want to hear what I want to hear, sometimes they don't. The main . . . value of being a performer is that I get to listen to the audience the whole time. I listen very carefully to them. It's not about listening to them clapping—it's about listening to them breathing. What are their bodies doing right now in relation to what I'm doing, and are we connecting? It's that kind of question I'm always asking. If I always listen to that, then it's not about success in terms of album sales or awards. It's actually about meaning something to people and reaching people and making a difference."

In the same way, a career is never fully finished. We must each keep working, not obsessively but patiently, toward mastery in our work. How are we connecting to people? Can you hear not only the appreciation, but also feel the resonance in response to your work? What does it feel like when you achieve a goal or acquire a new skill? Listening at this level to yourself and to others around you can be the greatest stretch exercise of all.

Onward

You have brains in your head. You have feet in your shoes. You can steer yourself any direction you choose. You're on your own. And you know what you know. And YOU are the one who'll decide where to go. . . ."

—Dr. Seuss

Our goal as authors was to give you the capacity to be fully engaged, enjoy fulfillment in your work, and be ready to stretch to the next level. We believe you can do this no matter where you are in your career, whether 22 or 82. We have provided an overview of tomorrow's workplace and practical advice, including:

1. Career management tools that you can implement on your own, without the need for big financial or company resources.

2. A broad set of options and strategies on how to approach work and develop your career, so that you have the flexibility to pick what works within your own situation.

3. Ways for you to assess your current reality and plot a path to achieve your dreams for tomorrow's workplace.

The future beckons. Will you be one of the disengaged, or will you stretch to new capabilities, extending your sell-by date? The fulfillment of dreams doesn't happen by luck. Stretch to become your best self—the person who you know you can be.

Supplemental Materials

Acknowledgments

List of Figures and Tables

Appendix A: Research Methodology

Appendix B: Essential Books to Learn More

Notes

ACKNOWLEDGMENTS

We are happy to say that one of the great pleasures of researching and writing a book with a co-author is the opportunity to stretch. Not only did we stretch each other, but also countless of our friends, family, and colleagues who helped us see new ways to approach the material, shared stories that gave us new angles, and provided feedback generously.

People Who Shaped Us

Since we met at Case Western Reserve University and shared years of doctoral work together, our many professors were constantly in our thoughts. We thank them all, in particular for serving as advisors for some of the earliest research of this book: John Aram, Richard Boyatzis, Paul Salipante, Jagdip Singh, Diana Bilimoria, and Dick Boland. The class of 2003 also provided great insight into our research on types of network strategies discussed in Chapter 4. Sue Nartker, you helped us stay sane.

Connectors and Experts

We are sure that we used way more than Dunbar's number in terms of people who actively helped us with this book. We may not have used their stories, but their conversations shaped our thinking. Our page numbers are limited, but to just mention a few: Dan Pontefract, brilliant thinker, expert on learning, author, change agent, and partner in reviewing the book; Bill Byham, visionary leader and talent management pioneer, for his encouragement and advice; Joseph Grenny, author and behavioral science guy, who has provided years of invaluable advice; Kevin Oakes, entrepreneur, leader, and connector, for providing connections and feedback on the broad topic; Charles Jennings, one of the most respected learning leaders in Europe, or the world for that matter, who provided connections to stories in the book; Barbara Pollack, gifted coach at The Center for Creative Leadership, who shared her incredible insights and inspired us to reach deeper into the meaning of work; Karen Kocher, extraordinary CLO with a balance of theory and practicality; Jenny Dearborn, for continuing to model growth and the ability to stretch; Joe Campbell, deep thinker and astute learning expert; Kelly Palmer, who shared her LinkedIn story and just keeps on pushing the limits of what it means to stretch a career; Linda Babcock, CMU colleague, for introducing us to Mark Fortier; Sameer Patel, social collaboration guru, for connecting us to stories; Jay Cross for years of advocacy on informal learning; Daniel Gray and Marga Biller of the Harvard Learning Innovations Lab for sharing their time and research; Gwen Havern, fun, insightful friend whose belief that people can own and change their world views inspired sections of the chapter on being open; John Ambrose, who connected us to stories to help the book stay global; and Mike Dulworth, who shared his passion for networks. For the many, many more who helped us, and whose stories are told in this book—to name a few Alexis Antes, Helen Volkov Behn, Bob Cancalosi, Rick Harwell, Chris James, and Nathaniel Koloc—our deepest appreciation. Champagne is on us the next time we meet any of you.

Supporters and Research Team

A number of people provided direct support during the creation of this book. We thank SAP for allowing us to be involved in the shaping and analysis of their global research study. Here's a big shout out to Deb Lyons, Mona Farah, and Bri Vellis, who lived through the weeds of a nearly year-long study. Thanks to Marketing at SAP for sponsoring the budget for the survey, as well as Julie Knight, David Ludlow, Steve Hunt, Mike Ettling, Ashley Colombo, Geraldine Lim, and the team at PAN Communication for promoting the results. Our appreciation to the brilliant Oxford Economics team—Debra D'Agostino, Ed Cone, Ben Wright, and Adrianna Gregory; Sanchita Sur of Emplay for providing additional analytics on the survey; also appreciation to Josh Bersin of Deloitte and the SAP HR senior leadership team for providing early reactions and feedback on the survey results; the Athena Foundation for allowing access to its award winners during our doctoral work; Henry van Wagenberg—world traveler and all around interesting person—who found and interviewed people to collect stories for the book; Megan McFarland, who researched skills of the future for us; to the team at Wilson for their enthusiasm, especially Melissa Imes, who was always willing to do whatever it took; Brian Speer, cover and graphics advisor and master of icons and fonts; Brain Ecker, Elissa Heil, Mary Ann Naso, Camilla Rawleigh, and Mary Beth Williams, who willingly tested mindsets around campus.

Family, Friends, and Readers

Some of our closest ties were the people we prevailed upon to critique ideas and various drafts. We endlessly stretched their patience, whether as readers or for bowing out on fun adventures, but thankfully, *Stretch* is better as a result. Our partners: Andy Bonnewell, for that initial staycation, his love, endless patience, and abundant zeal for the book, and Steven Gerson, for his quiet support, reinforcement, and being the resident scientific advisor; our children and their partners, who gave up family time and travel, jumped on board enthusiastically, and linked us to their connections and world, whether about social media, being a Millennial or healthcare in Cuba: Sloane and Taylor Davidson, Tori Mistick, Addy Mistick, Charis and Chris Ackerson, Rena Jones and Marc Sciglimpaglia; our trainers who kept us stretching literally so that we would have the energy for the long hours this book required: Eric Lugg and Sara Sheets; David Swanson, most excellent HR advisor and reader; Teresa Roche, for being a friend, expert, reviewer, and extraordinary human being; Cindy Skrzycki, friend, fellow author, and most excellent listener; Robin Bernstein for her enthusiasm and great connector capabilities; the "Women Who

Read Too Much" book club; Jayne Huston and Becky Campbell, great sources of inspiration: Larry Peters, long-term advisor, reader and friend; Rick Von Feldt, for sharing ideas and conducting interviews on an earlier vision of the book and Dr. Rene Gonzalez for building extraordinary expertise and using it when most needed.

Team Stretch

From the beginning, Katie Kotchman, our agent, believed in the content of the book and remained an enthusiastic and tireless champion even when we had to pivot; Tori Winters, book assistant, for making the details work, maintaining a sense of humor, and sticking with us right up to the frantic deadline; Trai Cartwright, development editor, who provided candid and supportive feedback on at least three versions of the book; the very responsive team at Wiley, especially Matt Davis, who, despite the shifting tides in publishing, remains a positive force and great guitar lover; Heather Brosius; Dawn Kilgore, and Rebecca Taff for production patience; and finally Mark Fortier and Courtney Nobile, who are helping us make *Stretch* come alive and share it with the world.

Stretch Inspiration

Barbara I owe thanks, most of all, to my parents, Bill and Georgiana, for whom work and life were one journey. This is a book about the meaning of work, and I learned from them how meaningful work and partnership could be, along with a work ethic that inspires joy and resolve. Those early memories of accompanying my father to work and watching the way in which he interacted with people inspire me still.

Karie At the other end of the age spectrum, I owe my inspiration to my two young grandchildren, Aidan and Zoe. My deepest wish is that they find meaning and happiness in their lives through beautiful relationships and important work. The future is theirs, and I hope I can provide them some guidance as they venture into the world.

LIST OF FIGURES AND TABLES

A RESEARCH METHODOLOGY

Our research mission was to discover how changes in the global economy and shifting demographics would impact the employment and talent marketplace, from both the employer and employee perspectives. By understanding both views, we would be able to offer advice to both companies and employees on how to prepare to meet each other's expectations for the future. In 2014, we collaborated with SuccessFactors, an SAP company, and Oxford Economics to conduct twin studies of executives and employees across 27 countries to find out what the future workforce wants.

Altogether we polled 2,800 employees and polled or interviewed 2,700 executives, with even distribution across countries. Employees were working professionals in white-collar jobs, and executives were largely senior executives in a direct-reporting relationship to a CEO or company president. The respondents came from across many thousands of companies, encompassing industries such as retail, public sector, finance, healthcare, consumer goods, and others. An independent polling firm selected all respondents. Since our focus was on the future, half of our employee respondents were Millennials–people born after 1979. Countries in which we surveyed are shown in Figure A.1.

FIG A.1 Countries Surveyed

Legend: Lighter shaded areas indicate surveyed countries.
Source: SAP

A little more than 53 percent of the employee respondents were men, and almost 47 percent were women. Executives were not sorted by age or gender, since we did not anticipate there would be enough females or Millennials in top jobs to help us sort the data. Each survey asked a broad range of questions covering over 90 items focusing on factors such as contributors to their job satisfaction, their company benefits and offerings, development opportunities, benefits, culture, manager quality, and skills.

We also inserted variables to sort the respondents by work performance or job satisfaction. In the case of employees, we asked for their last performance review rating, their intention to leave, and their overall job satisfaction. In the case of executives, we asked how profitable and how fast their companies were growing compared to others in their industry. As one of our data sorts, we compared high performers to low performers in both surveys. When we refer to high-performing employees in the book, they are the people who said their performance rating was above average or excellent. As an example, high performers were 26 percent more likely than low performers to say that self-directed learning was one of the top three ways they have experienced the most professional development. That insight helped inform our practice "Learn on the Fly" and inspired us to look further at how high performers direct their own learning.

In addition to the global surveys, we estimate we interviewed and talked to hundreds of people and consulted with dozens of academic or corporate learning experts to refine and validate our practices. We reviewed more than 1,000 academic papers, kept Amazon in business with book deliveries, and clicked through countless of the web's estimated trillion pages. As partners, we have researched together since we started our doctoral programs together in 1999. Our first project was interviewing award-winning people to determine how they used their networks in achieving their success. This long research partnership enabled us to span a broad array of research topics and translate those into actionable career development practices.

Key Workplace 2020 Survey Findings

Overall, our survey findings fall into five broad themes, outlined below:

1. The face of the workforce is shifting to be more diverse and global. Executives agreed strongly that they will be hiring more contingent, part-time, and contract labor, meaning the future of work will be comprised of a more flexible workforce.

2. Millennials are not as different as widely reported, at least when it comes to what they want at work. By and large, people of all ages want meaningful work, aspire to make a difference, and value the same benefits. Millennials are different in that they want more feedback and more development than their non-Millennial peers, understandably so since they are earlier in their careers.

3. Executives and employees don't see eye to eye on what matters to job satisfaction. Compensation was the most important factor to both satisfaction and loyalty, but executives reported a low focus on competitive compensation. The one exception where compensation was not ranked first was in the United States. There Millennials rated development as their top factor driving satisfaction and loyalty. Rosabeth Moss Kanter, Harvard professor, based upon her research says that when companies provide an environment that offers employees a chance to gain mastery, be a highly connected member, and experience meaningful work, money becomes a distant fourth. This may be true in more stable economic times, or perhaps our study's respondents aren't experiencing the first three in a consistent way, as money has risen to the top of their agenda. Executives also highly value loyalty and commitment from their employees, which is surprising given that out of the Fortune 500, fewer than 100 companies have an average employee tenure greater than five years. Gallup routinely reports that most employees are disengaged, so no wonder options elsewhere seem attractive. Even at Google, one of the most desired companies to work for in the world, average employee tenure is just a little over a year, partially attributable to growth, but low nonetheless.

4. To be prepared for the future, both employees and executives agreed that more preparation is needed for leaders. Even though executives said they anticipated having more diverse employees, only 34 percent of executives said their leaders were prepared to lead a more diverse workplace. Less than half of executives—47 percent—said their organizations were prepared to lead in a global environment.

5. Finally, employees were clear that they need development to be prepared for tomorrow's workplace. The number one concern employees around the world share is that their position will change or their skills will become obsolete, shown in Figure A.2. Additionally, only 50 percent of the employees from our survey believe the skills they have today will be the skills they need just three years from now. Only 34 percent say their company provides the training they need to stay current.

FIG A.2 What Concerns Employees Most About Their Jobs

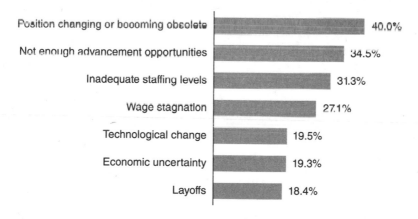

- Position changing or boooming obsolete — 40.0%
- Not enough advancement opportunities — 34.5%
- Inadequate staffing levels — 31.3%
- Wage stagnation — 27.1%
- Technological change — 19.5%
- Economic uncertainty — 19.3%
- Layoffs — 18.4%

B ESSENTIAL BOOKS TO LEARN MORE

Act Like a Leader, Think Like a Leader, Herminia Ibarra
Ibarra, a professor at INSEAD, provides insightful and practical advice including a step-by-step guide for managers and executives interested in leadership positions.

Crucial Conversations: Tools for Talking When Stakes Are High, Kerry Patterson, Joseph Grenny, Ron McMillan, and Al Switzler
This bestseller draws our attention to the defining dialogues and conversations that literally shape our lives, our relationships and our world.

Curious: The Desire to Know and Why Your Future Depends on It, Ian Leslie
Drawing on fascinating research, Leslie makes a passionate case that everyone is born curious and encourages the cultivation of our "desire to know."

Decisive: How to Make Better Choices in Life and Work, Chip Heath and Dan Heath
In tackling the topic of how to help people make better decisions, this book covers our biases and irrationalities and provides a four-step process to counteract these biases.

Drive: The Surprising Truth About What Motivates Us, Daniel H. Pink
Based on scientific research on human motivation, this provocative and fascinating book will change how you think about your life and our world.

HBR's Guide to Getting the Mentoring You Need, Harvard Business Review Press
This guide provides powerful and efficient tools for identifying how to build relationships with influential sponsors and stand out in your organization.

How We Learn: The Surprising Truth About When, Where, and Why It Happens, Benedict Carey
A wonderful practical, playful, and fascinating guide to what we really know about learning and memory and how we can apply it to our own lives.

Lean In: Women, Work, and the Will to Lead, Sheryl Sandberg
In this landmark and sometimes controversial manifesto, Sandberg poses a set of ambitious challenges to women, to create the lives we want.

Mindset: The New Psychology of Success, Carol S. Dweck
Stanford's Dweck distills her decades of research on achievement and success into a groundbreaking idea—the power of our mindsets. If you can only read one book from this list, start here.

No Ordinary Disruption: The Global Forces Breaking All the Trends, Richard Dobbs, James Manyika, and Jonathan Woetzel
Based on years of research by the directors of the McKinsey Global Institute, this book examines and provides rigorous illustrations of the four forces transforming the global economy.

The Power of Full Engagement: Managing Energy, Not Time, Is the Key to High Performance and Personal Renewal, Jim Loehr and Tony Schwartz
In order to read all the books we've included here, you are going to need plenty of energy, and this is the book that can unlock the key to high performance as well as health, happiness, and life balance.

Primal Leadership: Unleashing the Power of Emotional Intelligence, Daniel Goleman, Richard Boyatzis, and Annie McKee
Drawn from decades of analysis, this book unveils and explores the role of emotional intelligence in leadership and provides a road map for how to connect with others.

Rise of the Robots: Technology and the Threat of a Jobless Future, Martin Ford
Ford details what accelerating technology means for our economic prospects and details how past solutions to technological disruptions aren't going to work.

The Start-Up of You, Reid Hoffman and Ben Casnocha
This book, by the co-founder of LinkedIn, provides insights into how the Internet has fundamentally changed business and society and how you can live and thrive in a networked world.

NOTES

Preface

1. *T.H. White:* White, T.H. "Book 2." *The Once and Future King.* New York: Putnam, 1958.
2. *Barbara Mistick and Karie Willyerd met.* Because we wrote this book together, when we describe incidents from our own lives, we refer to ourselves by our first names, Barbara and Karie.
3. *We also know from Gallup:*, "State of the Global Workplace," Gallup, 2013.

Chapter 1

1. *Langston Hughes:* Langston Hughes. Dreams from *The Collected Poems of Langston Hughes,* edited by Arnold Rampersad with David Roessel, Associate Editor, copyright © 1994 by the Estate of Langston Hughes. Used by permission of Alfred A. Knopf, an imprint of the Knopf Doubleday Publishing Group, a division of Penguin Random House LLC. All rights reserved. Reprinted by permission of Harold Ober Associates Incorporated.
2. *Jade stepped out on her apartment's patio:* Jade is a composite character of a few people we know. David is a person we know, fictionalized a bit to keep him anonymous. Throughout, when we use first names other than our own, we are telling the real stories of people with whom we have talked. Sometimes a character may be a mash-up of more than one person. We have taken some artistic license in the use of names or identifying situations. In some cases, people offered to use their full names, which are so indicated.
3. *growth hacker:* Ryan Holiday, "Everything Is Marketing: How Growth Hackers Redefine the Game," *Fast Company* (December 17, 2012).

4. *Gallup reports that most of us are disengaged*: "Gallup State of the American Workplace Report 2013," Gallup, 2013.

5. *Studs Terkel, author and Pulitzer Prize winner*: Studs Terkel, *Working* (The New Press, 1997).

6. *"Learn to play the accordion"*: Steve Chawkins, "Leonard Nimoy dies at 83; 'Star Trek's' transcendent alien Mr. Spock," *Los Angeles Times* (February 27, 2015).

7. *McKinsey estimates*: Yuval Atsmon, Peter Child, Richard Dobbs, and Laxman Narasimhan, "Winning the $30 trillion decathlon: Going for Gold in Emerging Markets," *McKinsey Quarterly* (August, 2012).

8. *By 2030, nearly two-thirds*: Mario Pezzini. "An Emerging Middle Class," *OECD Observer* (2012).

9. *US GDP, double what it was in 1955*: Alan Murray, "5 Things You Didn't Know About the Fortune 500," *Fortune* (June 4, 2015).

10. *resulting in the loss of thousands of jobs*: Daniel Roberts, "Here's What Happens When 3G Capital Buys Your Company," *Fortune* (March 25, 2015).

11. *"like most large U.S. visual-effects firms"*: Ben Fritz, "Rival Visual-Effects Firm Wins Rhythm & Hues Auction," *The Wall Street Journal* (March 31, 2013).

12. *Paraphrasing John Donne*: John Donne, *Devotions Upon Emergent Occasions* (1623). www.poemhunter.com/poem/no-man-is-an-island.

13. *People are living and working longer*: Amy Langfield, "Average US Retirement Age Is 61—And Rising," *CNBC* (May 16, 2013).

14. *Among those people over 55*: Dave Burdick, "Retirement Savings Low? It Doesn't Take a Catastrophe to Be Part of the Retirement Crisis," *The Denver Post* (July 1, 2013).

15. *According to the United Nations Population Division*: Karie Willyerd and Jeanne Meister reported on these statistics in their book, *The 2020 Workplace*. Also see W. David Delong, *Lost Knowledge: Confronting the Threat of an Aging Workforce* (Oxford University Press, 2004).

16. *Millennials replacing the exiting older workers*: Paul Taylor and the Pew Research Center, *The Next America* (Public Affairs, 2014).

17. *Women Compromise*: "Women in the Labor Force in 2010," U.S. Department of Labor, July 19, 2011.

18. *outnumbering men in college attendance*: Mark Hugo Lopez and Ana Gonzalez-Barrera, "Women's College Enrollment Gains Leave Men Behind," Pew Research, March 6, 2014.

19. *non-whites will be the majority by 2040*: Jennifer M. Ortman and Christine E. Guarneri, "United States Population Projections: 2000 to 2050," U.S. Census Bureau.

20. *data will grow 4300 percent annually*: "Big Data Universe Beginning to Explode," *CSC*, 2012.

21. *the entire Internet in 2008*: Dave Evans, "The Internet of Things," *Cisco Blogs* (July 15, 2011).

22. *In 2015, IBM estimated*: "What Is Changing in the Realm of Big Data?," ibm.com/big-data.

23. *The United Nations has declared*: David Kravets, "U.N. Report Declares Internet Access a Human Right," *Wired* (June 3, 2011).

24. *first driverless car to cross the United States*: Chris Isidore, "Driverless Car Finishes 3,400-Mile Cross-Country Trip," *CNNMoney* (April 3, 2015).

25. *Japan is expecting one in three*: Naoko Muramatsu and Hiroko Akiyama, "Japan: Super-Aging Society Preparing for the Future," *The Gerontologist* (May 24, 2011).

26. *serving as the check-in staff*: Adrian Bridge, "Robots to Serve Guests in Japanese Hotel," *Telegraph* (February 3, 2015).

27. *The OECD anticipates*: "Water: Governments Must Deal with Rising Risks," OECD, February 9, 2013. The Organization for Economic Co-operation and Development (OECD) sets as a mission to promote policies that will improve the economic and social well-being of people around the world.

28. *South-to-North Water Diversion Project in China*: Lily Kuo, "China Has Launched the Largest Water-Pipeline Project in History," *The Atlantic* (March 7, 2014).

29. *land degradation, freight impact, and other factors*: Richard Dobbs, James Manyika, and Jonathan Woetzel, *No Ordinary Disruption* (Public Affairs, 2015), 121.

30. *freelancers or contractors*: Richard Greenwald, "A Freelance Economy Can Be Good for Workers: Let's Make It Better," *The Atlantic* (November 16, 2012). Richard Greenwald, a sociologist of work and professor at St. Joseph's College in Brooklyn, estimates that up to half of all workers may be freelancers in the next decade.

31. *increasing regulations*: Alan Murray, "5 Things You Didn't Know About the Fortune 500," *Fortune* (June 4, 2015). Executives told us in our separate survey with them that increasing regulatory requirements was their number one business concern. *Fortune* reported it as the number two global concern of executives, behind technological innovation.

32. *stressors that affect overall health and wellness for employees*: Shana Lynch, "Why Your Workplace Might Be Killing You," *Stanford Business* (February 23, 2015).

33. *"What got you here won't get there"*: Marshall Goldsmith, and Mark Reiter, *What Got You Here Won't Get You There* (Hachette Books, 2007).

34. *Now It's 15 years*: Steve Denning, "Peggy Noonan on Steve Jobs and Why Big Companies Die," *Forbes* (November 19, 2011).

35. *Only 67 companies stayed on the Fortune 500 list*: Mark J. Perry, "Fortune 500 Firms in 1955 vs. 2011; 87% Are Gone," AEI Carpe Diem, November 23, 2011.

36. *According to Scott Timberg*: Scott Timberg, *Culture Crash: The Killing of the Creative Class* (Yale University Press, 2015).

37. *36 percent decline in inflation-adjusted net worth*: Anna Bernasek, "The Typical Household, Now Worth a Third Less," *New York Times* (July 27, 2014).

38. *The most notorious of these was Al Capone*: "Al Capone." Bio. A&E Television Networks, 2015.

39. *"we been in the wrong racket all along"*: John William Tuohy, "The Milk Men," AmericanMafia.com, *Feature Articles*, 178 (December 1, 2001).

40. *The first time sell-by-dates were used on milk*: Al Zagofsky, "Milk Expiration Dates—Courtesy of Al Capone," *Carbon County Magazine* (August 2011).

41. *George Crane*: Crane is an author and writer, as quoted in Dennis Swanberg and Criswell Freeman, *Dr. Swan's Prescription for Job-itis* (Broadman and Holman Publications, 2005).

42. *Had he actually just said that out loud*: Karie attended this conference and heard the comments directly.

43. *In a review of the 17,000 leaders*: Jack Zenger, "We Wait Too Long to Train Our Leaders," *Harvard Business Review* (December 17, 2012).

44. *might mean starting your own business*: "Mind the Gaps: The 2015 Deloitte Millennial Survey Executive Summary," Deloitte, 2015. Millennials are increasingly expressing interest in starting their own businesses, especially in emerging economies, according to a Deloitte 2015 study.

45. *the 70-20-10 model*: Ron Rabin, "Blended Learning for Leadership: The CCL Approach," Center for Creative Leadership, 2014.

46. *"constant learning is more valuable than mastery"*: Liz Wiseman, *Rookie Smarts* (Harper Business, 2014).

47. *"Human beings, who are almost unique"*: Douglas Adam, *The Hitchhikers Guide to the Galaxy* (Del Rey, 1995).

48. *Michael Webb*: From a conversation in December 2014.

49. *how much grit you have*: Angela L Duckworth, Christopher Peterson, Michael D. Matthews, and Dennis R. Kelly, "Grit: Perseverance and Passion for Long-Term Goals." *Journal of Personality and Social Psychology*, 92 (June 2007), 1087–1101.

50. *a strong predictor of success*: Malcolm Gladwell, *Outliers: The Story of Success* (Back Bay, 2011).

51. *Bad is stronger than good*: Roy F Baumeister, Ellen Bratslavsky, Catrin Finkenauer, and Kathleen D. Vohs, "Bad Is Stronger Than Good," *Review of General Psychology*, 5 (2001), 323–370.

Chapter 2

1. *Alvin Toffler:* From an interview with Herbert Gerjuoy, Alvin Toffler, *Future Shock* (Bantam, 1984).

2. *Jonah:* This story is from an interview conducted in October 2013, but identity details have been changed at the request of the interviewee.

3. *Like a good portion of his generation:* U.S. Chamber of Commerce Foundation, "The Millennial Generation Research Review."

4. *Tenure doesn't guarantee expertise*: Steve Sonnentag, "Excellent Software Professionals: Experience, Work Activities, and Perceptions by Peers," *Behavior & Information Technology*, 14 (1995), 289–299.

5. *we must all learn a living:* Chris James featured in Chapter 3 has used this phrase for a number of years as a reminder for himself of what he must do to stay current and up to date at work.

6. *"On a daily basis, who cares for your learning?"*: Gianpiero Petriglieri, "Learning Is the Most Celebrated Neglected Activity in the Workplace," *Harvard Business Review* (November 6, 2014).

7. *Companies that provide opportunities*: James L. Heskett, W. Earl Sasser, and Leonard A. Schlesinger, *The Service Profit Chain* (The Free Press, 1997). The service-profit chain theory is well established. A number of other studies have shown that training leads to employee satisfaction, such as "The Effects of Employee Satisfaction, Organizational Citizenship Behavior, and Turnover on Organizational Effectiveness" by Daniel J. Koys, Department of Management, DePaul University, 2001.

8. *nearly 80 percent of employees*: "Accenture Study Finds U.S. Workers Under Pressure to Improve Skills, But Need More Support from Employers," *Accenture* (November 16, 2011).

9. *spent per employee is still just over $1200*: ATD Research, *2014 State of the Industry* (Association for Talent Development, 2014).

10. *organizations indicating they will spend more on formal training*: *Global Human Capital Trends 2015* (Deloitte University Press, 2015).

11. *providing extraordinary development opportunities:* ATD BEST Awards. The BEST Awards recognize organizations that demonstrate enterprise-wide success as a result of employee talent development.

12. *Raymond Wlodkowski*: Raymond J. Wlodkowski, *Enhancing Adult Motivation to Learn* (Jossey-Bass, 2008).

13. *"But if anyone else tried to give advice"*: Plato (Translated by C.C.W. Taylor), *Protagoras* (Oxford: Clarendon Press, 1991).

14. *Figure 2.2*: Table adapted from Michelene T.H. Chi, "Two Approaches to the Study of Experts' Characteristics," *Cambridge Handbook: Expertise and Expert Performance* (Cambridge University Press, 2006).

15. *Benjamin Barber*: Benjamin Barber, *The Reader's Digest*, 140 (1992).

16. *Even teachers or masters*: Richard E. Clark, "Cognitive and Neuroscience Research on Learning and Instruction," The 11th International Conference on Education Research, whitepaper, September 29–October 1, 2010.

17. *The first strategy to learn how to learn*: Carol Dweck, *Mindset* (Ballantine Books, 2007).

18. *A person with a growth mindset*: Carol Dweck, *Mindset* (Ballantine Books, 2007).

19. *find yourself more open to new experiences*: Don VandeWalle, "Are Our Students Trying to Prove or Improve Their Ability? Development and Validation of an Instrument to Measure Academic Goal Orientation." Paper presented at the Academy of Management's national meeting, Cincinnati, Ohio, August 1996.

20. *skill improvement goals you set out for yourself*: Joan F. Brett and Don VandeWalle, "Goal Orientation and Goal Content as Predictors of Performance in a Training Program," *Journal of Applied Psychology*, 84 (1999).

21. *Stretch Break 2.2*: Table excerpted from Don VandeWalle, "Development and Validation of a Work Domain Goal-Orientation Instrument," *Educational and Psychological Measurement* (December 1, 1997). The instrument has three components; this is part one. Copyright © 1997. Reprinted by Permission of SAGE Publications.

22. *checking his phone constantly*: Linda Stone, "Continuous Partial Attention," lindastone.net.

23. *Mindfulness applied to learning involves focusing*: Bauback Yeganeh and David Kolb, "Mindfulness and Experiential Learning," *OD Practitioner* (2009).

24. *By observing in the moment*: Ellen J. Langer, *The Power of Mindful Learning* (Da Capo Press, 1998).

25. *"Wrong, it's not when you understand them. It's when they feel heard."*: As told by Dave Ulrich at a conference in São Paulo, Brazil, March 2015. Karie was also a speaker at this forum.

26. *"Try to be one of the people upon whom nothing is lost"*: Published in *Longman's Magazine*, 4 (September 1884) and reprinted in *Partial Portraits* (Macmillan, 1888).

27. *"Not being satisfied is what makes curiosity so satisfying"*: Ian Leslie, *Curious: The Desire to Know and Why Your Future Depends on It* (Basic Books, 2014). 33.

28. *Todd Kashdan of George Mason University*: Elizabeth Svoboda, "Cultivating Curiosity," *Psychology Today* (September 1, 2006).

29. *"The more accurate the machine gets, the lazier the questions become"*: Tim Adams, "Google and the Future of Search: Amit Singhal and the Knowledge Graph," *The Guardian* (January 19, 2013).

30. *Bob Cancalosi*: This story is from an interview conducted with Bob Cancalosi in March 2015.

31. *strength training for the brain*: Pam A. Mueller and Daniel M. Oppenheimer, "The Pen Is Mightier Than the Keyboard: Advantages of Longhand Over Laptop Note Taking," *Psychological Science* (April 23, 2014).

32. *Reflection leads to learning*: Lillian A. Rafeldt, Heather Jane Baden, Nancy Lesnick Czarzasty, Eilen Freeman, Edith Ouellet, and Judith M. Snayd, "Reflection Builds Twenty-First-Century Professionals," Association of American Colleges & Universities, 2014.

33. *knowledge is doubling every 13 months:* David Russell Schilling, "Knowledge Doubling Every 12 Months, Soon to Be Every 12 Hours," *Industry Tap* (April 19, 2013).

34. *more data bits available now than there are stars in the universe:* "Executive Summary: Data Growth, Business Opportunities, and the IT Imperatives | The Digital Universe of Opportunities: Rich Data and the Increasing Value of the Internet of Things," EMC, April 2014.

35. *Samuel Arbesman*: Samuel Arbesman, "The Half-Life of Facts," *The Economist* (November 28, 2012).

36. *the need to learn:* A special thanks to the Learning Innovations Laboratory at Harvard for sharing their research on unlearning.

37. *how we think about the world*: Karen Becker, "Individual and Organizational Unlearning: Directions for Future Research," *International Journal of Organizational Behavior,* 9 (2005), 659–670.

38. *discourage us from changing:* Katie Heikkinen, "Unlearning to Learn: Changing Mindsets," President and Fellows of Harvard College, October 2013.

39. *Expect to be frustrated when you are unlearning*: Julee H. Hafner, "A Conceptualization of Unlearning in Organizational Employees," The Chicago School of Professional Psychology, 2014.

40. *Dunning-Kruger effect:* Justin Kruger and David Dunning, "Unskilled and Unaware of It: How Difficulties in Recognizing One's Own Incompetence Lead to Inflated Self-Assessments," *Journal of Personality and Social Psychology,* 77 (December 1999), 1121–1134.

41. *biggest steps you can take to avoid this trap:* Carol Dweck, *Mindset* (Ballantine Books, 2007), 11.

42. *we rely on technology to do our jobs for us*: Nicholas Carr, "Automation Makes Us Dumb," *The Wall Street Journal* (November 21, 2014).

43. *Captain Sullenberger*: Andrew Prince, "Experience, Training Make for Smooth River Landing," NPR, January 16, 2009.

44. *"it takes courage, not just time"*: Gianpiero Petriglieri, "Learning Is the Most Celebrated Neglected Activity in the Workplace," *Harvard Business Review* (November 6, 2014).

45. *"I had to seek out advisers and learn quickly"*: Adam Bryant, "Brian Chesky of Airbnb, on Scratching the Itch to Create," *The New York Times* (October 11, 2014).
46. Table excerpted from: Don VandeWalle, "Development and Validation of a Work Domain Goal Orientation Instrument," *Educational and Psychological Measurement* (December 1, 1997). The instrument has three components, and this is part three. We elected not to use the second part for this book. Copyright © 1997. Reprinted by Permission of SAGE Publications.
47. *Lewis Lapham*: Lewis H. Lapham, "Old Masters," *The New York Times* (October 23, 2014).
48. *path of learning, then learn:* Thanks to Larry Peters for this phrase he uses with his students at Texas Christian University.
49. *failure rate in new roles:* Anne Fisher, "New Job? Get a Head Start Now," *Fortune* (February 17, 2012).
50. *Andi Litz was hired into human resources: HBR Guide to Getting the Mentoring You Need* (Harvard Business Review Press, 2014), 79. See chapter "Accelerate Your Development: Tips for Millennials Who Need Mentoring" by Jeanne C. Meister and Karie Willyerd.
51. *Don't be a jerk:* Lars Dalgaard, the colorful former CEO of SuccessFactors, built the entire culture of the company around simple rules such as these and a few others. To this day, Karie avoids using bcc on emails as a result of his rules.
52. *Kelly Palmer:* This story is from an interview conducted with Kelly Palmer of LinkedIn in February 2014.
53. *Vinolia Singh:* This story is from an interview conducted with Vinolia Singh in May 2015.

Chapter 3

1. *Daniel Pink*: Daniel H. Pink, *Drive* (Riverhead Books, 2011).
2. *Chris James*: This story is from an interview with Chris James conducted in January 2015.
3. *Bill Gates said*: Bill Gates, *The Road Ahead* (Viking, 1994).
4. *calls this the "success delusion"*: Marshall Goldsmith, *What Got You Here Won't Get You There* (Hachette Books, 2007). A must read for anyone in a senior-level role changing to a new position or a new company.
5. *Ron Wayne*: Andrew Couts, "Why Apple Co-founder Ronald Wayne Threw Away His Golden Ticket," *Digital Trends* (February 24, 2012.)
6. *"I saw for myself," he said*: Ron Wayne, "Why I Left Apple Computer After Only 12 Days." Facebook post, February 22, 2012.
7. *Eric Ries*: Eric Ries, *The Lean Startup* (Crown Business, 2011).
8. *"I spent more time thinking about my iPhone purchase"*: Leigh Mcmullan Abramson, "The Only Job with an Industry Devoted to Helping People Quit," *The Atlantic* (July 29, 2014).
9. *People who are slow to decide are also ineffective*: Karen M. Taylor and Nancy E. Betz, "Applications of Self-Efficacy Theory to the Understanding and Treatment of Career Indecision," *Journal of Vocational Behavior*, 22 (1983), 63–81.
10. *identity crisis:*: Kenneth Gergen, *The Saturated Self* (Basic Books, 2000).

11. *zooming in and zooming out*: Rosabeth Moss Kanter, "Managing Yourself: Zoom In, Zoom Out," *Harvard Business Review* (March 2011).

12. *access to the big picture*: Globally, 52.5 percent of employees told us they are interested in learning more about the entire business.

13. *how to collaborate with others*: Jens Förster, "Relations Between Perceptual and Conceptual Scope: How Global Versus Local Processing Fits a Focus on Similarity Versus Dissimilarity," *Journal of Experimental Psychology: General*, 138 (2009), 88–111.

14. *People who can step away from the details of their work to see the big*: Jens Förster, "Relations Between Perceptual and Conceptual Scope: How Global Versus Local Processing Fits a Focus on Similarity Versus Dissimilarity," *Journal of Experimental Psychology: General*, 138 (2009), 88–111.

15. *Colin Baden*: This story is from an interview with Colin Baden conducted in April 2013. Baden has been involved in topics as wide-ranging as Bubba Watson's hovercraft golf cart and the importance of education with Michele Obama. Yet he is a surprisingly modest person, as testified to by multiple interviewers. If you haven't seen the hovercraft golf cart, view it here: https://youtu.be/z5u_2bGPdUY

16. *Blade Runner post-apocalyptic set*: *Blade Runner*. Warner Bros., 1982. From the moment you walk in the front door of Oakley, you know you must expect the unconventional. The waiting chairs in the lobby are recycled ejection seats, and visible to anyone in the lobby is the extreme product testing area.

17. *economist Joseph Schumpeter argued*: Joseph Schumpeter, *Capitalism, Socialism, and Democracy* (Start Publishing LLC, 2012).

18. *Listen to Novices*: Liz Wiseman, *Rookie Smarts* (Harper Business, 2014). Wiseman argues that having a rookie approach beats being an expert since rookies are in constant learning mode. We think that both approaches have their merits: constantly learning and becoming expert.

19. *CEO Ken Olson*: Ken Olsen, "10 Most Memorable Tech CEOs of the Digital Era," *PC Magazine* (January 21, 2011). Decades later he claimed he meant that people would not want a Jetson-like computer controlling their home functions, but his company failed to enter the market, and home computing continues to advance.

20. *online resources*: http://www.ted.com

21. *even if they are very capable*: Tiziana Casciaro and Miguel Sousa Lobo, "Competent Jerks, Lovable Fools, and the Formation of Social Networks," *Harvard Business Review* (June 2005).

22. *highly valued by executives around the world*: We asked executives what employee attributes were most important to them. The most important was having a high level of education or training, and second highest was loyalty and long-term commitment to the company. See Appendix A.

23. *You will get less feedback*: Douglas T. Hall, Karen L. Otazo, and George P. Hollenbeck, "Behind Closed Doors: What Really Happens in Executive Coaching," *Organizational Dynamics*, 27 (1999), 39–53.

24. *people only apply the feedback they are given 30% of the time*: Scott Halford, "Five Steps for Giving Productive Feedback," *Entrepreneur Magazine* (April 7, 2011).

25. *"grow skin like a rhinoceros"*: Eleanor Roosevelt (1884–1962), American politician, diplomat, activist, and First Lady of the United States (1933–1945).

26. *the feedback you need*: Kerry Patterson, Joseph Grenny, Ron McMillan, and Al Switzler, *Crucial Conversations* (McGraw-Hill, 2011). Excellent advice on how to have difficult conversations when the stakes are high.

27. *you would never have guessed what lay in front of him*: Jim Bates, "John Paul De-Joria . . . From Homeless to Billionaire," *Winners Win* (November 6, 2013).

28. *Dick Boland learned that first hand*: Karl E. Weick, "Organizational Design and the Gehry Experience," *Journal of Management Inquiry*, 12 (March 2003), 93–97.

29. *Zappos*: Tony Hsieh, *Delivering Happiness* (Grand Central Publishing, 2013).

30. *Deliberately Developmental Organizations*: Robert Kegan, Lisa Lahey, Andy Fleming, and Matthew Miller, "Making Business Personal," *Harvard Business Review* (April 2014).

31. *promotion-ready candidates*: Jay A. Conger and Robert M. Fulmer, "Developing Your Leadership Pipeline," *Harvard Business Review* (December 2003).

32. *Human Resources group at Oakley*: This story is from multiple interviews conducted in April 2013 with the Human Resources staff at Oakley HQ.

33. *People who understand the strategy*: Robert S. Kaplan, David P. Norton, *The Strategy-Focused Organization* (Harvard Business Review Press, 2000).

34. *sports such as golf and tennis*: W. Timothy Gallwey, *The Inner Game of Tennis* (Random House, 1997).

35. *helping employees understand how their work*: Aaron De Smet, Monica Mc-Gurk, and Marc Vinson, "Unlocking the Potential of Frontline Managers," McKinsey & Company, August 2009.

Chapter 4

1. *Tony Schwartz*: Tony Schwartz, "What I Learned from My Daughter's Wedding," *The New York Times* (June 28, 2013). This quote is from Tony Schwartz, CEO of The Energy Project.

2. *Zach Altneu*: This story is from an interview with Zach Altneu conducted in October 2013.

3. *We don't invest in networking*: Herminia Ibarra, *Act Like a Leader, Think Like a Leader* (Harvard Business Review Press, 2015). Herminia Ibarra, along with Mark Lee Hunter, discuss how leaders use networks in several *Harvard Business Review* articles, including "How Leaders Create and Use Networks" in the January 2007 issue of *Harvard Business Review*.

4. *further our personal or professional goals*: Charles Kadushin, *Understanding Social Networks* (Oxford University Press, 2011). The Oxford English Dictionary Online (June 2011) included a definition of networking as a noun to cover the usage. "The action or process of making use of a network of people for the exchange of information, etc., or for professional or other advantage." While network theory has been discussed since the 1970s, the advent of social networking websites in the 2000s accelerated the ability to make connections.

5. *Close or strong ties are usually defined as*: Mark Granovetter, *Sociological Theory* (Wiley, 1983), 201–233. See also, Mark Granovetter, *Getting a Job: A Study of Contacts and Careers* (Harvard University Press, 1974). Mark Granovetter, "The Strength of Weak Ties: A Network Theory Revisited," in P.V. Marsden & N. Lin (Eds.), *Social Structure and Network Analysis* (Sage Publications, 1982).

6. *your closest work friends*: "Item 10: I Have a Best Friend at Work," *Gallup Business Journal* (May 26, 1999). In its annual workplace survey, Gallup even uses one of twelve survey items to determine whether "you have a best friend at work."

7. *In his landmark work:* Mark Granovetter, "The Strength of Weak Ties," *American Journal of Sociology* (May 1973), 1360–1380. Sociologist Mark Granovetter examined the importance of weak ties in this study in which he found that most people obtained their jobs through acquaintances, not close friends. See also Mark S. Granovetter, *Getting a Job: A Study of Contacts and Careers* (2nd ed.) (University of Chicago Press, 1995).

8. *recognize an entrepreneurial opportunity*: Candida G. Brush, Patricia G. Greene, Myra M. Hart, and Harold S. Haller, "From Initial Idea to Unique Advantage: The Entrepreneurial Challenge of Constructing a Resource Base," *Academy of Management Executive*, 15 (February 2001), 64–80.

9. *Nathaniel Koloc*: This story is from an interview with Nathaniel Koloc, co-founder of ReWork, conducted in January of 2015.

10. *reach and connect with dissimilar people:* For a more in-depth understanding of the research on social networks, see Charles Kadushin, *Understanding Social Networks* (Oxford University Press, 2011).

11. *Helen Volkov Behn*: This story is from an interview with Helen Volkov Behn conducted in April of 2015.

12. *it took only six different stops*: Jeffrey Travers and Stanley Milgram, "An Experimental Study in the Small World Problem," *Sociometry*, 35 (1969), 425–443.

13. *the degree of separation is just three contacts*: John D. Sutter, "On Facebook, It's Now 4.74 Degrees of Separation," CNN, November 22, 2011.

14. *"Your network is bigger than you think"*: LinkedIn founder Reid Hoffman makes this point well. See Reid Hoffman and Ben Casnocha, *The Start-Up of You* (Crown Business, 2012).

15. *we see everyone our network knows*: David Smith, "Proof! Just Six Degrees of Separation Between Us," *The Guardian* (August 2, 2008).

16. *average of eleven job changes between our first job and our last*: Bureau of Labor statistics, "US Department of Labor USDL-12-1489: Number of Jobs Held, Labor Market Activity, and Earning Growth Among the Youngest Baby Boomers." July 25, 2012.

17. *adults on Facebook average over 300* "friends": Aaron Smith, "6 New Facts About Facebook," Pew Research Center, February 3, 2014.

18. *people share too much*: Aaron Smith, "6 New Facts About Facebook," Pew Research Center, February 3, 2014.

19. *more than two-thirds of American adults*: Paul Taylor and Pew Research Center, *The Next America* (Perseus Books Group, 2014). This is part of a Pew Research Center series of reports exploring the behaviors, values, and opinions of the teens and twenty-somethings who make up the Millennial generation.

20. *Prolonged time online can increase our working hours:* Lee Rainie and Barry Wellman, *Networked, The New Social Operating System* (MIT Press, 2014). See also Kenneth Gergen, *The Saturated Self* (Basic Books, 2000).

21. *arms race for the biggest network*: Lee Rainie and Barry Wellman, *Networked, The New Social Operating System* (MIT Press, 2014). When our loose tie networks dominate our close tie networks, this shift in relationship structure is called "networked individualism," a term created by University of

Toronto NetLab Director Barry Wellman and Lee Rainie, director of the Pew Research Center. There are several implications for this new network structure where our close tie networks no longer dominate. People with a larger number of loose ties are less likely to have a close tie network they can depend on when they need a lifeline. Many are worried that this digital life is leaving us isolated and lonely. See also, Paul Taylor and the Pew Research Center, *The Next America* (Perseus Book Group, 2014).

22. *His work relies on an understanding:* Robin Dunbar, "The Bright Stuff," *New Scientist* (May 24, 2014) 34–36. Robin Dunbar, "Social Networks," *New Scientist* (April 7, 2012).

23. *we discovered two distinct and broad categories:* The examples provided are based on interviews conducted as part of our doctoral research using thematic analysis, see R.E. Boyatzis, *Transforming Qualitative Information: Thematic Analysis and Code Development* (Sage Publications, 1998). In order to protect the confidentiality of those interviewed, the names we use have been changed, although we use direct quotes. Barbara Mistick and Karie Willyerd, "Comparison of the Network Strategies of Successful Entrepreneurial and Professional Women," Case Western Reserve University (submitted in partial fulfillment of the requirements for the degree of Doctor of Management, May 2003).

24. *Introverts might prefer a smaller network:* Dorie Clark, "Networking for Introverts," *Harvard Business Review* (August 15, 2014). See also, Dorie Clark, *Stand Out* (Portfolio, 2015).

25. *"You're not going to do this forever":* Adam Bryant, "Knock-Knock: It's the C.E.O.," *The New York Times* (April 11, 2009).

26. *different network composition was needed:* Herminia Ibarra and Mark Lee Hunter, "How Leaders Create and Use Networks," *Harvard Business Review* (January 2007). To read further, check out Herminia Ibarra's *Act Like a Leader, Think Like a Leader* (Harvard Business Review Press, 2015).

27. *Warren Buffet:* William Green, "I've Followed Warren Buffett for Decades and These 10 Quotes Are What I Keep Coming Back To," LinkedIn, April 29, 2015.

28. *When people collaborate across organizations:* Morten T. Hansen, *Collaboration* (Harvard Business Review Press, 2009).

29. *people who have been in their careers a long time:* Jeanne C. Meister and Karie Willyerd, "Mentoring Millennials," *Harvard Business Review* (January 2007).

30. *Bjorn Atterstam:* This story is from an interview with Bjorn Atterstam conducted in January of 2015.

31. *Speed dating helps people save time and money:* Eli J. Finkel, Paul W. Eastwick, and Jacob Matthews, "Speed-Dating as an Invaluable Tool for Studying Romantic Attraction: A Methodological Primer," *Personal Relationships* (April 19, 2007) 149–166.

32. *Lisa O'Donnell:* This story is from an interview with Lisa O'Donnell, vice president of Global Learning Services at Marriott, conducted in April of 2015.

Chapter 5

1. *Albert Einstein:* Albert Einstein (1879–1955), German-born theoretical physicist.

2. *Oliver Wendell Holmes*: Oliver Wendell Holmes, Jr. (1841–1935), American judge.

3. *two very different ways*: This story is from interviews conducted in September of 2013. Jarred's story is used with his permission. Julie's name has been changed at her request, although the details of the story are as conveyed to us.

4. *John Keats*: Letter to George and Georgiana Keats (February 14–May 3, 1819).

5. *"I had no choice but to grow with it"*: Bill Strickland and Vince Rause, *Make the Impossible Possible* (Crown Business, 2009). Bill Strickland is the founder and CEO of Manchester Craftsman Guild and a MacArthur Foundation Genius Grant winner.

6. *having an excellent quality of life*: Susan Sorenson, "How Employees' Strengths Make Your Company Stronger," *Gallup Business Journal* (February 20, 2014).

7. *Randy Pausch*: Randy Pausch, *The Last Lecture* (Hachette Books, 2008).

8. *The average salaried worker puts in 49 hours a week:* Lydia Saad, "The '40-Hour' Workweek Is Actually Longer by Seven Hours," Gallup, August 29, 2014. Salaried workers on average have longer hours than hourly workers, thus the difference between the article title and the number we use.

9. *According to researchers at Harvard:* David Perkins, Michele Rigolizzo, and Marga Biller, "Learning Better from Work: Three Stances That Make a Difference," Learning Innovations Laboratory at the Harvard Graduate School of Education, January 2013.

10. *Surmounting these challenges leads to learning*: For additional information, see Carol Dweck, *Self Theories* (Psychology Press, 2000), and Carol Dweck, *Mindset* (Ballantine Books, 2007).

11. *In a study of software engineers*: Sabine Sonnentag, "Expertise in Professional Software Design: A Process Study," *Journal of Applied Psychology*, 83 (1998), 703–715.

12. *"Our clients are demanding more"*: Dan Schawbel, "How 2012 Graduates Can Get Jobs and Advance Their Careers," *Forbes* (May 29, 2012).

13. *Vivek Gupta, CEO of Zenzar Technologies*: Adam Bryant, "Vivek Gupta of Zensar Technologies: Beware of Hiring People Just Like You," *The New York Times* (March 7, 2015).

14. *Alexandra Ames*: This story is from interviews with Alexandra in September and October of 2013.

15. *"Well, you've gotta try everything once. . . "*: The Doors, "Variety Is the Spice of Life," *Other Voices* (Elektra Records, 1971).

16. *Lori Goler*: Sheryl Sandberg, *Lean In* (Knopf, 2013).

17. *limits a little more*: Katty Kay and Claire Shipman, "The Confidence Gap," *The Atlantic* (May 2014). Also see, Tara Sophia Mohr, "Why Women Don't Apply for Jobs Unless They're 100% Qualified," *Harvard Business Review* (August 25, 2014). Some attribute women's reluctance to apply to lack of confidence. Others suggest a more complex set of dynamics that contribute to the difference between men's and women's willingness to apply for stretch positions.

18. *Elastigirl*: *The Incredibles* (Walt Disney Home Entertainment, 2005).

19. *applied 30 percent of the time*: Scott Halford, "Five Steps for Giving Productive Feedback," *Entrepreneur Magazine* (April 7, 2011).

20. *more than 60 million people*: Jeffrey Neuner, "40% of America's Workforce Will Be Freelancers by 2020," *Quartz* (March 21, 2013).

21. *Andy Claiborne*: Karie and Andy worked together in a small startup, and this account is from multiple live conversations and email exchanges in 2014 and 2015.

22. *Studies show that people with more education*: "Employment Projections," U.S. Bureau of Labor Statistics, April 2, 2015. Based on 2014 Bureau of Labor Statistics data, the unemployment rate for those without a high school degree is 9 percent, with a high school degree 6 percent, and with a professional degree 1.9 percent.

23. *earn more money over their careers*: Jennifer Cheeseman Day and Eric C. Newburger, "The Big Payoff: Educational Attainment and Synthetic Estimates of Work-Life Earnings," U.S. Census Bureau, July 2002. This report found that over an adult's working life, high school graduates can expect, on average, to earn $1.2 million; those with a bachelor's degree, $2.1 million; and people with a master's degree $2.5 million. Therefore, a person with a master's degree should see $1.3 million in additional earnings over a person with a high school degree.

24. *funding from the United States Trade Adjustment Assistance*: "What Is Trade Adjustment Assistance?," U.S. Department of Labor, June 22, 2012. Trade Adjustment Assistance (TAA) is a federal program of the U.S. government to act as a way to reduce the damaging impact of imports felt by certain sectors of the U.S. economy. The current structure features four components of Trade Adjustment Assistance: for Workers, Firms, Farmers, and Communities.

25. *Being loyal increases our sense of*: Albert O. Hirschman, *Exit, Voice and Loyalty* (Harvard University Press, 1970). The basic concept of organizations and businesses forming human groupings and then acting by exiting (withdrawing from the relationship) or using their voice (to repair or improve the relationship) is strongly moderated by loyalty. In Hirshman's application in organizations where there are strong loyalty bonds (similar to brand loyalty) exit is reduced and members are more likely to feel that their voices are heard.

26. *ruined by a massive accounting scandal*: Alan Deutschman, "Is Your Boss a Psychopath?," *Fast Company* (July 2005). Also see, John A. Byrne, *Chainsaw* (Harper Business, 1999). Dunlap's style has been widely reported.

27. *advice for those working for bully bosses*: Rob Walker, "Workologist," *The New York Times*.

28. *as long as you know the tradeoff*: Sheryl Sandberg, *Lean In* (Knopf, 2013).

29. *Dan Pontefract, chief envisioner*: This story is from interviews conducted with Dan Pontefract and Paul Bleier in March of 2015.

30. *employees have a variety of interests*: Stefan Sagmeister, "The Power of Time Off," TED Talk, July 2009.

31. *Art Fry was trying to mark places*: "An Idea That Stuck: How a Hymnal Bookmark Helped Inspire the Post-it Note," NPR, July 26, 2014. Arthur Fry, a 3M chemist, invented the Post-it Note, and Spencer Silver invented the glue.

32. *"apprenticeship program at Barclays"*: Anne Tergesen, "'Internships' for 40-somethings take root on Wall Street," MarketWatch.com, March 3, 2015.

33. *higher levels of employee job satisfaction*: For Deci's classic work, see Edward Deci, *Intrinsic Motivation* (Plenum, 1975). Bandura's work on self-efficacy can be found in Albert Bandura, *Self-Efficacy* (Worth Publishers, 1997). Also

see Jay A. Conger and Rabindra N. Kanungo, "The Empowerment Process: Integrating Theory and Practice," *Academy of Management Review*, 13 (1988), 471–482. Conger and Kanungo build on the intrinsic need for self-determination (Deci, 1975) and Bandura's (1986) model of personal self-efficacy.

34. *provide employees targeted coaching and advice*: Julie Cook Ramirez, "Rethinking the Review," *Human Resource Executive* (July 24, 2013). According to Morris, Adobe abolished the one-time-a-year formal written performance review in 2012 for a review process called "The Check-In," an informal system of ongoing real-time feedback.

35. *wouldn't have a chance to interact with*: Cynthia D. McCauley, D. Scott Derue, Paul R. Yost, and Sylvester Taylor, *Experience-Driven Leader Development* (Jossey-Bass, 2013).

Chapter 6

1. *J.K. Rowling*: Carmel Hagen, "9 Reasons Why Failure Is Not Fatal," *99u*, 2011.

2. *an officer in the Italian Airforce*: Christopher Lee, "From Child on Street to Nobel Laureate," *Washington Post* (October 9, 2007).

3. *Aldous Huxley*: Aldous Huxley, *Texts and Pretexts* (Norton, 1960).

4. *instead he became chairman of Walt Disney Studies*: Brooks Barnes, "Disney Film Boss Alan Horn Finds Success After Ouster by Warner," *New York Times* (November 9, 2014). Also see, "Alumni Interview: Alan Horn, Chairman of Walt Disney Studios," Harbus, November 27, 2012.

5. *"You can recover from most experiences"*: "The 2015 meaning of life—Jill Abramson," *Esquire* (January/February 2015). Abramson's profile in the *Forbes* list of the most powerful people of 2014 can be found at www.forbes. com/profile/jill-abramson/. See also, Ken Auletta "Why Jill Abramson Was Fired," *The New Yorker* (May 14, 2014) and Jill Abramson, "Struck on the Street: Four Survivors," *New York Times* (May 2, 2014).

6. *Acton netted over 40 million shares*: Sarah Buhr and Frank Barbieri, "40 People Who Are Living Proof You Can Make It in Silicon Valley After 40," *Tech Crunch* (July 15, 2014). See also, "WhatsApp founders Jan Koum and Brian Acton Own Nearly $9 Billion in Facebook Stock," *The Economic Times* (October 30, 2014).

7. *without getting stuck in grief or blame*: Andrew Zolli and Ann Marie Healy, *Resilience: Why Things Bounce Back* (Simon & Schuster, 2012).

8. *Truman Capote*: "Truman Capote: About the Author," *PBS American Masters*, July 28, 2006.

9. *whose theory on mindsets*: Carol S. Dweck, *Mindset* (Ballantine Books, 2007).

10. *what we can achieve*: Steven M. Southwick and Dennis S. Charney, *Resilience* (Cambridge University Press, 2014).

11. *A mentor was just what Spielberg needed*: Jeff Stibel, "A Profile in Failure," LinkedIn, January 30, 2015.

12. *seek advice or try a different strategy*: Carol S. Dweck, "The Secret to Raising Smart Kids," *Scientific American* (January 1, 2015). Also, "How Companies Can Profit from a Growth Mindset," *Harvard Business Review* (November 2014), and Carol S. Dweck, *Mindset* (Ballantine Books, 2007).

13. *Rivers had to break through the conventions*: "Joan Rivers: A Piece of Work," PBS, September 22, 2014.

14. *"Love the process."*: "Joan Rivers: Why Johnny Carson Never Ever Spoke to Me Again," *The Hollywood Reporter* (December 6, 2012). Joan Rivers is famous for the full quote, "Don't worry about the money. Love the process."

15. *we are living in crazy and intense times*: Nathan Bennett and G. James Lemoine, "What VUCA Really Means for You," *Harvard Business Review* (January–February 2014).

16. *everyone is redefining how they think*: Emily Esfahani Smith and Jennifer L. Aaker, "Millennial Searchers," *The New York Times* (November 30, 2013).

17. *"most important factors defining career success"*: Alexandra Levit and Sanja Licina, "The Future of Millennial Careers," The Career Advisory Board, March 2011.

18. *By adopting a way of thinking*: Alexandra Levit and Sanja Licina, "The Future of Millennial Careers Research," The Career Advisory Board, March 2011.

19. *Shift Index validates this way of thinking*: John Hagel III, John Seely Brown, and Tamara Samoylova, *Unlocking the Passion of the Explorer* [film] (Deloitte University Press, September 17, 2013).

20. *Rising above the noise in your company*: Donald Sull and Kathleen M. Eisenhardt, *Simple Rules* (Houghton Mifflin Harcourt, 2015). To read more about how to manage complexity at work, consider this book from which we drew some insights for the questions included in the Stretch Break.

21. *Martin Seligman*: Martin E. P. Seligman, *Flourish* (The Free Press, 2011).

22. *take relaxation seriously*: Manfred Kets De Vries, "The Importance of Doing Nothing," *Forbes* (July 1, 2014).

23. *Unknown:* This quote is often attributed to Theodor Seuss Geisel (pen name Dr. Seuss) without a citation of source, as an anonymous proverb, or attributed to Gabriel García Márquez, in Spanish: "No llores porque ya se terminó... sonríe, porque sucedió."

24. *all those hours multiply your progress*: Martin E. P. Seligman, *Flourish* (The Free Press, 2011).

25. *older people have more grit*: Angela Lee Duckworth and Patrick D. Quinn, "Development and Validation of the Short Grit Scale," *Journal of Personality Assessment* (2009), 166–174.

26. *"The only thing that is constant is change"*: Heraclitus of Ephesus (535 BC–475 BC) Greek philosopher.

27. *Jack Dempsey*: William Harrison "Jack" Dempsey (1895–1983), American boxer who held the world heavyweight title between 1919 and 1926.

28. *Diane Coutu*: Diane Coutu, "How Resilience Works," *Harvard Business Review* (May 2002). Therefore, by definition, resiliency is not just possessing one set of characteristics or skills, but rather the ability to employ these skills cumulatively, with the result being "bouncing back."

29. *Melody Gardot*: "Melody Gardot's Road to Recovery," NPR, March 8, 2008.

30. *resilient people invest*: Coutu, "How Resilience Works."

31. *negative impact on intrinsic motivation*: Tomas Chamorro-Premuzic, "Does Money Really Affect Motivation? A Review of the Research," *Harvard Business Review* (April 10, 2013). Chamorro-Premuzic cites meta-analysis studies of 120 years of research to substantiate that money is not the answer. See also Edward Deci, *Intrinsic Motivation* (Plenum, 1975).

32. *Jack Ma*: Ashley Lutz, "Alibaba Founder Jack Ma Was Rejected from 30 Jobs, Including KFC, Before Becoming China's Richest Man," *Business Insider* (February 17, 2015).

33. *five sources of meaning for humans at work*: Carolyn Dewar and Scott Keller, "Four Motivation Mistakes Most Leaders Make," *Harvard Business Review* (October 17, 2011).

34. *"The idea that your job is going to make your heart sing"*: Adam Bryant, "Cindi Leive of *Glamour* on Harnessing the Power of Praise," *The New York Times* (April 2, 2015).

35. *Brian Ray*: Brian Ray, "The Lessons of Failure," *The Chronicle of Higher Education* (January 7, 2015).

36. *advocates adopting a curiosity habit*: Al Siebert, *The Resiliency Advantage* (Berrett-Koehler, 2005).

37. *"discovering the truth about ourselves"*: Fred Rogers, *The World According to Mister Rogers* (Hyperion Books, 2003).

38. *Adapted from* The Resiliency Advantage: Al Siebert, *The Resiliency Advantage* (Berrett-Koehler, 2005).

39. *"forget about the last shot"*: "UConn-Georgetown Post Game Quotes," UCONN Huskies, February 11, 2012. Kaleena Mosqueda-Lewis quote on Connecticut's shooting: "We don't want to be one of those teams that have to keep relying on our outside shooting to win games. We have to get the ball inside. If we aren't making shots as shooters, we have to make sure that we forget about the last shot and keep shooting. If we keep missing we will have to find other ways to score."

40. *Max Levchin's*: "FailCon: Failing Forward to Success," NPR, October 29, 2009.

41. *start with a few miles at a time*: Jeff Galloway, *Marathon: You Can Do It!* (Shelter Publications, 2010).

42. *"Meaning is not something you stumble across"*: John Gardner, "The Road to Self-Renewal," *Stanford Alumni Magazine* (March 1994).

43. *James Robertson*: James Robertson, *And the Land Lay Still* (Hamish Hamilton, 2011). Reproduced by permission of Penguin Books Ltd.

44. *James B. Stockdale*: Much has been written about Admirial Stockdale. We used multiple sources for this story. Jim Collins in his book, *Good to Great* called Stockdale's dilemma "The Stockdale Paradox." His story is also included in Steven M. Southwick and Dennis S. Charney, *Resilience* (Cambridge University Press, 2014).

45. *BACK US*: While a prisoner of war, Stockdale supported and united the other POW officers with the sticky acronym BACK US. It stood for "Don't Bow in public; stay off the Air; admit no Crimes, never Kiss them goodbye. 'US' could be interpreted as United States, but it really meant 'Unity over Self.'" Although the POWs were broken down daily, they were inspired by Stockdale. Jim Stockdale and Sybil Stockdale, *In Love and War* (Bantam Books, 1985).

46. *Gianpiero Petriglieri*: Gianpiero Petriglieri, "Learning Is the Most Celebrated Neglected Activity in the Workplace," *Harvard Business Review* (November 6, 2014).

47. *Return on investment*: Tim Lane, David Snow, and Peter Labrow, *Learning to Succeed in Business with IT* (NNC Education, 2000).

48. *five sources for meaning at work*: Carolyn Dewar and Scott Keller, "Four Motivation Mistakes Most Leaders Make," *Harvard Business Review* (October 17, 2011).

49. *When employees feel proud*: Nitin Nohria, Boris Groysberg, and Linda-Eling Lee, "Employee Motivation: A Powerful New Model," *Harvard Business Review* (July 2008).

50. *business brain that gets smarter*: Bill Murphy, Jr., "Write Down Your Failures. You Just Might Learn Something," *Inc.* (January 9, 2014).

Chapter 7

1. *Henry David Thoreau*: Henry David Thoreau, *Walden, or Life in the Woods* (Ticknor and Fields, 1854).

2. *pink noise being filtered into the room*: Neva Grant, "Using 'Pink Noise' in a Loud Workplace," NPR, January 30, 2008.

3. *virtual command of drone trucks*: "Unmanned Drone Technology for Mining Trucks in Australia," Eideard Group, June 9, 2011.

4. *advanced drone submarines*: Eric Larson, "Underwater Drones Might Soon Map the Ocean Floor," *Mashable*, July 11, 2014.

5. *Angry Bird users*: Carl Benedikt Frey and Michael Osborne, "Citi GPS: Global Perspectives & Solutions," Citigroup, February 2015.

6. *come to fruition*: Sarah Zhang, "Why *Scientific American's* Predictions from 10 Years Ago Were So Wrong," GIZMODO, May 4, 2015. Just one example is *Scientific American*'s 2005 predictions, which by one blogger's count, only predicted 2 of 16 medical future forecasts accurately.

7. *up to 67 percent of Millennials surveyed*: "The Prepared: U Project's Report on Millennial Minds," Bentley University, November 11, 2014.

8. *Top talent will enjoy a seller's market*: Rainer Strack, "The Workforce Crisis of 2030—and How to Start Solving It Now," TED, October 2014.

9. *25 percent of US jobs are at risk*: Martin Ford, *Rise of the Robots: Technology and the Threat of a Jobless Future* (Basic Books, 2015).

10. *and another 19 percent at medium risk*: Carl Benedikt Frey and Michael A Osborne, "The Future of Employment: How Susceptible Are Jobs to Computerization?," Oxford Martin School, September 17, 2013.

11. *written by a human versus a computer*: Christer Clerwall, "Enter the Robot Journalist: Users' Perceptions of Automated Content," *Journalism Practice* 8 (2014), 519–531.

12. *By your authors*. Steven Levy, "Can an Algorithm Write a Better News Story Than a Human Reporter?," *WIRED* (April 24, 2012). As reported in *WIRED* magazine, Narrative Science is the company behind an increasing number of financial and sports reports. We can assure you that your authors are not robots. Currently, software is able to take a finite set of data and construct it into sentences, write reports, or synthesize into abstracts. Software is not yet able to conceive a new topic across broad categories, interview people, design surveys based on a selection of academic models, etc. At least not yet.

13. *Answer*: An algorithm developed by the company Narrative Science wrote the first one.

14. *"their mental model"*: Julie Bort, "Bill Gates: People Don't Realize How Many Jobs Will Soon Be Replaced by Software Bots," *Business Insider* (March 13, 2014).

15. *menial work we detest*: From an interview with Katy DeLeon, Narrative Science, in June 2015.

16. *end of management as a profession*: Gary Hamel and Bill Breen, *The End of Management?* (Harvard Business Press, 2007).

17. *China, threatened mass suicide*: Steven Musil, "Microsoft Probing Report of Foxconn Mass-Suicide Threat," CNET, January 11, 2012.

18. *replace hundreds of thousands of workers*: Jason Dorrieron, "Million Robot Revolution Delayed—iPhone Manufacturer Foxconn Hires More Humans," Singularity Hub, October 12, 2014.

19. *25 percent more productive*: Jacques Bughin, Michael Chui, and James Manyika, "Capturing Business Value with Social Technologies," *McKinsey Quarterly* (November 2012).

20. *As Wired reports*: David Pierce, "We're on the Brink of a Revolution in Crazy-Smart Digital Assistants," *Wired Magazine* (September 16, 2015).

21. *pursuing augmentation*: Thomas H. Davenport and Julia Kirby, "Beyond Automation," *Harvard Business Review* (June 2015). An excellent article on how people can reposition themselves for the coming robot revolution.

22. *Georgia Tech:* You can read about the program at https://www.udacity.com/georgia-tech.

23. *Figure 7.1*: Chart credited to The Hamilton Project at the Brookings Institution, 2013.

24. *is growing starker*: Claire Cain Miller, "From Microsoft, a Novel Way to Mandate Sick Leave," *The New York Times* (March 26, 2015).

25. *large corporations like Microsoft*: ibid.

26. *"the creative process."*: Morten T. Hansen, "IDEO CEO Tim Brown: T-Shaped Stars: The Backbone of IDEO's Collaborative Culture," *Chief Executive* (January 21, 2010).

27. *according to researchers*: John D. Mayer, and Peter Salovey, *What Is Emotional Intelligence?* (Basic Books, 1997). As authors, we owe much of our knowledge of emotional intelligence to one of our professors, Richard Boyatzis, co-author along with Daniel Goleman and Annie McKee, of *Primal Leadership: Unleashing the Power of Emotional Intelligence* (Harvard Business Review Press, 2013).

28. *navigating organizational politics*: Gerald R. Ferris, Darren C. Treadway, Pamela L. Perrewé, Robyn L. Brouer, Ceasar Douglas, and Sean Lux, "Political Skill in Organizations," *Journal of Management* (June 2007), 290–320.

29. *Nobody wants to work with a jerk*: Robert I. Sutton, *The No Asshole Rule* (Business Plus, 2010).

30. *Lady Gaga*: Cynthia Germanotta, "Raising Lady Gaga: Cynthia Germanotta on Why It's Time for an Emotion Revolution," *The Daily Beast* (April 15, 2015).

31. *traits such as intellectual honesty*: Thomas L. Friedman, "How to Get a Job at Google," *The New York Times* (February 22, 2014).

32. *we must all learn how to persuade*: Daniel H. Pink, *Drive* (Riverhead Books, 2011).

33. *personal board of directors*: *HBR Guide to Getting the Mentoring You Need*, (Harvard Business Review Press, 2014). See chapter titled "Employ a Personal Board of Directors" by Priscilla Claman.

34. *Mike Ettling*: This story is from an interview conducted with Mike Ettling in March of 2015.

35. *insensitive tweet can blow up your life*: Jon Ronson, "How One Stupid Tweet Blew Up Justine Sacco's Life," *The New York Times* (February 12, 2015). Her tweet was: "Going to Africa. Hope I don't get AIDS. Just kidding. I'm white!" She regrets the tweet, which she says was meant to take aim at the insulated bubble of her world.

36. *front-desk receptionist:* Karie met a woman working in the Silicon Valley as a receptionist who hoped to retire that year before her 100th birthday. She had worked in the federal government until she was 55 and had worked in a mainstay technology company for the subsequent 44 years in the same receptionist role.

37. *will be done virtually*: Jenna Goudreau, "The Best-Paying Jobs You Can Do from Anywhere," *Forbes* (October 19, 2012).

38. *skills and competencies*: Siwan Mitchelmore and Jennifer Rowley, "Entrepreneurial Competencies: A Literature Review and Development Agenda," *International Journal of Entrepreneurial Behaviour & Research*, 16 (2010), 92–111.

39. *make the time*: Morgan W. McCall, Jr., and Robert E. Kaplan, *Whatever It Takes* (Prentice Hall, 1989). In one study, there was no relationship between managers' priorities and how they actually spent their time.

40. *"stop doing" list*: Jim Collins, "Best New Year's Resolution? A 'Stop Doing' List," *USA Today* (December 30, 2003). Author Jim Collins recommends making an annual "stop doing" list as part of your New Year's resolutions.

41. *on and off seasons*: Jim Loehr and Tony Schwartz, *The Power of Full Engagement* (The Free Press, 2003).

42. *short-term engagement*: *HBR Guide to Getting the Mentoring You Need* (Harvard Business Review Press, 2014). See chapter titled "Accelerate Your Development: Tips for Millennials Who Need Mentoring" by Jeanne C. Meister and Karie Willyerd.

43. *composer and pianist*: KC Ifeanyi, "Pianist Vijay Iyer's Insights on Getting Comfortable with Creative Improvisation," *Fast Company* (December 11, 2014).

44. *Dr. Seuss:* Excerpt from OH, THE PLACES YOU'LL GO! by Dr. Seuss ™ and copyright © by Dr. Seuss Enterprises L.P. 1990. Used by permission of Random House Children's Books, a division of Penguin Random House LLC. All rights reserved.

Appendix A

1. *Future workforce wants:* More detailed findings on the 2014 survey can be found at www.successfactors.com/workforce2020.

2. *the web's estimated trillion pages:* Jesse Alpert and Nissan Hajaj, "We knew the web was big. . . ," *Google Official Blog*, July 25, 2008.

3. *when companies provide an environment*: Rosabeth Moss Kanter, "Three Things That Actually Motivate Employees," *Harvard Business Review* (October 23, 2013).

4. *fewer than 100 companies*: "Employee Loyalty: Full List of Employee Tenure," *Pay Scale* (2013).

5. *most employees are disengaged*: "State of the American Workplace," Gallup, 2013.

6. *average employee tenure is just a little over a year*: Leonid Bershidsky, "Why Are Google Employees So Disloyal?," *Bloomberg View* (July 29, 2013).

INDEX

Page references follow by *fig* indicate an illustrated figure; followed by *t* indicate a table; followed by *s* indicate a Stretch Break.

to reach, 37–40; levels of, 37–38*t*; non-conscious, 40–41; by pursing mastery after failure, 159–160; 10,000 hours of practice to achieve, 40; where to focus efforts toward, 39*s*–40. *See also* Skills

F

Facebook: big data produced through, 11; Lori Goler's hiring at, 134, 135; 300 "friends" average on, 105; Whataspp acquired by, 158
Failure: the brain as a "failure engine," 180; finding silver linings in, 157–158; getting over false starts and initial, 160–161; having the resilience to adapt after, 157, 158–159; how success can come out of, 159–160
Feedback: gift feedback strategy to gain experience, 129, 135–136*s*; Mark's story on value of, 77–78; measure whether managers are giving, 86–87; seeking honest, 75, 76–80; Streak Breaks on gifting, 136*s*; Stretch Break on getting needed advice and, 79
Fellowship programs, 151–152
Find a need—solve a problem strategy, 129, 132–134
Fixed mindset, 41–44, 159
Flexible workforce trend, 187–188
Flourish (Seligman), 163
Fortune 500: changes over the last fifty years, 16; globalization of the, 9
Foxconn plant strike (China), 192
Freelancer, 14
Fry, Art, 150
Functional excellence capability, 197, 204*s*

G

Galloway, Jeff, 172–173
Gallup reports: on engagement scores, 6; on work disengagement, 5–6
Gallwey, Tim, 88
Gardner, John, 173–174
Gardot, Melody, 167–168
Gates, Bill, 63, 74, 191
GE Crotonville, 46

Geek acumen capability, 200, 204*s*
Gehry, Frank, 82
General Electric (GE), 36
Generation X (born 1964 and 1979), 10, 161
Generation Y. *See* Millennials (Generation Y)
George Mason University, 45
Georgia Tech, 194
Get global experience strategy: for Be Greedy About Experiences practice, 129, 131–132; Stretch Break on increasing your global awareness, 132*s*
Gift feedback strategy, 129, 135–136*s*
Global Learning Services (Marriott International), 121
Globalization: McKinsey estimates on business, 9; as work environment megatrend, 9–10
GoFundMe.com, 132
Goldman Sachs, 151
Goldsmith, Marshall, 16, 63
Goler, Lori, 134, 135
Good bosses: getting honest feedback from, 144; Stretch Break on assessing if your boss is a, 144*s*; as talent developers and career makers, 143
Google, 187, 198; definitions of jobs on, 13–14; Jarred's story on his experience at, 124, 126; sabbaticals offered by, 150
Google Now, 193
Google Search, 45
Government human capital development/training policy, 194–195*fig*
Granovetter, Mark, 99
Greg's story, 82–83
Grit: definition of, 157; developing endurance by fostering, 166; springing back from setbacks through, 165, 166
Groom a clan strategy: build a diverse network using, 105, 106–107; Stretch Break on network goal statements, 108*s*
Growing approach to network building, 110–111, 113*t*

social collaboration and, 121; "Six Degrees of Kevin Bacon" game applied to, 104–105; Zach Altneu's story on becoming an entrepreneur through, 93–94, 96

Networks: Close Tie and Loose Tie types of, 97–100*fig*, 102–104; "Dunbar's Number" theory on the size of, 107; importance of both personal and professional, 99–100*fig*; increasing your options through a healthy, 115; Stretch Break on assessing quality of your, 97*s*; understanding the nature of, 95–97. *See also* Build a Diverse Network practice

The New York Times, 158

The New York Times' Workologist columns, 145

Nimoy, Leonard, 7

Nimoy, Max, 7

Non-compensation rewards, 180

Non-conscious expertise, 40–41

Novice expertise level, 38*t*

O

Oakley, 87

Obsolete job trends, 190–191

Ochsner, Kevin, 78

O'Donnell, Lisa, 121

OECD countries: climate change predictions by the, 13; labor market training expenditures as percentage of GDP in the, 195*fig*

Olson, Ken, 74

On-boarding training: for facilitating transitions by creating "success maps," 56–57; provide training on how your organization operates, 87

Online social collaboration tools, 121

On-the-job training. *See* Learn on the Fly practice

Opportunities: Be Open practice strategy to see, 65, 80–81; "Chutes and Ladders" (career game) on finding, 62, 84, 85; consider yourself a learn startup looking for, 65, 66–69; getting over the setback of missed, 163–164; providing employees with "learning a living,"

35*fig*, 36–37; see them everywhere, 65, 80–81

Organic talent management, 119–120

Organizations: Be Greedy About Gaining Experiences practice facilitation by, 149–152; Be Open practice facilitation by, 86–89; Bounce Forward practice facilitation by, 178–180; Build a Diverse Network facilitation by, 118–121; changing the traditional career track, 191–192; creating a developmental culture in your, 86; employment categories spectrum within, 188, 189*t*; Learn on the Fly facilitation by, 56–59; trend toward becoming increasingly virtual, 188, 190

Over-managing risk trap, 52–53

Overseas experience, 131–132

Oxford Economics, 8, 75

P

Pacific Cinemas, 86

Palmer, Kelly, 58

"Passion of an explorer" trait, 162–163

Patron, 81

Paul Mitchell, 81

Pausch, Randy, 128

PayPal, 172

Peace Corps, 131

People and Places (Adobe), 151

Performance stance, 129

Performing approach to building networks, 110

Perkins, Elizabeth, 104

Persisting strategy for building network, 109

Personal advocacy capability, 198–199, 204*s*

Petriglieri, Gianpiero, 36, 37, 52, 178

Pew Research Center, 105, 106

Pink, Daniel H., 61, 198

Pontefract, Dan, 150

Pounce strategy, 170, 171*s*

Priestly, Miranda (*The Devil Wears Prada* character), 145

Private–sector employment net changes, 17*fig*

Problem solving: capability for creative, 202, 204*s*; expand your experience